The Genealogy Forum on America Online

The
Genealogy Forum
on
America Online
The Official User's Guide

by

George G. Morgan

Ancestry.com

Library of Congress Cataloging-in-Publication Data

Morgan, George G., 1952
    The genealogy forum on America Online : official user's guide / by George G. Morgan.
    p. cm.
  Includes Index.
  ISBN 0-91-648987-6
  1. Genealogy - - Data processing. 2. Internet (Computer network) - - Handbooks, manuals, etc. 3. America Online, Inc. I. Title.
  CS21 .M66 1998
  910'.285--dc21

98-41009
CIP

Copyright ©1998
Ancestry Incorporated
P.O. Box 476
Salt Lake City, Utah 84110-0476
www.ancestry.com

All Rights Reserved

Windows and Windows 95 are trademarks of the Microsoft Corporation. Macintosh is a trademark of the Apple Corporation.

No part of this publication may be reproduced in any form without written permission of the publisher, except by a reviewer, who may quote brief passages for a review.

First Printing 1998
10 9 8 7 6 5 4 3 2 1

Printed in the United States of America

This book is dedicated to Drew Smith,
whose patient, caring support and clear perspective
have sustained me through the good, the bad,
and the many in-betweens.

Acknowledgments

Writing a book is an enormous undertaking. It is much different than writing a magazine article or a weekly, online genealogical column. It requires great self-discipline and sacrifice. The former comes with time and practice; the latter at a much greater price.

The authoring of this book taught me that the writing can take up a greater part of one's life than might be imagined. Important occasions and life events can float out of perspective and take on less importance if you aren't careful. Much of my personal life was placed on hold while I worked days, nights and weekends at all kinds of odd hours. Family, friends and colleagues were loving and supportive throughout the birth of this book. I know, however, that there was a cost to them too. I would like to acknowledge my debt of gratitude to these people.

First, I must thank George Ferguson, owner of the Genealogy Forum, for having long ago given me the opportunity to work with some of the most talented genealogists in the U.S.—the staff and volunteers of the Genealogy Forum. It is this group of wonderful people who really make the forum the interesting, informative and fun place that it is. So many of these talented individuals have become my online family, as well as part of my extended, chosen family.

Next, many thanks to my editor, Loretto Szucs, at Ancestry, Inc., for her gentle guidance and support in the creation of this book. Her openness to ideas and her belief in the viability of the project inspired me to give it my all. Thank you, Lou!

Let me next express my thanks to America Online for the strength of a tremendously robust service, and for its kind permission to capture the screen shots that, I hope, make this book such a visual delight.

I must also thank Penelope Weatherly, my elegant and eloquent aunt, for her unfailing love and support, not only during the creation of this book, but throughout my life in nearly everything I have accomplished. It's my turn for the next long-distance call.

My heartfelt thanks to my brother, Carey T. Morgan. I am there for you no matter what fate brings. Thank you for being there for me.

Many thanks to the many dear friends and colleagues whose gentle hearts and kind words kept me going throughout the project: Carl Johansson, Pat Richley, Karen Roth, Terry Morgan, Betsey "Tish" DeVane, Beth Herrod, Julia Christiansen and Karen Pfeister. To Kim Myette and Pam Koch, I owe you a cheesecake! To Candy Ziebell, thanks for keeping the FB running! To Kathleen de la Peña McCook, thanks for the opportunity to work with the talented group at USF while doing my "real" jobs.

And thanks to our stunningly beautiful Tosca for keeping me company during all the days and nights.

George G. Morgan
Odessa, FL
Fall 1998

Table of Contents

Introduction 1

Chapter 1: Introduction to Genealogy and the Online Environment 7
- Where Do I Begin? 8
- Primary and Secondary Sources 10
- How Do I Know What to Believe? 12
- Documenting the Information You Find 14
- Types of Online Environments 14
- Citing Your Electronic Sources 15
- Should You Use the Information You Find Online? 16

Chapter 2: Introduction to America Online 18
- Getting Help 19
- Using Keywords 22
- Favorite Places 24
- Electronic Mail (E-mail) 26
- Read 26
- Write 26
- Mail Center 30
- Instant Messages (IMs) 31
- The Member Directory 33
- Downloading Files and E-mail Attachments 34

Chapter 3: The Main Screen: Gateway to the Genealogy Forum 37
- Touring the Main Screen 37
- Beginners 39
- Messages 41
- Chats 42

- Files 42
- Resources 43
- Internet 44
- Surnames 45
- Reunions 46
- Golden Gate Store 46
- AOL Members' Choice Award 46
- Phone Numbers 47
- Search the Forum 47
- Main and Help 47
- Feature Button 48
- The Listbox 49
- Member Welcome Center 49
- Genealogy Forum NEWS 50
- DearMYRTLE Daily Column 50
- "Along Those Lines…" Column 51
- Genealogy Conferences & Events 51
- Genealogy Classes 52
- Advertisement Box 53
- Keyword 53

Chapter 4: The Beginners' Center: Beginners Start Here 54
- FAQ/Ask the Staff 56
- The 5-Step Research Process 57
- DearMYRTLE's Beginner Lessons 58
- Beginners' Tool Kit 59
- "For Starters" Conference Room 63
- Contents in the Listbox 64-68
  - New—Introduce Yourself
  - Choosing a Genealogy Program
  - Genealogy Classes
  - Genealogy Chat Topics
  - How-to Guides
  - New to AOL
  - No More Brick Walls
  - Parents & Teachers
  - Suggested Reading

Chapter 5: The Resource Center 69
- Regions of the World 70
- United States 72
- Canada 77
- Mexico 83
- British Isles 83
- Scandinavia 87
- Western Europe 88
- Eastern Europe 90
- Southeastern Europe 93
- Ethnic Resources 95
- African American Resource Area 96
- Hispanic Resources 101
- Jewish Resources 103
- Native American Resource Area 104
- Huguenots 110
- Vital Records/Other Records 110
- Addresses 111
- Other Resources 113
  - Ancestral Seasonings (The Cookbook) 113
  - Perpetual Calendar Connection 114
- Other Items of Interest in the Resource Center 114

Chapter 6: The Message Board Center 116
- Setting Your Personal Preferences 119
- Organization of the Message Boards 121
- Surnames 121
- The United States 122
- Countries of the World 123
- Ethnic and Special Groups 123
- Computer and General 124
- Working With a List of Messages 126
- Reading Messages 130
- Replying to Messages 132
- Creating a Properly Formatted and Effective New Subject . 134
- Examples of How to Use the Message Boards 136

Chapter 7: The File Libraries Center 139
- Organization of Material in This Chapter 141
- How Do Files Get Into the Libraries? 141
- How to Upload a File 143
- Guidelines for Uploading Files 148
- How Do I Locate Files to Download? 150
- Decompressing Files 157
- All about the Libraries (Major File Groups) 157
- Ancestors 157
- History and Culture 159
- Records 161
- Logs, Newsletters, and More 163
- Software and Tools 164
- How You Can Get the Most from the Libraries 165

Chapter 8: The Surname Center 167
- Surname Areas 168
- Top 100 U.S. Surnames 179
- Mayflower Surnames 179
- Message Board Center 180
- Input Surname Web Sites 180

Chapter 9: The Chat Center 183
- The Chat Center Screen 184
- Check the Schedule 185
- Inside a Chat Room 187
- How a Chat Works 192
- Lecture Chats and the Use of "Protocol" 193
- Chat Etiquette 194
- Logging a Chat 195
- Making the Most of the Chats 197

Chapter 10: The Internet Center 199
- Sites by Topic 202
- Sites by Region / Ethnic Group 206
- Mailing Lists/Newsgroups 208
- Mailing Lists 208

- Usenet Newsgroups...210
- Locating Mailing Lists and Usenet Newsgroups........211
- Reading Newsgroups on AOL...................................212
- Search Engines...216
- Internet Tour...217

Chapter 11: The Reunion Center..219
- Family Reunion Chat Room......................................221
- Family Associations..222
- Family Newsletters..223
- How Do I...?..225
- Plan a Family Reunion...225
- Publish a Family History..226
- Publish a Family Newsletter....................................227
- Surname Center..229

Chapter 12: The Genealogy Columns.....................................231
- Dear MYRTLE Daily Column..................................232
- "Along Those Lines..." Column...............................237
- The Genealogy Forum NEWS..................................242

Chapter 13: Search the Forum...246
- What Determines What Is Searchable?...................246
- Which Materials Are Searchable?............................248
- How to Use "Search the Forum"..............................250
- Ways of Narrowing Your Search.............................253

Chapter 14: Telephone Search Facilities................................258

Chapter 15: Other Related Forums on AOL..........................262

Glossary of Terms..267

Index...275

Introduction

GENEALOGY IS A MULTIDIMENSIONAL PUZZLE, ONE THAT CAN AND WILL OCCUPY YOUR ENTIRE LIFE. Genealogy is often defined as the study of lines of descent. More than that, however, it is the investigation and documentation of family history and traditions.

There are many reasons why people trace their genealogy. Genealogy gives us a sense of belonging. It provides a sense of stability in an era when people move freely across the country or world to pursue careers and other opportunities. There is comfort in the knowledge of where we came from and how we fit into our family and society. Genealogy sometimes provides answers to genetic-related questions such as, "Where did I get my green eyes?" or, "Is there a history of hemophilia in our family?"

Some people document only a single thread of their family, perhaps seeking admission into some society or satisfying a belief that they are descended from some famous person. Other people carefully study their ancestors and familial collateral lines so they can better understand their ancestor's place in the family and in history. Adoptees research their birth parents and siblings. Lawyers and paralegal professionals research inheritance claims. Others research their family's medical history. And for some, it's just the thrill of the chase or the challenge of solving the puzzle that drives them to genealogy. The reasons for genealogical research are many. Whatever the motivation, 42 million Americans are actively involved in genealogy today.

Online services, the Internet and free community networks have forever changed the way we approach information exchange and access. Tens of millions of people have joined the available online services. Web pages by the hundreds of millions have been placed on the Internet. Tens of thousands of Internet mailing lists have formed to allow groups of people with similar interests to exchange ideas and information. And Usenet newsgroups provide electronic bulletin boards whose information exchange functions are similar to mailing lists, without the clutter of E-mail mailboxes.

The Genealogy Forum on America Online (AOL) is, without a doubt, the preeminent genealogy facility among the online services. The AOL Genealogy Forum has over 150 people who contribute time, energy and extensive genealogical experience to help other America Online members make the most of their research experiences.

The Genealogy Forum contains an immense collection of diverse materials and tools. There is literally something for every type and level of genealogist, including:

- "How-to" articles and instructions for beginners
- Message boards where you can post and exchange information with other genealogists
- File libraries full of people's lineage files (GEDCOM), historical files, maps, software programs, tools, forms and many more types of information

- A resource area with articles for the intermediate and advanced genealogist
- Information about doing research in many areas of the world
- Resources for the African-American, Native-American, Hispanic, Jewish and Huguenot researcher
- Regularly scheduled real-time chats about different states, countries, ethnic groups, Internet research studies and a wide variety of other topics
- An in-depth Internet area with easy-to-understand explanations and links to Web sites, mailing lists and Usenet newsgroups
- Online columns that share information and tips on a daily, weekly and monthly basis

The people who work in the Genealogy Forum share a love of genealogy and a desire to help others. At the writing of this book, there are over 150 people working in the Genealogy Forum who volunteer their time to help people learn more about genealogy and do more effective research. They use their own considerable, personal knowledge and experience to guide others through research challenges. Many of them host or co-host live chats on specific topics in which they have strong backgrounds. GFS Karen, for example, who is of Native American descent, may lead a chat about Native American research; GFS Judi, GFS Ed, and GFS Mar host the French chat; GFS Drew hosts the South Carolina chat. Well-trained in the considerable resources of the forum and in how to use AOL facilities, these, and many other staff members, can direct you to the resources you need. They won't, of course, do your genealogical research for you, but they do offer you a tremendous resource.

This book will provide you with a strong understanding of the Genealogy Forum on America Online. But first, it's important that you understand the basic concepts of genealogy research. To that end, the next chapter, "Genealogy in the Online Environment," will discuss some of the basics—especially as they relate to online services and the Internet.

The chapter, "Introduction to America Online," will help both the person who is just beginning to use America Online and the experienced member to apply some essential AOL functions to genealogical research. The Member Directory, for instance, can be used to search for, and help you contact, other people who share your surname or people with another surname that you might be researching. That chapter will also help you understand some key concepts about how to get the most from the service.

You'll find numerous examples in this book of how to use a specific resource to research or solve a problem. In the chapter about the Message Board Center, you'll learn how to create an effective posting and how to determine where to post it. In the chapter about the Internet Center, you'll learn how to subscribe to a genealogy-related mailing list. These and many other practical examples will help you take maximum advantage of the Genealogy Forum *and* the Internet in your research.

One of the problems with writing a book pertaining to a computer service, a software program or the Internet is that they are so dynamic. Electronic materials change so quickly these days that they sometimes become unrecognizable or obsolete. In writing this book, I've worked closely with the Genealogy Forum's senior staff and programmers to capture the content and appearance of the forum as it should appear at the time of publication. However, you must realize that both America Online and the Genealogy Forum are constantly evolving. Their goals are to meet or exceed the needs of AOL members who use the facilities. Therefore, while every effort has been made to capture screen images that reflect Genealogy Forum screens and the various AOL functions, please be aware that there will be changes and variations over time. The principles, however, remain the same.

You really can further your genealogical research using the Genealogy Forum on America Online. Use this book as your personal guide. As a veteran genealogical researcher, I urge you to use the table of contents, the index, the glossary and everything in between to understand the contents of the book. Refer to the illustrations for specific examples of the screens and functions described in the text. All of these have been carefully crafted to help you become a master of the Genealogy Forum. By using these tools, you really will become an expert at using the Genealogy Forum on America Online to further your genealogical research.

I encourage you to experience each of the areas of the Genealogy Forum. You never know where you'll find that one missing piece that could fill an important gap in your family tree. The Genealogy Forum can help. And remember, you can do it!

Happy Hunting!
George G. Morgan

1 ▶ Introduction to Genealogy and the Online Environment

GENEALOGY INVOLVES RESEARCH. Sometimes the answers to your questions come easily. Other times, despite all your efforts, it may seem impossible to locate the information you seek. There are no substitutes for basic library research skills and a solid understanding of genealogical concepts and methods. These are the foundations of successful genealogical investigation. They also provide the foundation needed to transition into an online research environment. Once you understand these skills, you're well on your way to being able to use the Genealogy Forum on America Online and the Internet at large as helpful resources.

In an electronic, online environment, we've come to expect almost instant access to tremendous amounts of information. When we start researching online, we're very often bombarded with more information than we can assimilate. Today, anyone with a computer, a modem and some software can become an instant electronic publisher. The information disseminated—via E-mail, Web pages, and other media—may be accurate and concise, *or* it may be riddled with errors and misinformation. Therefore, it is important to learn to be selective about what information we choose to read. We must develop the skills necessary to carefully analyze what we read, and learn how to verify and corroborate that information. Finally, it is essential that we be able to document our sources for future reference.

Regardless of whether you're just beginning your quest into your family's history, or whether you're an accomplished genealogist just now learning about online genealogy, it's essential that you understand the basic concepts of genealogical research.

 ## *Where Do I Begin?*

Always begin with yourself and work backward. You know your name, your date of birth, and your gender. Unless you were adopted, you probably also know the names of your natural parents and any brothers or sisters you may have. This is where you start your research. Do you know where you were born? Do you know the dates and locations of the births of your parents and siblings? Are you sure? Do you have documentation of these dates? Do you know when your parents were married? Where they were married? Do you know the full name (including maiden name), birth date, place of birth, marriage date, marriage location, death date, place of death and place of burial of each of your grandparents? Great-grandparents? Great-great-grandparents? Do you know anything about your ancestors' arrival on this continent, such as where they were from, why they came and where and when they arrived? **Do you have any written proof?**

These can be some pretty perplexing questions—questions that require more than a little research. Where will you go for the answers? One of the best sources of information for a beginning genealogist is his or her family. By asking questions of family members and recording the answers in an orderly manner, you can build a framework of what your family tree looks like. You'll find that a great deal, but not all, of the information provided by family members is accurate. Sometimes the passage of time dims the memory and details become lost or obscured. Occasionally, you may receive intentional misinformation; someone may have an ulterior motive for providing incorrect dates, changing locations, or altering names. In the worst case, a family member may refuse to discuss anything to do with family history. In any event, you will want to verify or corroborate *every* single piece of information you receive, regardless of who in your family gave you the information.

There is a difference between verifying information and corroborating it. You should be clear about the difference.

When you **verify** a piece of information, such as a birth date, you are seeking some source of documentation that *confirms* that the event took place when and where you were told it did, and for/with the party(ies) whose name(s) you were given. If you were seeking to verify your mother's birth, you would want to see and/or obtain a copy of her birth certificate. That document would confirm that she was born on a certain date at a certain place, and typically would provide the names and ages of her parents.

If you want to **corroborate** information, you are seeking one or more *additional* sources of documentation that will confirm that the first document you located was, in fact, correct. For instance, a 1900 Federal census record might indicate the names of your great-grandparents at a certain place, the names of their children and any other people living with them, and the ages of all of those people. Perhaps your grandfather William Jones is listed as being 9 years old. How do you know that the census taker didn't make a mistake? You seek to corroborate your grandfather William's age by seeking other proof of his age. Perhaps you can locate your great-grandmother's Bible, in which she inscribed that William Conway Jones was born on the 22nd of December, 1890. You then have two sources of information that corroborate one another.

If you find sources of information that contradict one another, you must seek out one or more additional sources that corroborate one or the other of the original pieces of information. You are looking at what genealogists refer to as "a preponderance of evidence." What that means is that you want superior quality, authoritative materials that reconfirm your original material.

It may sometimes seem that you only require two or more pieces of evidence to corroborate one another. This can be a problem, however, if one piece of evidence was derived from another. Let's say, for example, that you are researching your great-grandfather's children's names. Perhaps you find the county genealogical society's newsletter that lists your grandparents' children with a notation that the names were taken from those listed in his will. Your first question should be, "Did the writer personally review the will or did he/she obtain the information from someone else's written abstract of the will?" If the latter was the case, the abstractor may have made an error, and the newsletter writer may have perpetuated the error.

You *always* want to examine the original document or an exact copy for yourself. Only then can you satisfy yourself that the information you have acquired from that source is accurate. You will also want to corroborate that information with at least one other source. The more sources that confirm the same piece of information, the more certain you can be that the information is, indeed, fact.

Primary and Secondary Sources

You must have a clear understanding of the types of informational sources that exist. Humans are documentation-crazy. We create documents for all type of events: birth certificates, birth announcements, christening announcements, *bar mitzvah* and *bat mitzvah* announcements, school records and diplomas, wedding announcements, marriage licenses, divorce records, military service papers, certificates of award, land records, tax records, health records, employment records, Social Security or Railroad Retirement records, death certificates, obituaries, published notices, wills, codicils, tombstones, plaques. The list goes on and on.

Usually, the most accurate record is the one that was created at, or near, the time the event occurred. For instance, a birth date found on a death certificate is much less likely to be correct than the date of death. Additionally, on the same death certificate, the names of the deceased parents may be missing or incorrect, depending on the knowledge of the informant—the person who supplied the information. In another example, the birth *and* death dates on a tombstone may both be incorrect. Why? Because the tombstone may not have been placed until some time—even years—after the burial. The person who ordered the stone may have given an incorrect date. The stonemason may also have made an error.

A genealogist is always dealing with records that are either a **primary source** or a **secondary source**. A primary source is usually a record that was made at or near the time of an event. It is always the original or an image copy of original record. It is sometimes certified by a government agency responsible for maintaining records such as birth, marriage, death, probate, land and other records. Examples of primary sources would include:

- vital records
- census records
- family Bibles, in which inscriptions were made at the time the event occurred
- journals and diaries maintained by the principals involved in an event or by eyewitnesses
- records maintained by religious institutions that document the events in the life of a member
- letters written by a witness to an event that describe and document details

A primary source record is *never* a transcription, an extract or an abstract of a document, as these are prone to human errors. To confirm the contents of a primary source, it is always best to view the original record and to obtain a copy of it for review and future reference.

A secondary source is usually a record created some time after an event took place. There is usually a good reason for the creation of the record. An example: a man born in North Carolina in 1909 would not have had a birth certificate. Birth certificates were not issued in North Carolina at that time. However, in order to make application for Social Security benefits, the man would have had to supplied some proof of his age. In that case, he may have presented his mother's family Bible, a copy of his primary school records, a copy of his employment records or an affidavit from a family friend to the State of North Carolina. The state, in turn, would have issued a delayed birth certificate for the man's use in applying for Social Security. The delayed birth certificate is considered a secondary source. Even though it was issued based on a number of primary and/or secondary sources, it is still not an original piece of documentation of the event. It is merely an "acceptable substitute" in the eyes of the U.S. government.

Is it possible for a record to be *both* a primary source *and* a secondary source? Of course! A death certificate is a primary source for the date of death because it was issued by an authority at the time of death. But is also a secondary source for the date of birth because it was not issued at the time of birth. The date of birth is merely hearsay evidence.

Materials you find on America Online and the Internet, E-mail you may receive and information found on genealogy-related CD-ROMs are all secondary sources. You will want to personally verify every fact yourself. Remember, genealogy is a research process, and the good genealogist takes nothing for granted. RESEARCH, VERIFY AND CORROBORATE EVERYTHING.

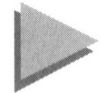 ## How Do I Know What to Believe?

Sometimes, when confronted with contradictory information, you need to determine which piece of information is more authoritative. The way to determine this is to analyze what you have in front of you. A good rule of thumb is to place more weight on a primary source than on a secondary source. Sometimes, however, you may have nothing but a collection of secondary sources. What do you do then?

In cases like this you must assess reliability of the documents. That means asking yourself a series of questions:

- What kind of document is this?
- What is the purpose of this type of document?
- What was the reason for the creation of the document?
- When was it created?
- Where was is created, and were there specific laws governing its creation?
- Who caused it to be created?
- Who provided the information?
- Was there any benefit to be obtained by anyone in falsifying information in the document?
- Is this the original document, or is it a transcript, extract or abstract?
- Can you verify or corroborate the information with another source?

By using what you know for certain, and through careful analysis of documents, both by themselves and against one another, you can come to an educated conclusion. Remember to ask yourself:

- How close was the record created to the time of the actual event?
- How credible or reliable was the source of information?
- Why was the record created?
- Can you verify and/or corroborate the information with other sources?

When in doubt about the reliability of information in one document, seek to verify or corroborate the information elsewhere.

Documenting the Information You Find

Once you obtain information from family members, obtain copies of records and come to some well-educated conclusions, you're going to want to record the information. For genealogists in years past, all this data was painstakingly recorded by hand on pedigree charts and family group sheets. Today, there are a great number of computerized genealogy database programs available for both PC and the Macintosh. These allow for the entry, storage and manipulation of great volumes of data. They also allow for the printing of detailed pedigree charts, family group sheets and a wide variety of other pre-defined and custom reports.

You will find much more information about how to perform research in the **Beginners' Center**, the **Resource Center**, and in other areas of the Genealogy Forum.

Types of Online Environments

The electronic, online environment isn't just a single area; it consists of a number of diverse means of communication using a variety of tools. These online areas include:

- **Online services** — The four major players are America Online, CompuServe, Prodigy and the Microsoft Network. These services offer connectivity to a wide array of services such as news, weather, sports, finance, online magazines, hobbies, games, entertainment, live chats and lectures, message boards, research resources, retailers and other vendors, software and other files, education and other topics.
- **Electronic Mail** — Also known as E-mail, this facility allows you to exchange messages with people from around the world.
- **Mailing lists** — Also known as "listservs," these are

groups of individuals who share a common interest and who exchange E-mail about that interest. An E-mail message created by one person is sent to the mailing list address where it is distributed to all subscribers.

- **World Wide Web (WWW)** — This is the ubiquitous Internet tool that provides access to those snazzy, colorful, exciting and informative Web pages.
- **Usenet newsgroups** — These are Internet bulletin boards where people post messages for others to read. They are similar to mailing lists, without the clutter of receiving E-mail that you must read and/or delete.
- **Internet Relay Chat** — Also known as IRC, these are the Internet equivalent of the online, real-time chats offered by the online services.
- **File transfer** — This is an Internet facility that allows you to access files on other computers and download them. Very little genealogical information is available in an organized manner, except through file libraries on the major online services.

As a genealogist, you may choose to participate in any or all of these options. What you will find is that America Online offers the best value for the money for genealogists. Not only does the Genealogy Forum offer you a vast array of information in a variety of formats, it gives you clever means and techniques to use the AOL functions to advance your genealogical research. (You'll learn more about AOL's features in the next chapter.)

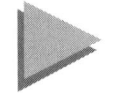 ## *Citing Your Electronic Sources*

The responsible genealogist <u>always</u> cites his or her sources of information. That means that, for every piece of information you have acquired, you provide information about where you obtained it. By citing your sources, you provide information about where you located the record, when the record was produced, who produced it and other details.

Do you remember creating bibliographies for research papers? Well, when you use books, magazines, newspapers and other print materials, you should be using standard bibliographic citations. If you're not sure or are out of practice about how to use them, check with your local library for reference books that describe citation formats.

Each of the new, electronic media that you will use will have its own citation format. When you access a Web page, you'll want to create a citation so that, if the page disappears, you will have recorded where you located the information. When someone shares a fact with you via E-mail, you'll want to create a citation the represents when, where and how you obtained the information. Sure, you can print a copy of the document and add it to your files, but a written citation will provide a trail for you and subsequent researchers.

An excellent resource for information about electronic citations is the Web page at http://www.cas.usf.edu/english/walker/mla.html. It is written and maintained by Janice R. Walker of the Department of English, University of South Florida at Tampa. Ms. Walker's work in this area has been endorsed by the Alliance for Computers & Writing and by a number of other organizations.

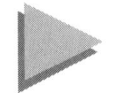 ## Should You Use the Information You Find Online?

You really do have to be selective in the online information you use. Everything—repeat, EVERYTHING—you discover online should be considered a secondary source. While you may find what appears to be *the* missing link that you've been seeking for years, don't assume that the information is accurate. Maintain a healthy skepticism. You will want to investigate each and every lead for the satisfaction of making absolutely certain that the information is correct. Even if it's not correct, though, it could be an important lead—a pointer to another source somewhere else.

In the electronic environment, CD-ROMs are produced that contain transcriptions of original documents, such as census indexes. People may publish their family trees on their Web pages or submit them for inclusion in mass compilations. People may post messages on bulletin boards with huge portions of their genealogy. They may send E-mail messages to each other or post to mailing lists with their genealogical information. These are just a few of the ways people communicate online.

Who is to say what is 100% accurate? What if there is a single typographical or transcription error? How will you know? Only if you verify and corroborate the research of others can you be confident that the information you have compiled is correct.

Regardless of whether genealogy is simply a hobby or whether you're a professional genealogist, you will want to make sure your research is correct. You will also want your information to be verifiable. As a serious genealogist, you're researching individuals, obtaining copies of records and documenting your sources. You're doing this for your own satisfaction, but you're also doing this for future scholars who may obtain and study copies of your work.

The Genealogy Forum on America Online is a terrific place to learn about genealogy techniques. It's the best place to meet and share information with other people worldwide who are researching the same surnames that you are. It's also one of the fastest growing repositories of secondary source materials for genealogists. Again, as with any other online resource, maintain a healthy skepticism of other people's work, but don't discount it. Take their work and perform your own research to verify and corroborate the details. You may, indeed, locate precisely the piece of information you need.

▶ 2 Introduction to America Online

AMERICA ONLINE (AOL) IS THE WORLD'S LARGEST ONLINE SERVICE. Its subscribers, or members, number in the millions. Among those millions of members are many thousands of other people searching for their genealogy.

The content available on America Online is staggering. You can access news, weather, sports, financial information, games, hobbies, shopping, magazines, newspapers, books, software, ethnic resources, international country information, travel services, encyclopedias, dictionaries, maps and much, much more. In addition, you can exchange electronic mail (E-mail) with people from around the world, and you can use AOL to access the tremendous resources of the Internet.

AOL has continued to develop and improve its service over the years. AOL has listened to its members and conducted usability tests in order to ensure functionality. Each new version of AOL has made it easier and more enjoyable to use AOL, while also expanding content and functionality.

There are several key functions you should understand that will quickly get you going on AOL. These are functions that, as a genealogical researcher, you will use again and again. They are:

- Getting Help
- Using Keywords
- Favorite Places
- Electronic Mail (E-mail)
- Instant Messages (IM)
- Member Directory
- Downloading Files and Attachments

This chapter will address each of these areas in some detail, for two reasons. First, each of these will help you successfully use AOL. Second, they supplement your use of the Genealogy Forum by providing additional resources for your genealogical research. (You will also want to learn about downloading files from the many library areas on AOL. The chapter about the **File Libraries Center** in the Genealogy Forum covers this process in great detail.)

The screen images used in the following illustrations are taken from AOL Windows Version 4.0. If you are using a Macintosh, or if you are using another version of the software, the screen images you see may differ. The screens are, of course, subject to updates and enhancement by AOL at any time. However, the essential functions are always a part of the service.

▶ *Getting Help*

There are two types of Help for America Online Users: Online Help and Offline Help. Online Help is available to you when you sign on to AOL. Offline Help is, in effect, the Help function of the software that is loaded on your machine. It is the documentation that came with the software when you loaded it on your computer. Let's talk about each type of Help.

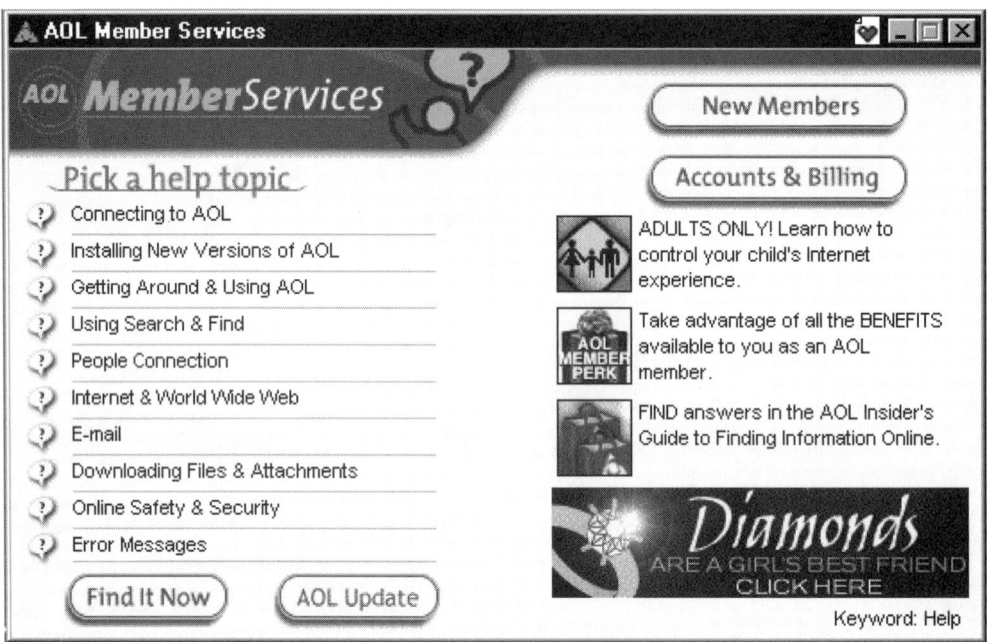

Figure 2.1

Online Help — AOL provides a number of areas that provide guidance on how to use the service. The online help area is a great place to start when you first sign on. You can easily access this by clicking your mouse on the word **Help** on the menu bar at the top of your screen and selecting **Member Services Online Help**. This will take you to a screen containing links to all sorts of great information and tutorials that can help you make the most of AOL. (See Figure 2.1.) One of the biggest mistakes made by most AOL users is not taking the time to tour this area. As a result, they sometimes miss using some of the features available to them, or they make errors while using them.

Offline Help — AOL has adopted the Windows standard of software Help. To access Offline Help, click on the word **Help** on the menu bar at the top of the screen and select **Offline Help**. You will be presented with the window shown in Figure 2.2. It's easy to find helpful information by simply selecting the Index tab at the top of the screen and entering a few letters in the box in area 1. As you type, you will see the entries in the box in area 2 scroll past.

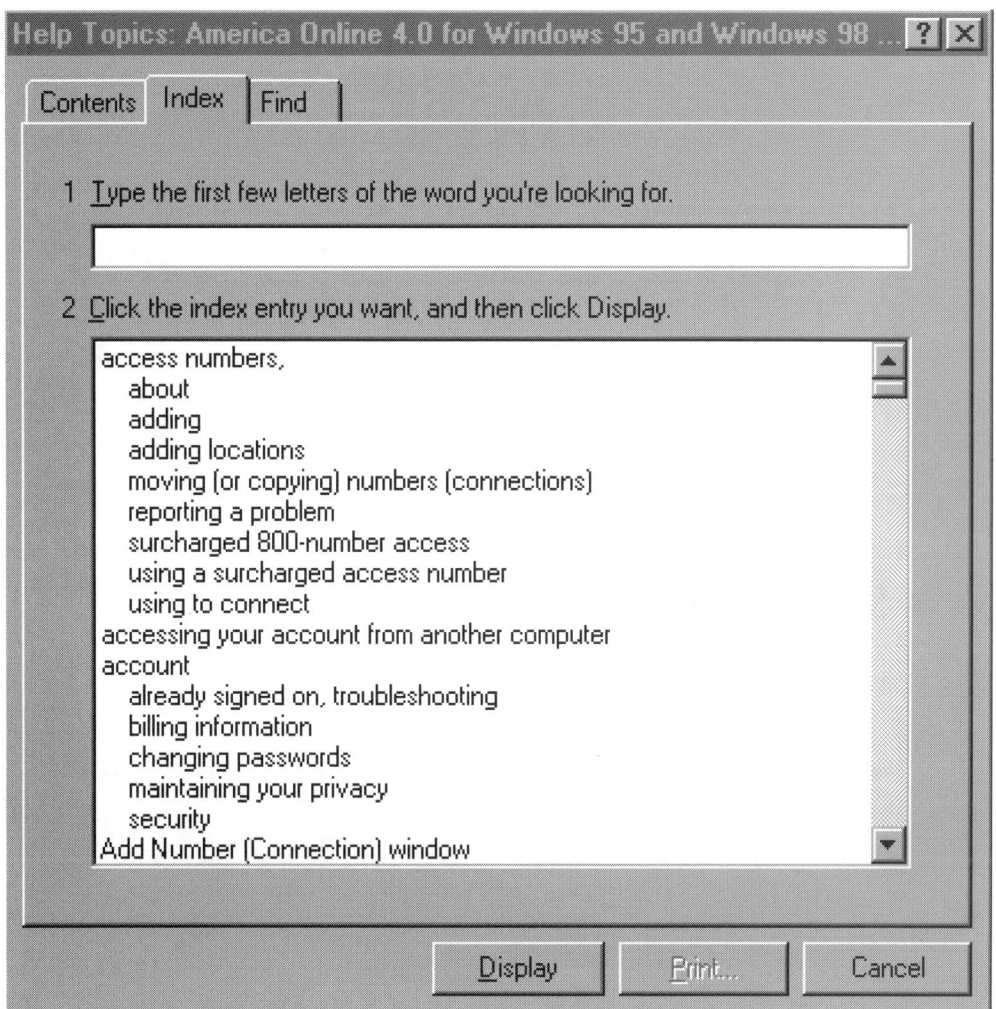

Figure 2.2

When you see a topic that looks like it may address your question, click once on the topic and click on the display button. (You also can just double-click on the topic.)

While you will find a great deal of information in Offline Help, the most detailed information will always be found in the Online Help.

▶ Using Keywords

AOL wants to make it easy for you to find your way to places that interest you. One of the ways they accomplish this is by providing Keywords. A Keyword acts as a nickname for a place on AOL and helps provide an easy-to-use link to move to a new area of the service.

At the center and near the top of the AOL screen, you will see a white box with text inside that reads "Type Keyword or Web Address here and click Go." (See Figure 2.3.) Here, you can type a Keyword, press the "Go" button, and AOL will take you directly to the site. You don't have to work your way through multiple menus and screens to get there, as long as you remember the Keyword. The two main Genealogy Forum Keywords are **roots** and **genealogy forum**.

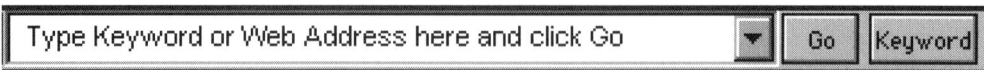

Figure 2.3

Another way to access a site using a Keyword is to use the Keyword window. If you look at Figure 2.3 again, you will see a button labeled "Keyword" to the right of the "Go" button. If you click on that button, the Keyword window (Figure 2.4) is displayed. You can type the Keyword in and click the "Go" button, or you can click on the "Keyword List" button. The latter will present you with a list of Keyword ranges in alphabetical order. (See Figure 2.5.) You can either use this list or click the "List by Channel" to see the list of AOL Channels. (Channels are logically organized groups of areas of similar types. For instance, the Shopping Channel contains all the commercial places on AOL. The Genealogy Forum is part of the Families Channel, located under Extended Family.) By using these lists, you can locate the Keyword you want. Then, go back to the Keyword window and type in the Keyword.

Figure 2.4

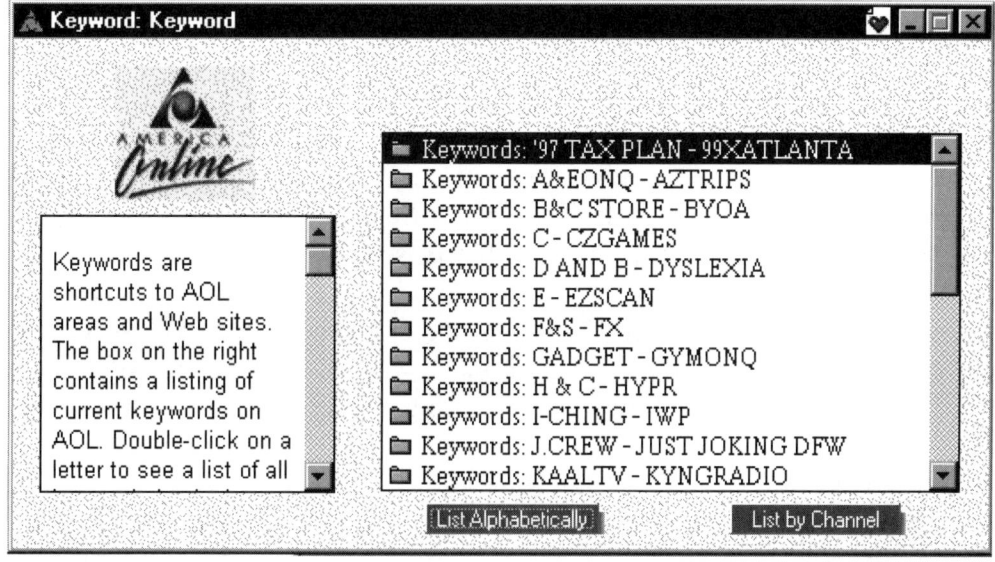

Figure 2.5

  What if you type a wrong Keyword? AOL will search for similar Keywords and display another window called "Keywords Found." All similar Keywords will be listed. If you see one that matches what you wanted, simply highlight the selection and click on the "Go" button. If you don't see a match, you can type a new Keyword, click on the "Keyword List" button discussed above, or click on the "Find" button.

The Genealogy Forum on America Online — 23

"Find" will take you to an AOL area called "Find Central." From there, you can search AOL or the Internet's World Wide Web, or you can access AOL's list of channels.

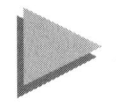

▶ Favorite Places

Another way that AOL makes it easy to get around is by providing a feature called "Favorite Places." A Favorite Place is a site that you decide you want to visit again and again without having to navigate through many AOL screens or remember its Keyword. In effect, it is like making a bookmark of the site and storing it in your own personal bookmark list. A Favorite Place may be either a site within AOL or a site on the Internet's World Wide Web.

When you find a site, such as the Genealogy Forum, that you want to mark as a Favorite Place, look for a small red heart on the right end of the blue title bar at the top of the site's window. To make it a Favorite Place, simply click on the heart. You'll be asked to verify that you want to make it a Favorite Place, and, when you do, the site will be added to your Favorite Places folder. (If you already have a Favorite Place with the same name in your personal list, you will be prompted to give the new one another name.)

Figure 2.6

Whenever you want to go to one of your Favorite Places, click on the icon at the top of your AOL screen called "Favorites." (See Figure 2.6.) A pull-down window will appear. From there, you can select the Favorite Place you would like to visit. They are listed at the bottom of the window. If you select the "Favorite Places" option at the top of the pull-down window, another window similar to the one shown in Figure 2.7 will be displayed. From here, you have several options:

- You can go to a Favorite Place.
- You can click on the "New" button and either manually

create a new Favorite Place or create a folder within your Favorite Places area.
- You can click on the "Edit" button to change the description of a site that appears in your Favorite Places list. You may also change the address of the site. (**NOTE**: The site is labeled "Internet Address" in this window. However, this term applies to either AOL's internal address for one of its sites or to the Web address of a site. AOL internal addresses are not accessible via the Internet.)
- You can delete the Favorite Place from your folder.

You will find that, using the "New" button, you can create folders in your Favorite Places area to help organize your favorite sites into categories. For example, you might decide to group all your Canadian genealogy places into a single folder. To do so, click on the "New" button, select the "New Folder" option on the window that is displayed, and type in a name for your new folder. You can now highlight a Canadian Favorite Place, then click-and-drag it with your mouse, and drop it on top of the new folder. The item should now be inside the folder. Organize your Favorite Places as you organize your genealogical materials, and you will become more efficient with your research.

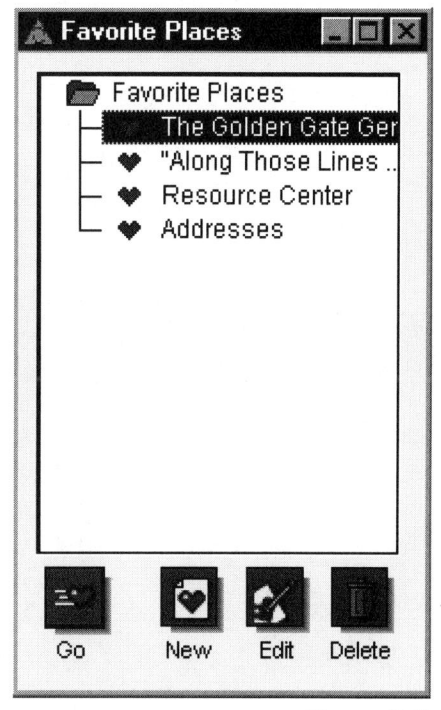

Figure 2.7

Electronic Mail (E-mail)

One of the most powerful tools at your disposal through AOL is electronic mail, also known as E-mail. E-mail is quick and economical, and it provides you with the ability to exchange messages with people worldwide.

As a genealogist, you will find that using E-mail on AOL is not only fun, but that it also provides you with a tremendous way to communicate with other people who are researching the same surnames that you are. You will see many examples throughout this book of how to use E-mail to improve your genealogy research.

First, let's look at the basics of how to use AOL's E-mail facility. At the top of the AOL screen, you will see three icons. One is a mailbox labeled "Read." Another is of a paper and pencil labeled "Write." The third is of a letter and is labeled "Mail Center." Let's discuss all three.

Whenever you have mail to be read, the flag on the mailbox icon will be in the upright position. If your computer has sound capability, each time you sign on to AOL and there is new mail, a voice will announce, "You've Got Mail." While you're signed on, if new E-mail arrives, you'll hear the voice announcement. To read your mail, click on the mailbox icon and a window will open the show your new, unread E-mail. You also have the option of viewing old E-mail that you've already read or viewing E-mail that you've already created and sent. **NOTE:** Old E-mail that you have read is aged by AOL and deleted from the system after a few days.

You will certainly want to compose E-mail and exchange messages with other people. Whenever you want to create a new E-mail message, click on the "Write" icon. AOL will present you with the window shown in Figure 2.8.

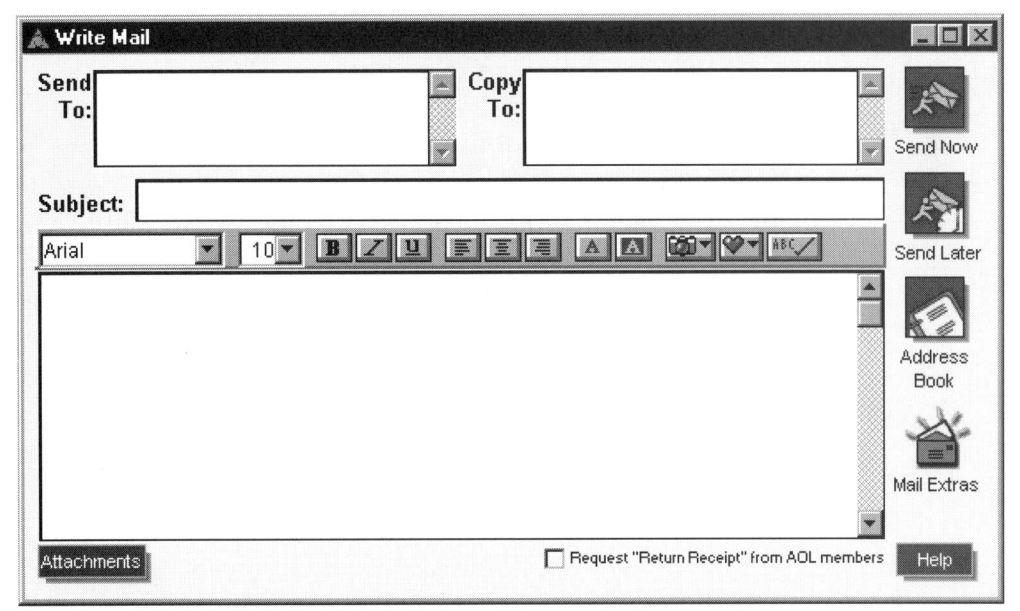

Figure 2.8

There are four areas of the E-mail form into which you can type:

- Send To:
- Copy To:
- Subject:
- The text area

In the "Send To:" box, you can address your E-mail to one or multiple addresses. If the addressee is on AOL, you simply type in his or her screen name. If the addressee is on another E-mail service somewhere on the Internet, you will need to type in their entire E-mail address. This consists of their E-mail ID, followed by the @ sign, followed by the machine (or domain name) where they have their E-mail account. The domain name consists of two or more names separated by periods (called dots). E-mail addresses have no spaces in them. A typical E-mail address looks like this:

jsmith1@abc.mailsys.net

You would read the address as follows: jsmith1 at abc dot mailsys dot net.

If you are not sure of someone's E-mail address, the best way to find out is to ask them. Your AOL E-mail address is your screen name, followed by the @ sign and closing with aol.com as the domain name. Let's say that your screen name is JohnD12a. If you are asked by someone outside AOL on the Internet for your E-mail address, tell them that your E-mail address is "johnd12a at aol l dot com"—and it would actually read as johnd12a@aol.com. **(NOTE:** Even though your screen name has one or more capital letters, most E-mail systems' addresses prefer it to be typed in lower case.)

If you are sending E-mail to multiple addressees, type the first one, follow it with a comma and a space, and then type the next one. Repeat the process for more addressees.

In the "Copy To:" box, you may send a courtesy copy to any number of addressees. Simply type the first address, follow it with a comma and a space, and then type the next one. Repeat the process for more addressees. If you want to send a BCC—blind courtesy copy—where the addressee(s) cannot see the address of the person whom you are copying, you can do so as follows:

- If there is only one "Copy To:" addressee, enclose the E-mail address in one set of parentheses. For example:

    (larry999@www.testnet.com)

- If there are multiple "Copy To:" addressees that you want to receive BCCs, group them together and enclose all of the E-mail addresses in two pairs of parentheses. For example, if you were sending BCCs to three people, you would list their three E-mail addresses, all enclosed in double parentheses as follows:

((larry999@www.testnet.com, marydoe7@abc.net, tommy19@luna.cas.usf.edu))

The next area is the "Subject:" line. Please be courteous to your recipients and type a thoughtful and informative subject. People receive many E-mail messages each day, and if the subject line reads, "Hi" or "Help", there is no indication of the contents of the message. Consequently, the recipient may or may not read your mail promptly. A better subject line might read, "Question About the MORGAN Family in NC."

The next area is the "Text" area. This is where you type the body of your message. When writing E-mail messages, remember that the written word carries no tone of voice, vocal inflection or body language. It can sometimes be misconstrued, so be careful when writing. Many a well-intentioned, innocuous statement in an E-mail has been misinterpreted and caused consternation or anger. Be careful!

A piece of Internet etiquette, also called "Netiquette," is that you should never write in all capital letters in E-mail. Typing words in upper case implies "shouting," and is considered rude. If you want to emphasize a word or phrase, enclose it in quotation marks or asterisks. In the AOL E-mail system, you can compose E-mail and use bold face, italics and underscoring. However, these types of emphasis are not communicated to other E-mail systems.

At the bottom of the E-mail screen is a button labeled "Attachments." As a genealogist, you may want to send a file to someone else. Perhaps it is one of your GEDCOM files from your genealogy database. (See the chapter about the **File Libraries Center** for details about different file types.) If you click on this button, a window will be presented that allows you to locate a file on your computer and attach it to your E-mail. For detailed information on how to do this, please click on the "Help" button on this window.

When you're finished creating your E-mail message and attaching any files, click on the button labeled, "Send Now." If you are signed on to AOL, the message will be sent. If you are not signed on, you can press the "Send Later" button. The next time you sign on, you will need to go to the Mail Center and select "Run Automatic AOL (Flashsessions) NOW."

Also on your E-mail message screen are two other buttons. One is labeled "Address Book" and can be used to save E-mail addresses of individuals or groups of people you write often. If you click on the "Help" button on this screen, you can read AOL's help facility containing detailed instructions on how to create and maintain your address book.

The other button is labeled "Mail Extras." This function is only available when you are logged on. It provides you with the ability to select style sheets for your E-mail messages, add colorful images and embed photographs. (**NOTE**: These functions only work on E-mail messages sent to other AOL members. They are stripped out of E-mail messages sent to people on other E-mail services, and these people will only receive text from you.)

The Mail Center is a focal point for every kind of information about E-mail on AOL. When you are logged on to AOL and click on the "Mail Center" button, you can access a variety of functions. (You can also access this area by using Keyword **Mail Center**.) There you will see the Mail Center itself, where you can learn more about using AOL's E-mail facility. There are the functions of Read Mail, Write Mail, Old Mail and Sent Mail discussed above. You can access your Address Book. You can also set your Mail Preferences for how your E-mail operates, including how long sent mail is retained for your review. There's also Mail Controls, where you may block junk E-mail and set Parental Controls. Take some time to explore this area and customize your E-mail operations.

One of the other exciting things that you can do as a genealogist is subscribe to E-mail mailing lists. A mailing list, also sometimes referred to as a listserv, is comprised of people who share an interest in a specific topic and who send messages to the entire subscriber base to discuss the topic. There are thousands of mailing lists on almost every topic imaginable. Among them are hundreds of genealogy mailing lists. We will discuss these in detail in the chapter about the **Internet Center.**

E-mail is a very powerful tool. It is important that you learn how to use it effectively.

▶ *Instant Messages (IMs)*

When you're signed on to AOL, you are one of tens of thousands of people online at that time. Among them, too, are your friends and perhaps other genealogists that you will encounter. Whereas E-mail is a great communication tool for exchanging information with others, AOL offers another tool called **Instant Messages,** also referred to as IMs.

An IM is a short, written communication that can take place between two people who are online at the same time. This is called "real-time" communication, because it occurs almost at once, similar to a telephone conversation.

To send an IM to another member online at the same time, all you need to know is his or her screen name. To initiate an IM, press the CTRL key and the letter I on your keyboard. (You can do this from anywhere in AOL.) A window will be displayed that looks like Figure 2.9. Simply type in the other person's screen name and the text you want to send, and click on the "Send" button. When he or she responds, you'll see a window that looks like Figure 2.10. You can reply by clicking on the "Reply" button, typing your text and clicking on the "Send" button again.

You'll use IMs frequently, so spend some time becoming familiar with them.

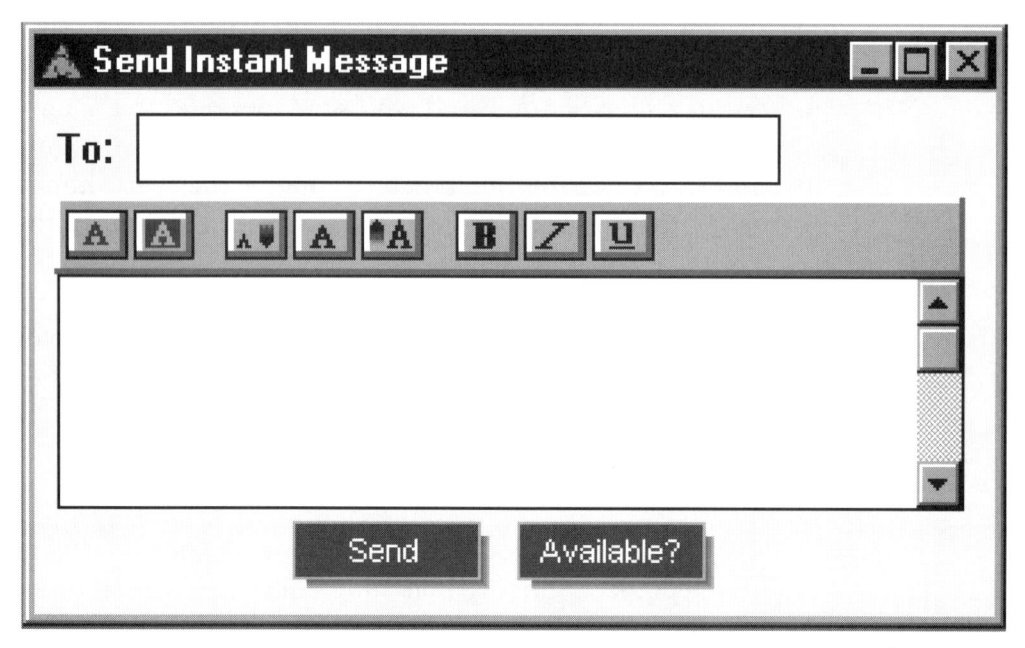

Figure 2.9

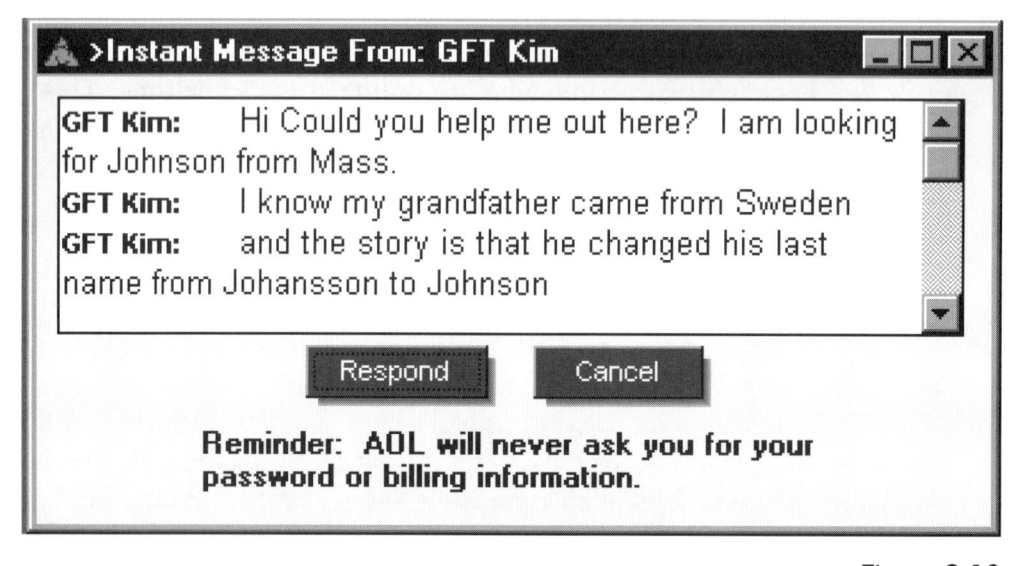

Figure 2.10

The Member Directory

The Member Directory is just like a telephone directory. It lists the screen names of everyone on AOL who has built a Profile for themselves. To access the Member Directory, enter Keyword **members**. AOL will display the window shown in Figure 2.11.

Figure 2.11

For a genealogist, a search of the Member Directory can provide plenty of new leads. In the box labeled "Search Entire Profile for the Following," you can enter one or multiple words. The search will look for the word(s) you specify and return a list of those members whose profiles contained the word(s). You can specify, for instance, a Boolean search phrase by using the connective operators of AND, OR and NOT. If you have a word that may have two spellings, such as grey and gray, you can use a "?" to indicate "anything that appears here." It would appear as gr?y when you enter it in the search box.

Please be aware that all members will be displayed that match your search inquiry. For instance, if you were searching for a surname spelled as HOLDER, your search results would include members who maybe had their surname, HOLDER, in their profile or something like "world record holder for the 100-yard dash." You will need to review each and every profile.

If you find a profile that contains information that leads you to think you have made a match with a relative or someone who has information you are seeking, you can certainly send them a polite E-mail inquiry.

In the meantime, you should set up your own profile on AOL. Other genealogists are using the search facility frequently to locate people with the same surnames that they are researching. You want to make it easier for them to find you, too.

Look at Figure 2.11 again. At the top of the window is a small icon labeled, "Create or Modify My Profile." Click here and you will be presented with your profile screen. Fill in whatever information you feel comfortable completing. However, please be sure to list the surnames you are researching. Also, be sure to include the word, "genealogy," somewhere in your profile so that people searching for other genealogists and their surname will locate your profile. Type them in upper case anywhere on the profile, but the fields for personal quote or hobbies seem to be the fields on the profile most commonly used. Remember that a search of the Member Directory will check all member profiles for the text entered on the screen shown in Figure 2.11. Therefore, make sure your profile contains information that others' searches will be seeking.

▶ Downloading Files and E-mail Attachments

There are tens of thousands of files on AOL. The Genealogy Forum, like other places on AOL, maintains file libraries that members can access. The chapter about the **File Libraries Center** in this book discusses in detail the categories and types of files available. However, you should be aware that you can access and download files from AOL to your own computer. You should know also that the Genealogy Forum and other areas on AOL are meticulous in checking files to ensure that they are not infected with viruses. You can be assured that files downloaded from the libraries on AOL have been checked and are virus-free.

Files that are attached to E-mail messages should always be viewed with skepticism. This is no assurance that these files do not contain viruses. Some rules of thumb:

- **Know your sender** — If you do not know the person sending you a file, do not download the file.
- **Do not download unexpected files** — If an E-mail arrives in your mailbox from someone, and there is a file attached that you were not expecting, do not download it.
- **Purchase, install and use a virus protection program** — It does no good to install a virus protection program if you don't use it. Install it and check <u>every</u> file you download. New viruses are developed all the time. Most reputable virus protection program vendors provide a free or low-cost update service. Once you install your virus protection program, check the vendor's Web site frequently for information about updates. Please take the time to download them!
- **Always download files to your A: or floppy disk** — By always designating a download to a floppy disk, you can significantly reduce the exposure of your hard disk to viruses. It's like putting a file in quarantine. Once you've downloaded a file to your floppy disk, immediately scan it with your virus protection program. If a virus is found, discard the disk. Do not reuse it.
- **Never run a file with an extension of .exe** — Files with

an extension of .exe are executable programs. These are a danger to PC users, but not to Macintosh users. There are a few "Trojan horse" viruses that affect Macs. If you receive an E-mail from someone and it has a file with an .exe extension, do not run the file. It may contain a virus that may damage or destroy data on your computer.

In the chapter about the **File Libraries Center**, we will discuss downloading files in great detail. We will also teach you to how to upload your genealogy files to the Genealogy Forum libraries.

▶ *Summing Up*

The functions described in this chapter are key to your success as a genealogical researcher in AOL's online environment. Please invest the time up-front to become familiar with each function, and read AOL's help text for each feature. You will immediately become a more effective communicator, and you will be able to find other people and information on AOL more quickly.

Now, with these basics out of the way, let's begin your discovery of the main screen of the Genealogy Forum on America Online. To go there, go to Keyword **roots**. When you get there, Favorite Place it. You're going to be using this one a lot!

3 The Main Screen: Gateway to the Genealogy Forum

IN THE LAST CHAPTER, WE TALKED ABOUT HOW TO USE THE AOL KEYWORD TO GET FROM PLACE TO PLACE. Once you log on to AOL, the fastest way to get to the Genealogy Forum is to go to Keyword: **roots**. Simply click once on the white area in the top center of your screen where it says, "Type Keyword or Web Address Here and Click Go." Then, type the Keyword **roots** and click on the button to the right labeled "Go." Another way to get there is to click on the button labeled "Keyword." A pop-up window will be displayed where you can type the word **roots** and click on the button labeled "Go." Either of these methods will take you directly to the Genealogy Forum's main screen, shown in Figure 3.1. This is the gateway into the vast resources of the Genealogy Forum on America Online. (Please note that The Genealogy Forum is owned and operated by Golden Gate Service, Inc. It is not owned by America Online. Rather, the forum leases space on AOL.)

Touring the Main Screen

The Genealogy Forum's main screen consists of text areas, clickable buttons and a listbox (scroll box) containing additional

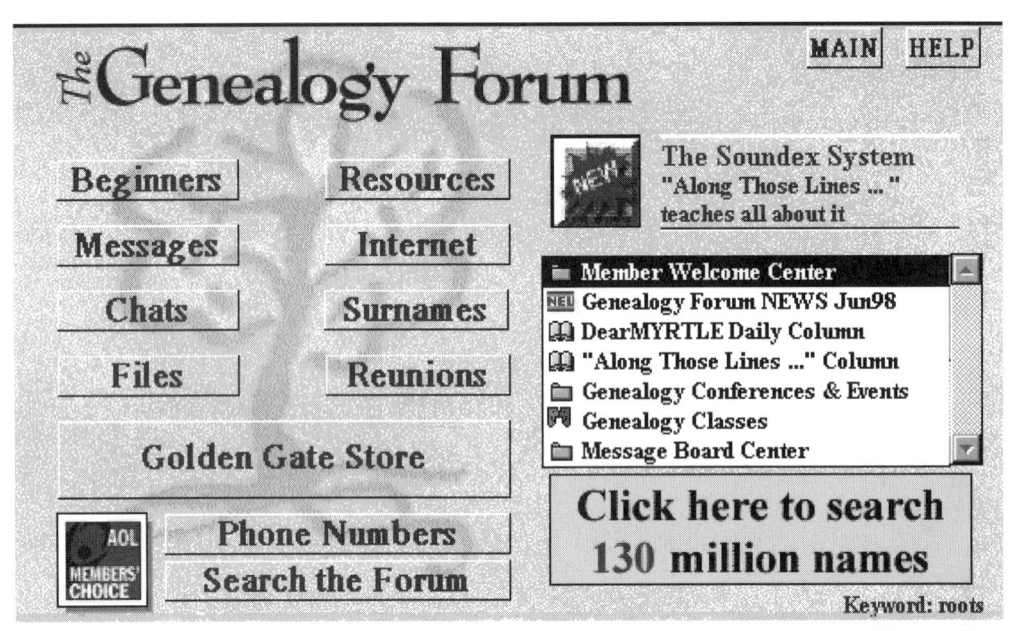

Figure 3.1

clickable selections. In this chapter, each of these items will be described, and then covered in detail in the following chapters. When appropriate, examples will be presented to show you how to use each option in your genealogical research.

Let's talk first about the buttons on AOL. Buttons are areas of a screen that, when clicked, take you to another area of AOL. By moving your mouse around the screen, you will be able to tell what areas are "hot", meaning buttons or places where you can click. You can always tell a "hotspot" because your mouse pointer will transform into a little hand with a pointing finger. Try it!

What happens when you open a window and then click to go someplace else? The next screen, or window, is opened on top of the previous one. Seldom on AOL does the new window replace the previous one; usually the new one opens on top and the previous one remains underneath. What that means is that you can "back up" by closing windows. You can also bring the previous window to the front by shifting the current one and clicking anywhere on the next one beneath it that becomes visible.

On the left side of the screen, under the banner that reads, "The Genealogy Forum," are the buttons that take you to the major areas of the forum.

▶ Beginners

This button is your gateway to the **Beginners' Center**. The Beginners' Center contains a huge collection of materials to get you started in genealogy. However, even seasoned researchers go there for information. There are "how-to" guides, articles on research methodology, an area of Frequently Asked Questions (FAQs), tips about selecting a genealogy database software program and a facility to ask questions of the very experienced forum staff. There's even a link available directly to the "For Starters" conference room, a place where you can meet with other genealogists in real-time to discuss questions and exchange information.

When you first click on the Beginners button, you will be presented with a screen of very helpful introductory information. It is titled, "Genealogy Quick Start" on the blue title bar, and says "Welcome!" on the top of the screen. Take time to read it. One thing you will discover here are items underscored and in blue. These are hyperlinks. As you move your mouse pointer over them, you will see the pointer transform into the little hand. That means you can click on these links and they'll take you to other places.

In order to print the contents of this informative window, simply click on the print icon at the top of your AOL screen.

At the bottom of the "Genealogy Quick Start" screen are two buttons. The first is labeled, "Introduce Yourself!" Please, don't be shy! When you click on this button, you will be presented with a screen from the Message Board center. (See Figure 3.2.) Scroll through the list of subjects to see if there are other new Genealogy Forum visitors who are researching the same surnames that you are. Maybe you will make a connection right off the bat. Be sure and

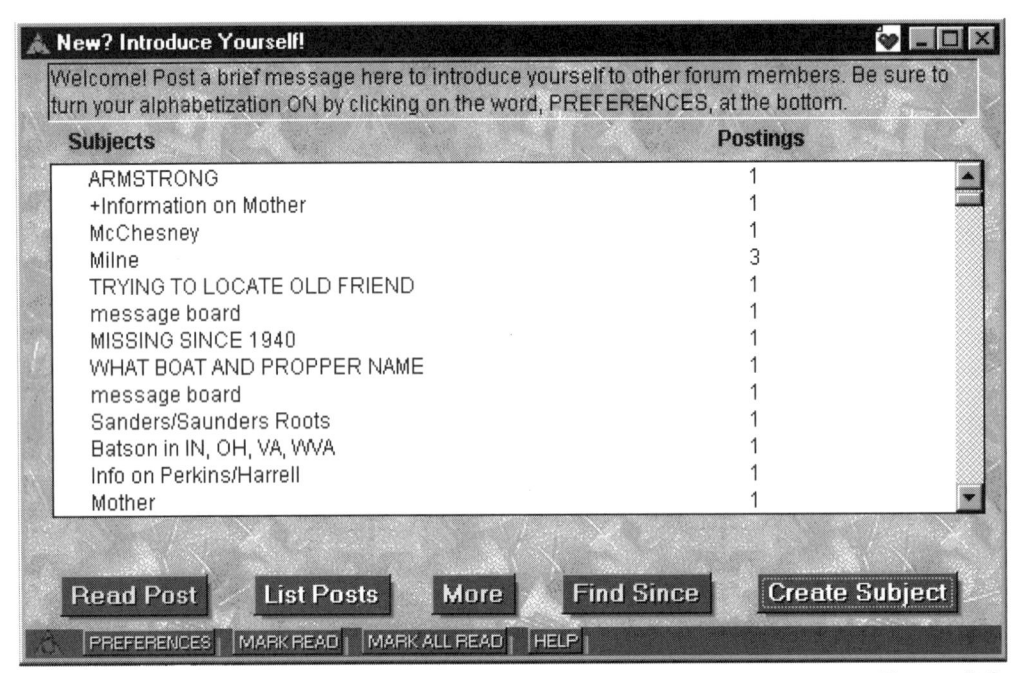

Figure 3.2

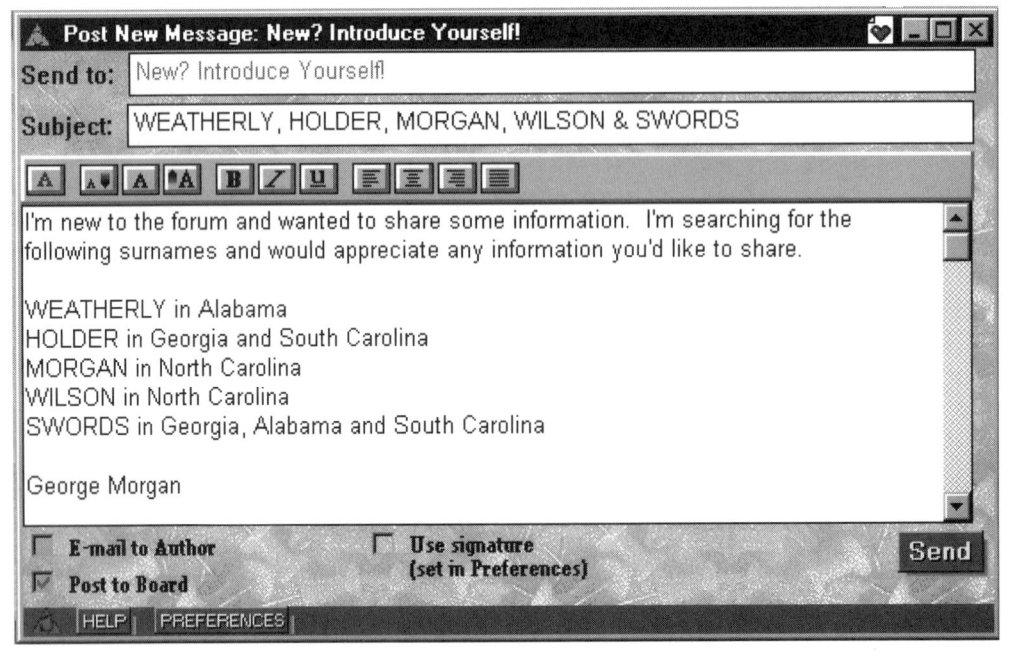

Figure 3.3

click on the **Create Subject** button at the bottom of the screen. You will be presented with an empty form where you can share some information about the research you are working on. Look at Figure 3.3 as an example. You can list the surnames you are researching and the areas where you believe the people might have lived. When you finish typing, press the "Send" button. Your message will be posted.

In addition to your message being posted, GFA Terry, a member of the Genealogy Forum's senior staff, will send you an E-mail containing lots of good information about using the Genealogy Forum.

Messages

The "Messages" button will take you to the Genealogy Forum's **Message Board Center**. Message boards are used throughout AOL in many forums to allow members to post information for others to read. This is a great way to exchange information.

In the Genealogy Forum, there are message boards available for surnames and geographical areas in the U.S. and around the world that you may be researching. There are also available boards for ethnic groups, historians and a number of other special interest groups. There are even boards available where people discuss the pros and cons of genealogy computer software programs, just in case you want details before you buy. And, of course, there are articles available that will help you use the message boards more effectively.

Many people have made connections on the message boards with lost or distant relatives and other genealogists researching their lines. Please see the chapter about the Message Board Center for more information about how to use this great communication facility.

▶ Chats

The "Chats" button will take you to the **Chat Center**. This is the departure point for real-time discussions about topics of interest to you. The Genealogy Forum offers more than 170 regularly scheduled chats each week. The chats are also referred to as "SIGs"—Special Interest Groups where people interested in specific topics come together to share information and ask questions in a "live" environment, referred to as a "chat room." These regularly scheduled chats are of two types:

- There are hosted chats with members of the Genealogy Forum staff acting as greeters, moderators, lecturers and helping to answer members' questions. The staff members are experts in the specific field covered in the chat.
- There are unhosted chats called Drop In Hours (DIHs), where members casually chat and exchange information.

There are five main chat rooms where the chats take place and, through the Chat Center, you can review the schedules and access the chat rooms.

Please see the chapter about the Chat Center for more information about how to use the chats to expand your genealogical research.

▶ Files

This button takes you to the **File Libraries Center**, a vast repository of files that can help you in your genealogical research. Here you will find files containing surnames and lineage information, ethnic genealogy, maps, history, forms, photographs and much, much more. Also available are archived newsletters and message boards from throughout the forum. You will also find vital records and library resources, as well as documents containing more tips and techniques for use in your research. Last but not least, there are also available software utilities for both the PC and Macintosh platforms.

You can read a description of the contents of each file and decide whether or not you wish to download it to your computer. Each file is meticulously checked to ensure that it is virus-free. You may also choose to share a file containing your own genealogical research from your database. In that case, you can create a file and then upload it to the Genealogy Forum. It will be virus-checked and made available for others to download.

You never know; another member may find a link in *your* file and contact you to share what they've found. And that may be just the piece of information you need!

Please see the chapter about the File Libraries Center for more information about how to locate, download and upload files, as well as about how to use information in the File Libraries Center in your genealogical research.

Resources

This button will take you to the **Resource Center**. This area contains a wide variety of materials to help the intermediate to advanced researcher. There are materials about every region of the world and materials devoted exclusively to African American, Native American, Hispanic and Jewish research, as well as to the Huguenots. An entire section of the Resource Center is devoted to information about vital records and other record types. If you are looking for addresses of genealogical and historical societies, there's a full collection of them available here. You'll also find a link to a perpetual calendar, and even a collection of old family recipes, called "Ancestral Seasonings."

The Resource Center is one of the most-visited places in the Genealogy Forum because its contents are so rich and varied. Please see the chapter about the Resource Center for more information about the types of information available in the Resource Center, and how to apply that information to your genealogical research.

▶ Internet

Nothing has changed the face of genealogy more drastically than the Internet. Today, there are Web pages with incredible amounts of information available, mailing lists to subscribe to and Usenet newsgroups to read. Locating the best of these resources can be a daunting task. The Genealogy Forum has selected the *créme de la créme* of genealogy research for you and consolidated it into the **Internet Center**.

The Internet button on the Genealogy Forum's main screen takes you to the Internet Center. Here, you will find the best of the general genealogy sites on the Internet consolidated into one collection. Another collection showcases groups of ethnic and regional sites.

Are you interested in subscribing to E-mail mailing lists about specific surnames, ships passenger lists, or research in a specific county, state or country? The Genealogy Forum's own GFS JohnF is the nation's acknowledged authority on mailing lists (or listservs). You will learn how to subscribe, as well as how to use the proper "netiquette" when posting and responding. And, if you are interested in Usenet newsgroups about genealogy, you can learn that here as well.

From this site, you also have available direct access to the best Internet search engines, which are powerful tools for searching the entire Internet for any subject word or phrase.

Finally, you can access an extensive AOL facility that provides a tour of AOL Internet functions. This facility contains extensive "how-to" information and answers most of the questions you will have about each of the Internet facilities.

The chapter about the Internet Center will cover each of the areas in detail, while also providing tips and strategies for using the Internet in your genealogical research.

▶ *Surnames*

This button will take you to the **Surname Center,** a specialized collection of information from all over the Genealogy Forum, grouped by surname. Here, you will find several presentations of surname collections.

In one collection, you will find the top 1,000 surnames in the U.S. (according to the U.S. census) arranged alphabetically with a variety of resources attached to each one. In another collection, only the top 100 surnames are listed. And a third collection contains specifically the surnames of the original colonists who came from England on the Mayflower and settled Plymouth Colony. If you can't locate your surname(s) here, there's a link available to the Message Board Center where you can post, read and respond to messages.

And, if you have created a Web page with information about any of the top 1,000 U.S. surnames, you can submit the URL (Web address) for inclusion in the Genealogy Forum's Surname Center. What a great way to increase your exposure and improve your chances to connect with another researcher!

The chapter about the Surname Center will discuss how to use each of the areas in the collection in conjunction with the Message Board Center and the Internet Center.

▶ Reunions

This button takes you to the **Reunion Center**, where you can learn all about how to plan, organize and host a successful family reunion. In addition, there are links to family associations and information about publishing a family newsletter, both of which are great tools for working on your reunion.

▶ Golden Gate Store

This button will take you to a place in the forum where you can purchase the very best materials available to the genealogy community. The Genealogy Forum's **Golden Gate Store** is the place to shop for reference books, CD-ROM products, software programs, charts and forms and other materials. You can shop in confidence that your purchasing information is secure and that you will be satisfied with the products you buy here.

▶ AOL Members' Choice Award

America Online frequently polls its members to find out which of its online areas are the most popular and which ones provide the best content. AOL tabulates the results and awards its prestigious **AOL Members' Choice Award** to each of the top 50 sites.

The Genealogy Forum consistently ranks among the top of the Members' Choice poll. The presence of the red Members' Choice button on the main screen is an indicator that the Genealogy Forum is consistently voted by AOL members to be a top quality site.

When you click on the Members' Choice button, you will go to the "AOL Top 50 Members' Choice" screen. Here, you can browse through and connect to the other award-winning AOL sites.

Phone Numbers

Have you ever wanted to try to locate your "lost" cousin? Perhaps you know he lives in Georgia, but you aren't sure where. How do you locate him?

The "Phone numbers" button takes you to a collection of Internet-based **Telephone Search Facilities**. With one or more of these facilities, you may be able to locate all the people listed with your "lost" cousin's name in the U.S. and then narrow it down to the best possibilities.

The chapter about **Telephone Search Facilities** will discuss how to use these Internet tools in your research.

Search the Forum

This button takes you to one of the most powerful tools in the forum. With it, you can enter a single word or several words linked with the Boolean operators AND, OR and NOT. Press the "List Articles" button and a list of all the items found in the Genealogy Forum containing your selected word(s) will be listed. It is then just a matter of investigating each one to see which provides information that might help you.

This facility will be discussed in more detail in the chapter, **Search the Forum**.

Main and Help

In the upper right-hand corner of the Genealogy Forum's main screen are two smaller buttons labeled **Main** and **Help**.

Clicking on **Main** will take you to the main AOL screen for its channels. The Genealogy Forum is part of AOL's "Families" channel, so when you click on **Main**, the Families channel screen is displayed.

When you click on the **Help** button, the AOL Member Services screen (Keyword: help) is displayed. This is the area described in Chapter 2 where you will find extensive AOL help information.

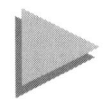

▶ The Feature Button

On the right side of the screen, above the listbox, is an area called the **Feature Button**. It consists of the two text areas enclosed in frames and the square icon to the left. See Figure 3.4 for an example of how it looks.

This area is used to tell you about new things in the Genealogy Forum, upcoming events, and features areas or items. The content of the Feature Button area changes daily. Look here for new ideas and information. One member reported that she had given up on locating one ancestor until she saw a notice in the Feature Button area about Huguenots. She clicked on the button, went to the Huguenot area, and found information that pointed her in another research direction. She reported that, after several weeks' work, she finally located records that pointed her to a town in France where she planned to conduct additional research.

Figure 3.4

The Feature Button provides access to features and promotions from all over the forum. Check there often for new and interesting items. Read the text and click on the square icon button. This will take you to the area described in the text box.

▶ The Listbox

The listbox is the next area to explore on the Genealogy Forum's main screen. See Figure 3.5 below for an example of what it looks like. It contains a combination of additional resources *and* links to all the forum's button areas on the left side of the screen discussed above. The reason for the redundant listings here is that there are AOL members still using old versions of AOL software that cannot accommodate AOL's new screen layouts and graphics. In order for these members to access the "centers" and other features of the forum, they must use scroll box entries.

Figure 3.5

Let's learn a bit about each of the new entries in the listbox. In order to visit one of these areas, simply highlight it with your mouse, and then either double-click or press the Enter key on your keyboard.

▶ Member Welcome Center

The Member Welcome Center is a great place to stop if you are a new visitor to the Genealogy Forum. Here you can learn more about the offerings in the forum, discover who the staff and volunteers are, browse a great collection of FAQs (frequently asked questions), learn about conferences that may be scheduled near you and view the copyright statement regarding use of materials you find in the Genealogy Forum.

The Genealogy Forum NEWS

Each month, a dedicated group of staff members prepares the "Genealogy Forum NEWS"—the official newsletter of the forum. You can always expect to find something interesting here. The team sets a theme for each month of the year. A typical month's newsletter will include articles written by staff members and members, a list of interesting new Internet sites, a list of staff milestones (birthdays and anniversaries within the forum), announcements of upcoming special presentations or lectures in the chats, upcoming conference announcements and a variety of special interest stories.

The "Genealogy Forum News" is normally posted on the first day of the month, and you will see it on the Feature Button. There is something available for everyone each month. You can learn more about the NEWS in the chapter entitled **The Genealogy Columns**.

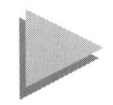

DearMYRTLE Daily Column

One of the most widely-read genealogy columns in the U.S. is written by DearMYRTLE. MYRTLE is a dynamic and prolific writer, and a long-time genealogy expert. She writes a daily genealogy column five days a week that is published in the Genealogy Forum. It is full of great information, and is written in an easy-to-understand manner.

In DearMYRTLE's area, you will find collections of articles, genealogy lessons and a wide variety of other materials that can enhance your genealogy experience.

For more information about DearMYRTLE's area, please refer to the chapter entitled **The Genealogy Columns**.

"Along Those Lines..." Column

"Along Those Lines..." is another regular column in the Genealogy Forum. [This column is written by the author of this book and is posted each Friday morning in the Genealogy Forum. It is also cross-posted at the Ancestry Web site (http://www.ancestry.com).] The column's weekly articles discuss genealogical research topics and provide insights based on personal experience. In addition, announcements of conferences and events are included so that you can locate educational opportunities close to where you might live.

For more information about "Along Those Lines..." and its area in the Genealogy Forum, please refer to the chapter, **The Genealogy Columns**.

Genealogy Conferences and Events

There is no better place than a genealogy conference or lecture to learn the right way to conduct your research. Not only will you hear good speakers, but you will also meet other genealogists. NEVER miss an opportunity to exchange information and share techniques with other genealogists. Many of these events also allow vendors to exhibit and sell their materials. This is a great opportunity to review and purchase books, CD-ROMs, software, forms and other genealogical supplies.

The "Conferences and Events Schedule" shows up in a number of places in the Genealogy Forum. When you click on this area, you will be presented with the screen shown in Figure 3.6. The conferences are listed in chronological sequence and include the name of the event and the city where they will be held. Browse down the list to look for events and places close to you. (If the "More" button is not grayed out, there are more events available. Click on the "More" button until it turns gray to ensure that you have seen all the listed events.)

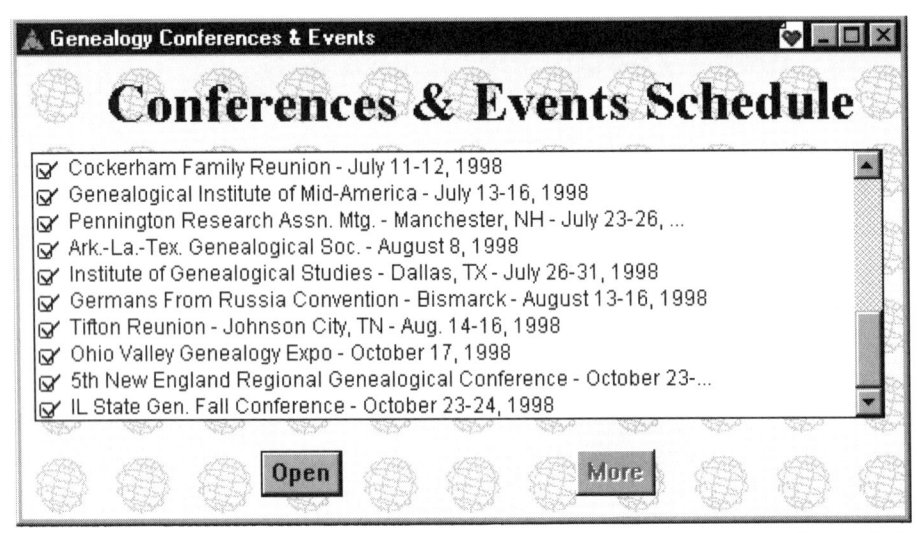

Figure 3.6

When you find an event that you'd like to learn more about, either double-click on the event with your mouse or highlight the item and press Enter.

Each event will contain information submitted by a representative of the organization(s) sponsoring the event. Often, you will see a blue, underlined hyperlink within the body of the text. By clicking on the hyperlink, you will be taken to another site. Sometimes this site may be a Web page for the organization(s). Other times, the link may open an E-mail form that you can use to send a request for a registration packet or for more information.

The Genealogy Forum does not endorse any of these events; it merely accepts the sponsors' advertisements. The forum also welcomes the opportunity to share this information with AOL members because it believes that genealogical education will make you a better, more effective researcher.

Genealogy Classes

If you're interested in taking a series of genealogy classes from one of the forum's most knowledgeable staff members, this is something you should investigate. The forum's own GFA Terry is a director at one of the LDS Family History Centers. She is an expert in research techniques and in the types of records that you can use to trace your family's genealogy.

Her course is conducted on AOL over four successive Monday evenings, and covers the extensive resources available in and through the Family History Centers. There is a nominal fee for this course.

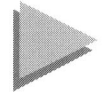

▶ The Advertisement Box

In the lower right-hand box on the Genealogy Forum's main screen is the advertisement box. Here, you will see ads from quality companies that provide genealogical materials, ranging from books and CD-ROMs to forms and online databases.

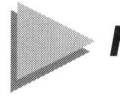

▶ Keyword

Finally, on the Genealogy Forum's main screen is its Keyword: **roots**. Whenever you want to come to the forum, simply go to the top center of the AOL screen, type **roots** and press the "Go" button. Better yet, click on the red heart at the top right-hand corner of the Genealogy Forum's main screen and add the forum to your Favorite Places folder.

Now that we've made the grand tour of the main screen, and you know what everything is in a general kind of way, let's explore each area individually. While chapters have been arranged in a sequence that helps you build on the previous chapters' materials, please feel free to skip around. Just be sure to refer to chapters mentioned as suggested reading for more details about new concepts or items you don't understand.

Let's go!

4 ▶ The Beginners' Center: Beginners Start Here

PERHAPS, WHEN YOU STARTED WORKING ON YOUR FAMILY TREE, THERE WAS NOBODY AVAILABLE TO GUIDE YOU. If you were like me, you may have started with a family Bible, a pad of paper, a pencil and some general idea of the family tree structure. And, if you were like me, you made mistakes because there was nobody available to answer your questions.

Fortunately, the Genealogy Forum is there to start you off in the right direction. The **Beginners' Center** provides a tremendous amount of material to get the beginning genealogist or family historian started. It's a place where you can learn basic research techniques, as well as a place you can return to again and again as you embark in new directions on your genealogy adventure.

When you're in the Genealogy Forum's main screen, click on the Beginners button. You'll be presented with a screen entitled, "Genealogy Quick Start Guide." This is your first introduction to the extensive resources available in the Genealogy Forum. Take a few minutes to read about "Search By Topic," "Surname Message Boards," "File Libraries Center," and "Special Centers Provide Additional Resources."

At the bottom of the Quick Start Guide are two small graphics. You'll find that these are buttons you can click on that will take you to other areas of the forum. These are common throughout the Genealogy Forum.

The first of the two buttons is labeled, "Introduce Yourself!" Here, you can post a message to introduce yourself to other members who use the Genealogy Forum. You can tell them what areas of the country or the world that you're researching, the surnames you're tracing and any other information you'd like to share. GFA Terry, one of the members of the forum's senior staff, and manager of the Genealogy Forum's message boards, will send you a welcome message with more information about how to use many of the forum's resources.

The second button is labeled, "Beginners' Center." This button is your gateway to the vast compilation of beginning genealogy resources. When you click on this button, the screen shown in Figure 4.1 will be displayed.

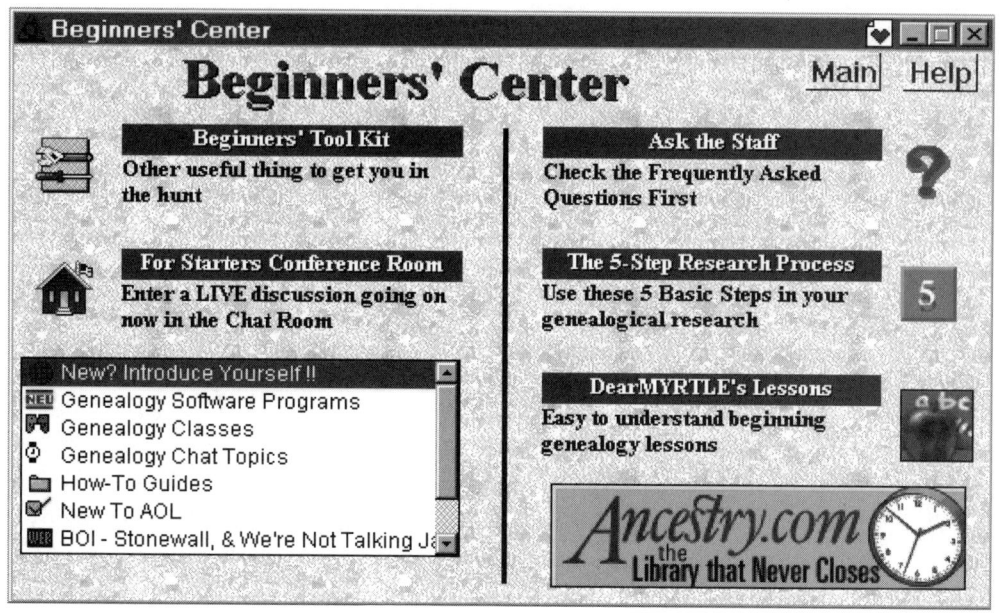

Figure 4.1

The Genealogy Forum on America Online — 55

The contents of the Beginners' Center screen can be said to be divided into two groups:

- There are five main topic areas with buttons accompanied by descriptive text. These contain collections of materials that are of a similar nature. We'll discuss each of these collections in detail.
- In the lower left corner is what is called a listbox. Here are additional important items that did not fit into the categories represented by the buttons on the screen. We'll discuss each of these in detail.

In addition, you will see buttons in the upper right corner labeled, "Main" and "Help." Clicking on Main will take you to the Family area of America Online; Help will take you to the AOL Help facility. Also, in the lower right corner of the screen, you will see a button representing one of the forum's advertisers. Clicking on the button will take you to the Web site for the advertiser or to another area on AOL where you can learn about that advertiser's products or services.

Let's now start our discussion of the Beginners' Center content with the buttons on the screen.

▶ FAQ/Ask the Staff

This area contains Frequently Asked Questions, or FAQs. There are a variety of topics introduced here, including:

- How do I download files?
- How do I upload files?
- Will the Genealogy Forum staff do research for me?
- Can I hire someone online to do research for me?
- Are the Mormon records available online?

Other topics are added over time as new questions arise.

If *you* have a question you'd like to ask the staff, there's an "Ask the Staff" option available as well. Here, simply fill in the box with your question and press the send button. Your message will be sent to members of the forum's senior staff. GFA Terry is usually the person who will send a response back to you via E-mail, and she will do so as quickly as possible. The E-mail includes information about scheduled chats available for your area of interest, message boards where you can post and share information of others and areas in the forum where you can find specific information. If there's something you're looking for and cannot find in the Genealogy Forum, be sure to use the "Ask the Staff" feature.

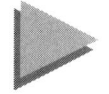

▶ *The 5-Step Research Process*

For a new genealogist, one of the most difficult tasks to undertake is understanding how to approach research. Locating the records that place an ancestor in a certain place at a particular point in time can be difficult, and attempting to substantiate dates and accuracy of content can seem a monumental task.

The 5-Step Research Process provides a terrific model for structuring your genealogical research. It represents a cycle that you will repeat again and again. There are articles available in the collection that address each of the following questions:

> What Do I Already Know?
> What Specific Question Needs to Be Answered?
> What Records Might Answer My Question?
> What Do The Records Actually Tell Me?
> What Conclusions Can I Reach Now?

You'll find detailed descriptions of each of these five steps and suggestions on how to make the best use of the process. Every beginning genealogist should understand and use this process.

Sometimes, when you come across a stumbling block, it helps to review the 5-Step Research Process. The process can prompt you to review or re-review material and look at it from another perspective.

▶ DearMYRTLE's Beginner Lessons

One of the best known, knowledgeable and prolific genealogists today is DearMYRTLE. MYRTLE is know nationwide as a kind and down-to-earth researcher. She has produced prodigious amounts of information in the Genealogy Forum for several years. You will find many of her articles sprinkled throughout the forum.

One of DearMYRTLE's more noteworthy areas is her compilation of genealogy lessons for beginners. Nowhere else will you find such a set of easy-to-read and easy-to-apply information.

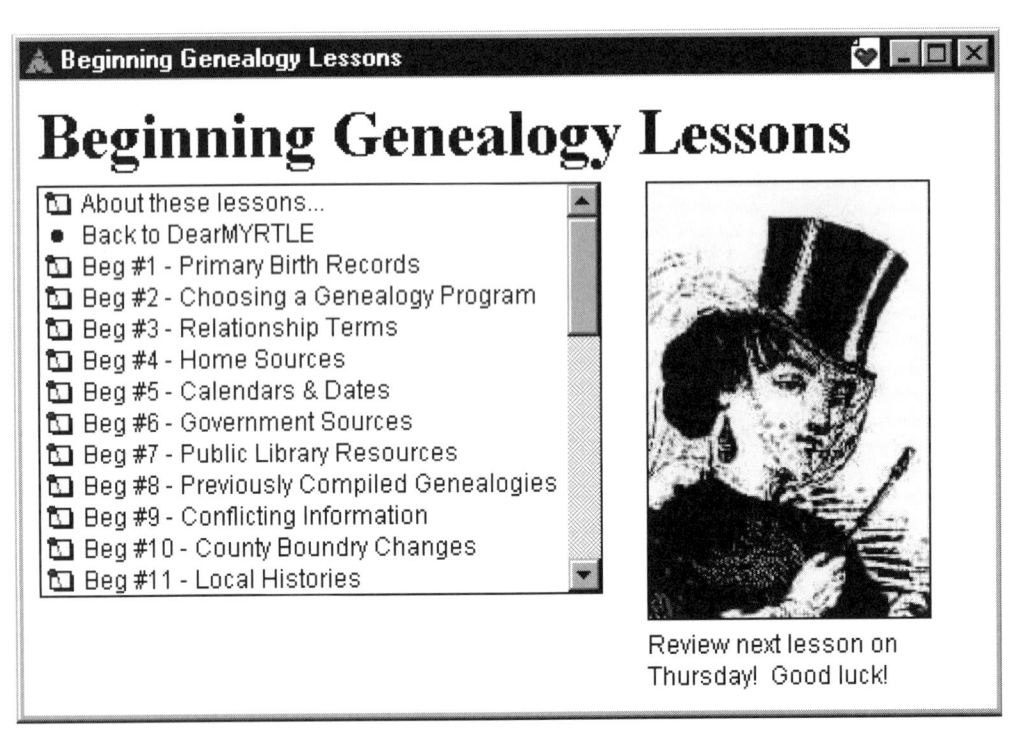

Figure 4.2

MYRT's writing style is easily accessible by genealogists of all ages. She will teach you the basics of research techniques, proper use of some research facilities, complete evaluation of materials and organization of the documents, photographs and other materials you collect.

To access the Beginning Genealogy Lessons, click on the Beginners' Center button labeled "DearMYRTLE's Lessons." The screen shown in Figure 4.2 will be displayed.

You may choose to proceed through these lessons in numeric sequence, but this is not required. You can just as easily read one lesson and skip to another somewhere else. Read whatever is most appropriate for you at the moment. What's important, though, is that you invest some time in familiarizing yourself with the content. DearMYRTLE is a most knowledgeable instructor, and she can be your personal mentor through the use of these lessons.

Beginners' Tool Kit

The Beginners' Tool Kit contains a massive variety of important resources you can use as you work on your genealogy. To access this area, click on the fourth button on the screen, labeled "Beginners' Tool Kit." You will be presented with the screen shown in Figure 4.3.

This area contains:

- **How-To Guides** — This is a large collection of miscellaneous materials available to help you either learn genealogical research techniques or connect you to other areas where you can gather more information. Compiled by DearMYRTLE, there are reference materials available throughout the Genealogy Forum and throughout the Internet. These also include a broad selection of genealogy courses available through the Internet.

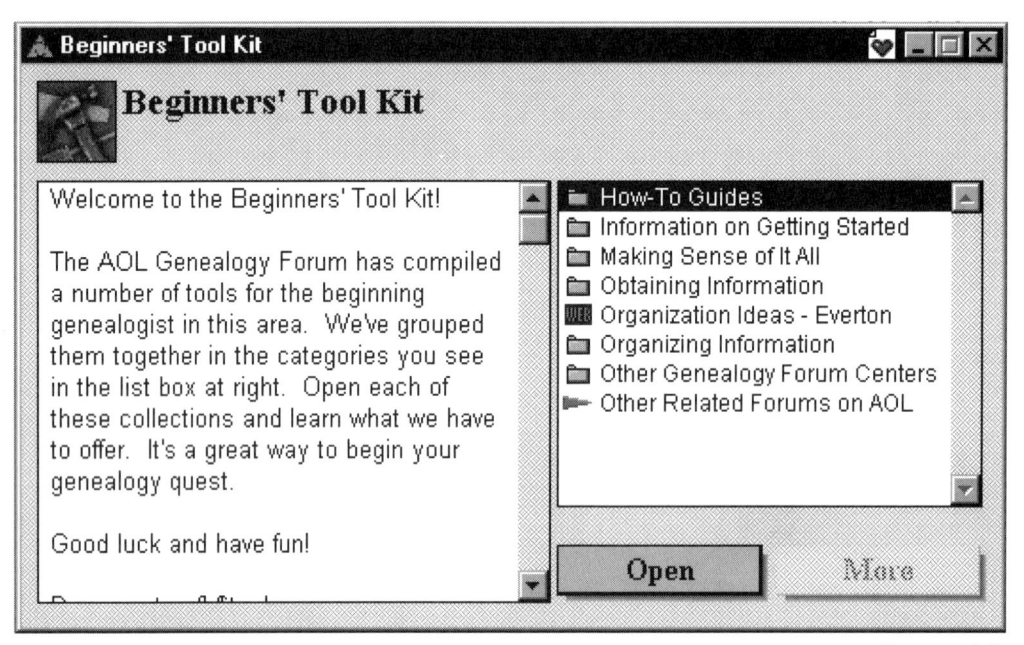

Figure 4.3

- **Information on Getting Started** — This collection contains a series of articles about getting started with research, in the Genealogy Forum and elsewhere. One article, "Avoiding Grief in Your Research," outlines 20 common pitfalls that the beginning genealogist will want to avoid. Another, "Naming Trends," provides insight into how parents named their children at different times in history. This can be important when tracing ancestors because it often can help you identify children and their place in the sequence of births in the same family.
- **Making Sense of It All** — This collection contains three very helpful resources:
  - **Days, Dates and Months** — This article contains a translation table of days of the week and months in English, German, Czech, Norwegian, Welsh and French. It also addresses the double-date calendar system that confuses so many genealogists. (The new calendar took effect 2 September 1752.)

- **Relationship Terms** — This article covers some common relationship terms and interpretations of their meanings.
- **Cousins Chart** — Do you know who your mother's second cousins twice removed are? You can download a file from the Genealogy Forum's file libraries that, when opened, will help you answer that question. These cousin relationships are often confounding, but this file can help you get through them.

- **Obtaining Information** — This collection contains guidance on how to locate and obtain copies of information. Included are:
  - **Some Possible Sources** — This article lists many types of information and alternative sources.
  - **Sample Letter of Request** — This is a sample of a letter you can use to request copies of vital records, photocopies and other materials. (You never know how far a well-written, courteous letter will get you!)
  - **Family Folklore Questionnaire** — Often, you may find it useful to obtain information from many people at the same time. In some cases, a questionnaire is a good vehicle. The link here allows you to download a questionnaire file from the Genealogy Forum's file library. You will want to customize this questionnaire for specific use with your family research.
  - **Records Cross Reference** —This is a link to the Internet's World Wide Web. This Web site describes the type of information you may wish to locate, where to check first and where to check next if you have no luck with your original search. You'll find that you'll return to this list again and again over the years.
- **Organization Ideas** — This is a link to Everton's site on

the Web, where they address pedigree charts, family group sheets and individual data sheets, as well as how you might want to organize your notes.
- **Organizing Information** — This collection is an important one, consisting of several sub-collections.
  - We all know how difficult it is to get organized and stay that way. The key to being able to review, assess and corroborate the information you've accumulated lies in being able to lay your hands on a record at a moment's notice. There's no enjoyment in research if you have to fight to locate materials. In this collection, you will find DearMYRTLE's **Finally Getting Organized Lessons**. These lessons provide a month-by-month approach that will help you organize that morass of material piled on the floor or stuffed in boxes. Follow her lead, and you'll have that mess organized in short order.
  - If you're tired of manually filling out and maintaining pedigree charts, family group sheets and other forms, it's time you considered computerizing your materials. In this area, you will find another collection to help you evaluate and select a genealogy software program (GSP). **Choosing a Genealogy Program** provides an overview of GSPs, describes four steps to selecting the right GSP for you and provides some descriptions and reviews of popular GSPs. This is a great place to learn more about what software is available and what features you should look for to suit your research style and needs.
  - Many of our ancestors kept journals or diaries. These treasured volumes tell us much about the political and physical climates in which they lived, their likes and dislikes, their joys, their problems. In this hurried era of computers and split-second communications, few take the time to keep a written account of our lives. But what a treasure

such records would be for our descendants! Another article in this area provides information about **Keeping a Journal**.
- Finally, you may be considering writing your family's history. This area also contains a short article, entitled **Compiling a Family History**. Perhaps this article will pique your interest and give you some ideas about how to lay out your own family's history.
- **Other Genealogy Forum Centers** — You can link to other areas of the forum from this collection without going all the way back to the main screen.
- **Other Related Forums on AOL** — This area contains links to other forums on AOL that may help you with your research. Please see the chapter entitled **Other Helpful Areas of AOL** for a discussion of what other areas on AOL can supplement the Genealogy Forum and help in your research.

For Starters Conference Room

Some of the most popular features of the Genealogy Forum are the scheduled chats. As mentioned in the previous chapter, the Genealogy Forum offers more than 170 regularly scheduled chats each week. Beginning Chats are offered every night of the week. These chats offer a venue where you can ask questions of knowledgeable hosts—forum staff and volunteers whose experience and expertise are available. In addition, other members can provide helpful information as a result of research they have conducted.

We will discuss the chats in detail in the chapter about the **Chat Center**. In the meantime, while you are in the Beginners' Center and looking at the button for the conference room, let's talk a little about it.

To check the schedule of all the Genealogy Forum chats—

Beginners and others—click on the item labeled **Genealogy Chat Topics** in the listbox in the lower left quadrant of the Beginners' Center screen. (Give it a few seconds to finish loading. It's a large list.)

Review the schedule for the topics that may interest you and for the times that are convenient for you. When you are ready to attend a Beginner's Chat, go to the For Starters Conference Room. You can access that room in one of three ways:

1. Come to the Beginners' Center and click on the **For Starters Conference Room** button.
2. Go to the **Chat Center** and click on the **For Starters Conference Room** button.
3. Review the **Chat Schedule** document and click on the blue, underscored hyperlink that reads "For Starters Conference Room," near the top of the schedule.

For complete information about chats, please see the chapter about the **Chat Center** later in this book.

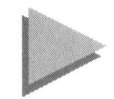

Contents in the Listbox

In the lower left quadrant of the Beginners' Center screen is the listbox. Here, you will find some materials already discussed, as well as some new items. You will find that a number of the most popular items in the forum are listed in multiple places. Many of these features have applicable information that you can use in different areas. The intent is to make them easily accessible in places where you may need them.

The listbox contains the following items:

- **New – Introduce Yourself** — You will remember this from earlier in the chapter. By double-clicking your mouse on this item, you have the opportunity to introduce yourself to other forum users. (You want as much exposure for yourself and the surnames you are researching as possible.) And, as an added benefit, GFA Terry will send you the informative E-mail discussed earlier.

- **Choosing a Genealogy Program** — This informative collection was discussed earlier in this chapter in the **Beginners' Tool Kit** area, under **How-To Guides**.
- **Genealogy Classes** — Discussed in the chapter about **The Main Screen**, this item takes you to one of the classes taught through the AOL feature, Courses Online (Keyword: **courses**). GFA Terry, under her alter-ego and screen name of Prof Terry, teaches a four-week class about genealogy research at the LDS Family History Centers.
- **Genealogy Chat Topics** — Here, you will find the schedule for every chat that meets in the Genealogy Forum throughout the week. For more detailed information about chats in the Genealogy Forum, please read the chapter about the **Chat Center**.
- **How-To Guides** — This area was discussed earlier in this chapter, and is also found under the **Beginners' Tool Kit** button. It's full of great information about how to get started, how to get the most out of your research, and where you can obtain general instruction.
- **New to AOL** — When you double-click on this item, the screen shown in Figure 4.4 is displayed. This collection is full of terrific general information about the forum and some of its most-visited areas. If you are new to using, uploading, downloading and working with files, there is much good information available here. Of course, you will learn more about this when you read the chapter about the **File Libraries Center**.
- **No More Brick Walls** — The article listed here includes a hyperlink to a Web resource at http://www.firstct.com/fv/stone.html. Available there are suggestions for alternative research paths

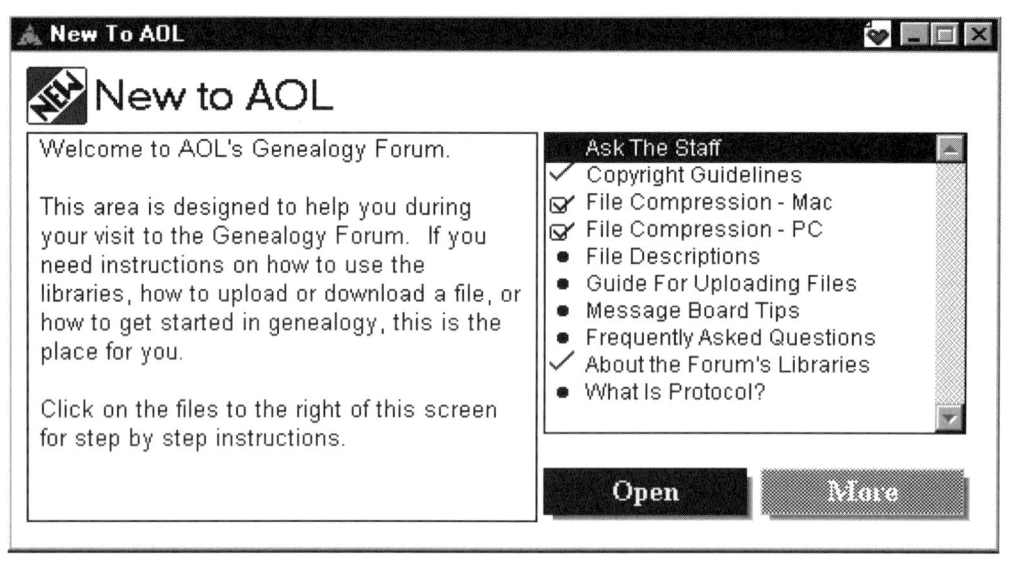

Figure 4.4

that you can take if you hit that "stone wall" or "dead end." Nothing is guaranteed, of course, but you should find some good ideas there.

- **Parents & Teachers** — If you want to help younger genealogists get a good start, you couldn't find a better place to begin! This collection is tailored to the younger set. It contains:

    - DearMYRTLE's Beginning Genealogy Lessons
    - Information and instructions for School Kids Genealogy Course Information
    - A wonderful Web-based resource to assist in interviewing and collecting oral history. (NOT just for kids!)
    - A collection of provocative E-mail messages from AOL member Somebody13 to DearMYRTLE, and her responses. (Somebody13 is a very active young member of the Genealogy Forum, and shows great promise as an up-and-coming professional genealogist!)

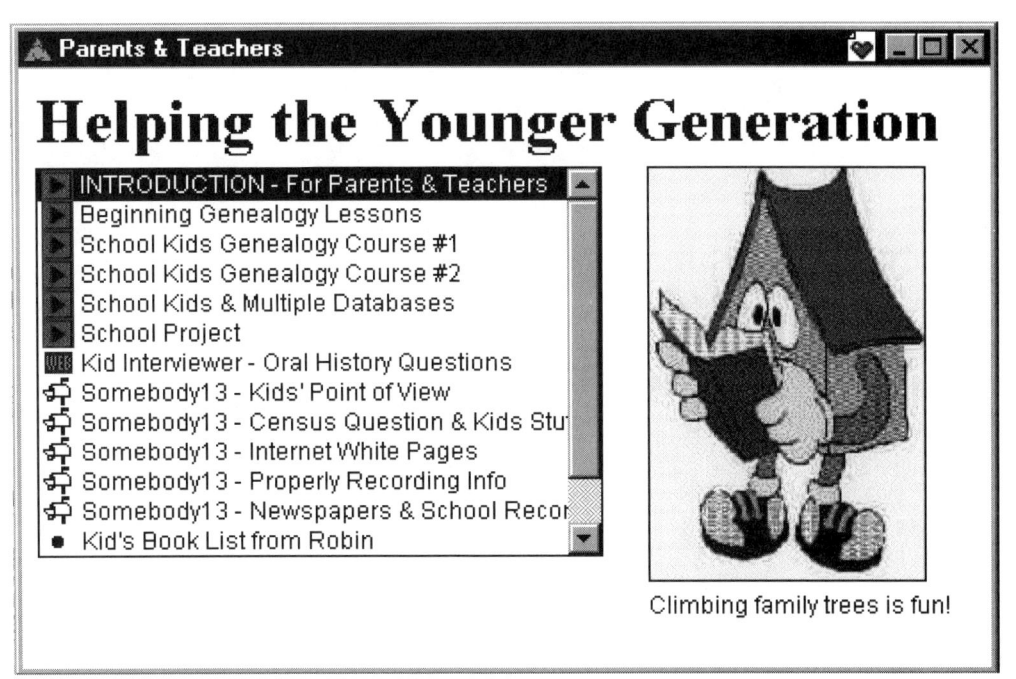

Figure 4.5

- Forum staff member GFA Robin has compiled a list of genealogy books for the younger readers. (Check with your local bookstore or your public library for a copy of "Books in Print" to determine the availability of these books.)
- Pedigree Trivia is another of the E-mail exchanges between Somebody13 and DearMYRTLE.
- The GEN-TEEN Mailing List is one of the E-mail subscription genealogy mailing lists available on the Internet. This article describes the list's content and how to subscribe. (For more detailed information about mailing lists and other Internet resources, please see the chapter about the **Internet Center**.)
- **Suggested Reading** — Genealogists and books are great friends. Not only are books necessary in the

research process, but they also provide excellent educational material about records and research methods. When you double-click on this item, you will see an article with a hyperlink to the National Genealogical Society's Web site. Available here is a list of books for purchase from the National Genealogical Society. However, you can also use this area as a suggested bibliography. It is, by no means, a complete list. A complete suggested reading list would include many more reference books, a list of periodicals and the suggestion that you contact the genealogical and historical societies in the states and localities you are researching. Most of these publish a newsletter or periodical with articles that can help place your ancestors and relatives into historical and geographical perspective.

Summary

Whew! There's a lot here in the Beginners' Center, isn't there? While you can't read and absorb everything at once, you should at least start by adding the Beginners' Center to your Favorite Places on AOL.

You will find that "the Beginners' Center" is something of a misnomer; genealogists of all skill levels use this area for education and reference. The Beginners' Center, coupled with **The Resource Center,** provides a complementary set of reference materials as you research your genealogy.

Make an appointment with yourself to come back to the Beginners' Center often for new information and techniques when you are starting a new area of research, or for a periodic review so that you keep on the right track.

Speaking of **The Resource Center,** let's make that our next stop.

5 ▶ The Resource Center

THE RESOURCE CENTER IS APTLY NAMED. It is an information hub in the Genealogy Forum that contains geographic, ethnic and reference resources, as well as a variety of other tools. The center has been geared towards intermediate and advanced genealogists. However, beginners can take advantage of the materials in the **Beginners' Center**, and then proceed directly into the Resource Center for more in-depth information.

To access this content rich area, simply click the Resources button on the Genealogy Forum's main screen. The screen shown in Figure 5.1 will be displayed. You will certainly want to click on the red heart in the upper right hand corner to bookmark this as one of your Favorite Places. You will find many areas within the Resource Center that you will bookmark as Favorite Places.

The contents of the Resource Center screen can be said to be divided into two groups:

- There are five main topic areas in the Resource Center with buttons and descriptive text. These

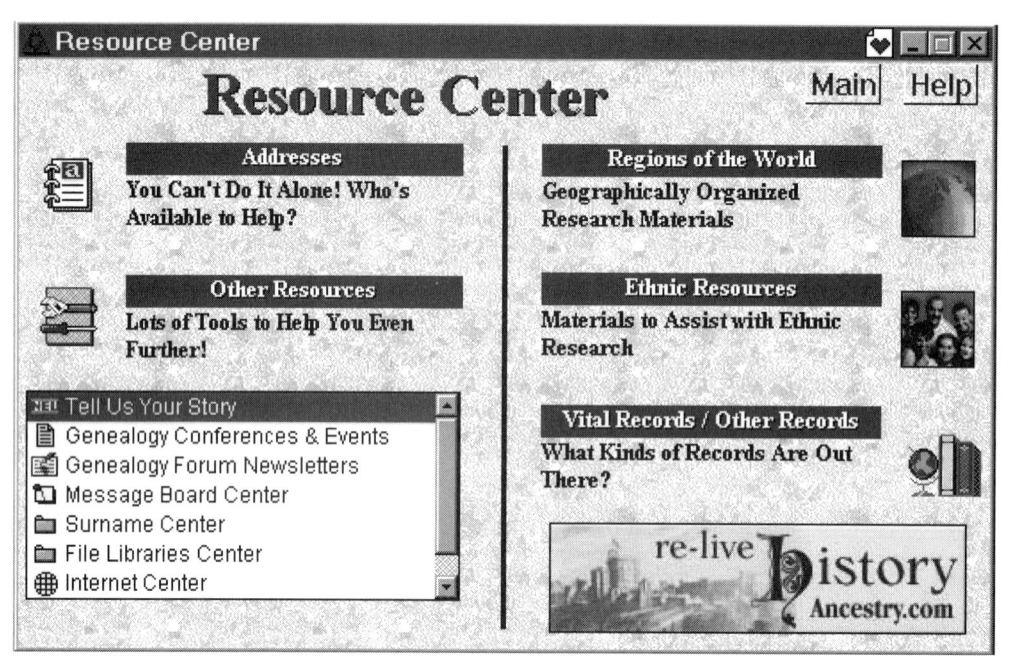

Figure 5.1

contain collections of materials that are of a similar nature. We'll discuss each of these collections in detail.

- The listbox in the lower left quadrant contains additional resources that do not fit into the button areas, as well as links to several of the other "centers'" in the Genealogy Forum.

Let's proceed with the buttons on the screen and their content first. We'll visit the items in the listbox later.

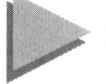

▶ Regions of the World

The Regions of the World is an impressive collection of materials, arranged geographically for your convenience, so that you can easily locate the area you are seeking.

The content of each area varies, depending on the interests of the Genealogy Forum members and the scope of AOL's connectivity. For instance, information about the United States, Canada and many areas of Europe is extensive. That is where most AOL genealogy members are located or where they are focusing their research. The South America, Asia, Africa and the Middle East, and Australia collections contain little or no material, either because member interest in those areas has been low or because there are few Genealogy Forum staff or volunteers with the knowledge or expertise about genealogy research in those areas. Best put, these areas are awaiting content, and there are plans to develop that content.

A great deal of the content in this area has been contributed by members and volunteers who have experience with particular geographic areas and who have a desire to see their material published online. (**NOTE:** If you are interested in contributing written articles for inclusion in any area of the Resource Center, please feel free to contact George Ferguson, leader of the Genealogy Forum, via E-mail at gflgeorge@aol.com.)

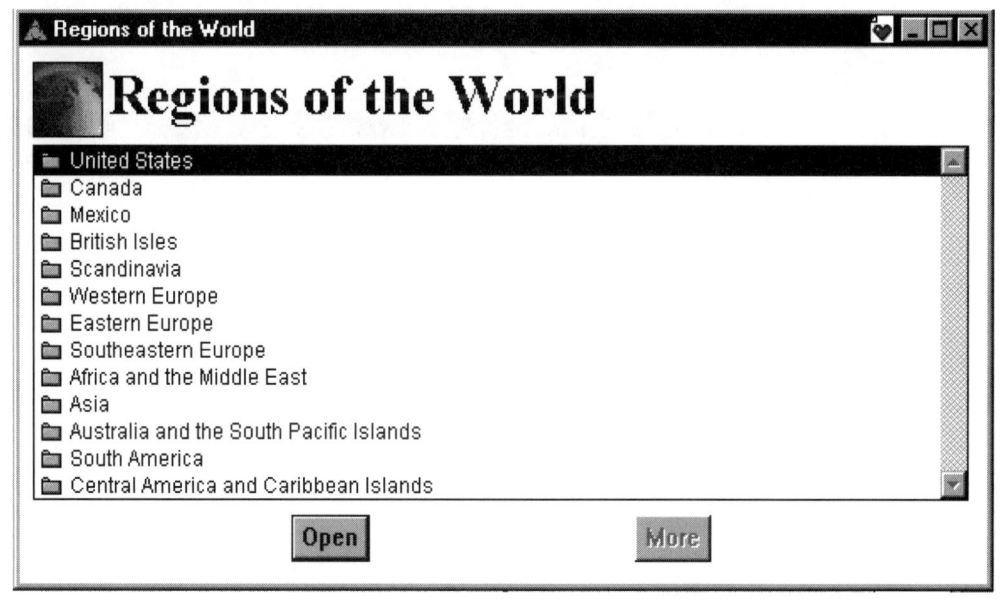

Figure 5.2

When you click on the Regions of the World button, the screen shown in Figure 5.2 will be displayed. As you can see, there are folders for all the major geographies available. Let's discuss each folder.

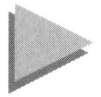

▶ *United States*

When you open the United States collection, the screen shown in Figure 5.3 is displayed. The collection contains, first of all, a current map of the United States. (You may also access maps of individual states by going to Keyword: **map**.) Maps are essential to genealogical research, and this one will help you locate the specific states through which your ancestors traveled and in which they settled. When you are researching a specific time period, please be certain that you use a map of the area *from that time*. You may otherwise waste time looking for records in a courthouse that did not exist or that did not have jurisdiction over an area at that point in history.

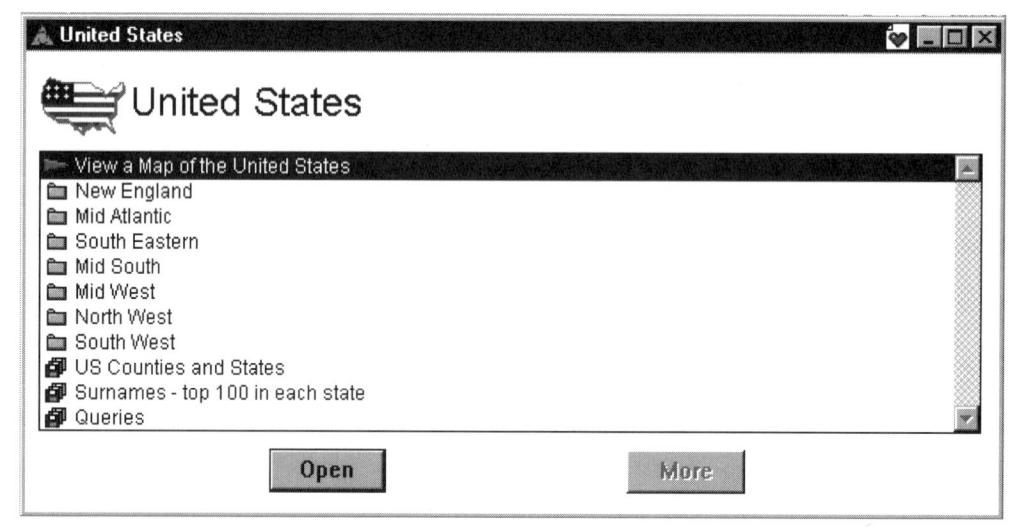

Figure 5.3

The next thing you see in this collection are folders for areas or regions of the United States. Each of these contains sub-folders for each state associated with that area. For example, when you

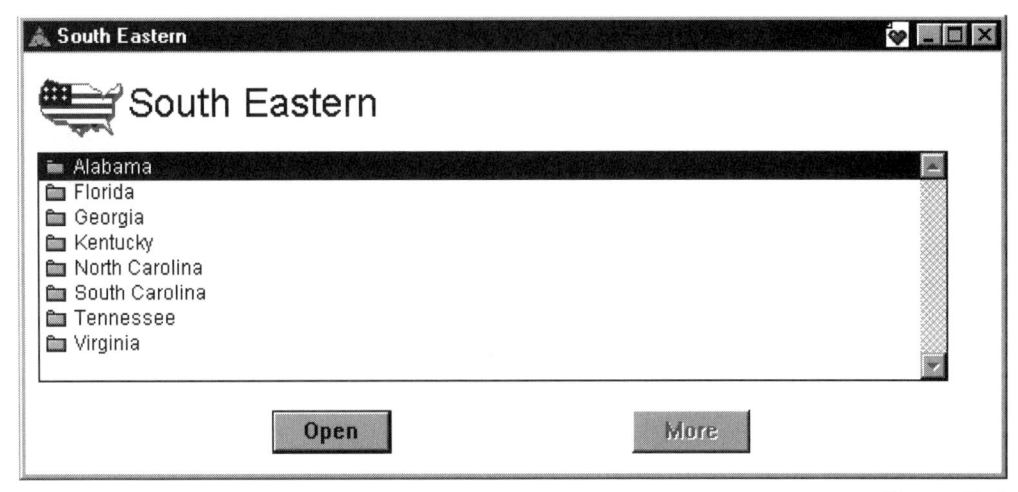

Figure 5.4

open the folder labeled "South Eastern," the screen shown in Figure 5.4 is displayed. It contains sub-folders for Alabama, Florida, Georgia, Kentucky, North Carolina, South Carolina, Tennessee and Virginia.

While the contents of each state's folder varies, the one for Georgia is representative of the type of content you might most often encounter. Figure 5.5 shows the types of information available. The mini-icons at the left of each entry tell you what to expect inside:

- The sheet of paper icon with the corner turned down is a single document.
- The file folder icon indicates there are a number of contents inside, including a collection of documents, files or more collections.
- The open book icon can represent a document containing a list or some other compendium of information.
- The pushpin icon indicates that that you can connect to the appropriate Message Board in the forum when you click it. (In this case, you would connect to the Georgia Message Board, where you can

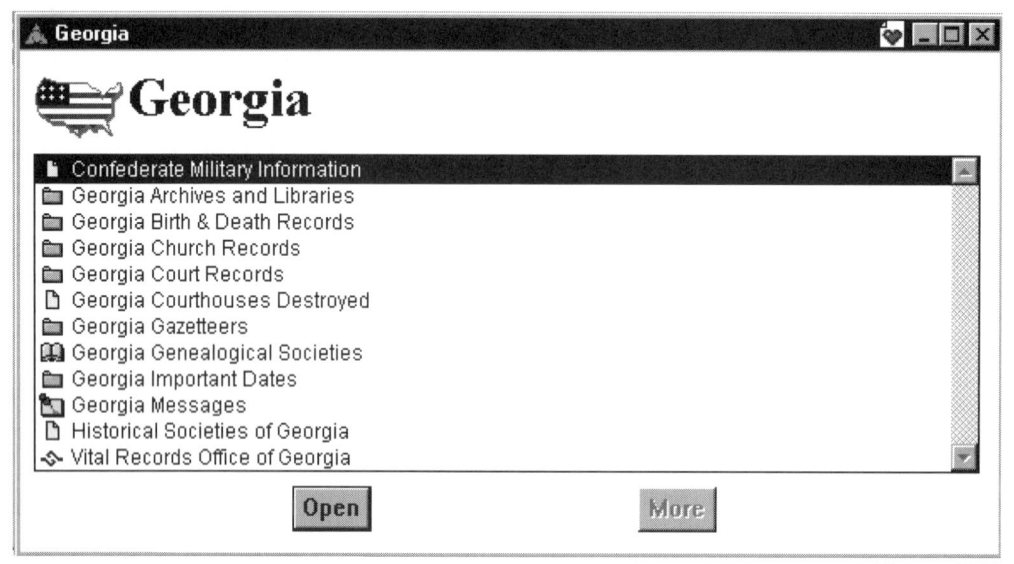

Figure 5.5

```
Georgia
  Confederate Military Information
  Georgia Archives and Libraries
  Georgia Birth & Death Records
  Georgia Church Records
  Georgia Court Records
  Georgia Courthouses Destroyed
  Georgia Gazetteers
  Georgia Genealogical Societies
  Georgia Important Dates
  Georgia Messages
  Historical Societies of Georgia
  Vital Records Office of Georgia
```

review messages posted by others who are researching in Georgia.)

- The diskette icon indicates that a file is available for download. (Clicking on one of these items will provide you with a description of the file, which you may review before deciding whether or not to download it.)

You may encounter miscellaneous mini-icons, but those listed above are the primary ones used in this area.

In the case of the Georgia collection, you will find:

- An extensive list of articles regarding Confederate Military Information
- A collection of addresses of important libraries and archives in Georgia
- A collection of the addresses in Atlanta, Savannah and Macon, to which you can write to obtain birth and death records for those cities
- A collection of addresses for obtaining the church

records of some denominations
- A collection of brief articles concerning the types of courts in Georgia and the types of records for which they were responsible
- An article listing 66 county courthouses in Georgia whose records were destroyed either partially or totally by fires, storms, tornadoes, etc.
- A collection of gazetteer books about Georgia towns
- A list of genealogical societies found in Georgia
- A list of historical societies found in Georgia
- A collection outlining important dates in Georgia history
- A link to the Georgia Message Board
- The address of Georgia's State vital records office

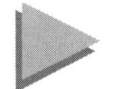

How Would I Use This Information?

Let's say you are researching your great-grandfather who was born in Gwinnett County, GA, on 22 December 1843. Your research to date has located him in the 1850 and 1860 censuses in Gwinnett County. You know that he served in the Confederate army, but you don't have details. You also know he married in Rome, GA, sometime in 1866, but you don't know the date of marriage or the maiden name of the bride. Your research of the 1870, 1880, 1900 and 1910 censuses indicate that he lived in Floyd County during those years. You know that the couple had ten children—five sons and five daughters. Your research also indicates that he died on 18 June 1931 in Rome, GA.

The information in the Genealogy Forum's collection about Georgia can help you in the following ways:

1. The article entitled "Confederate Military Information" provides a significant amount of information about the microfilm holdings at the

Georgia State Archives in Atlanta, GA. You might decide to research the possibility that there are military records available, and that microfilm of your great grandfather's Compiled Service Record might provide details about his parents' names, his dates of service, where he served and the rank he attained. Perhaps he or your great-grandmother applied for a Confederate pension, in which case there might be a microfilm record of the application.

2. Based on the information you found above, you would want to write to the Georgia State Archives. Their address can be found in the collection of libraries and archives.

3. Since you know that your great-grandparents were married in Rome, GA, in 1866, your research to date has found that Rome was (and still is) in Floyd County. A check of the list of courthouses whose records may have been destroyed by fire would indicate that Floyd County is not on that list. This tells you that you might want to write a letter to the Floyd County Courthouse and ask them to search for a marriage record. (A preliminary telephone call is advisable, to help you determine whether they have the necessary records, as well as to check on the cost of the search.)

4. Perhaps you are interested in determining if the local genealogical or historical society in the Rome area has information available about your ancestor. By checking the lists of genealogical and historical societies, you can determine that there is the Northwest Georgia Genealogical Society in Rome. A letter of inquiry to them would be a good idea. (Remember to include an SASE to encourage prompt response.)

5. Your great-grandparents had ten children. If you want to learn more about those family lines, a great way to test the waters would be to post a message on the Georgia Message Board. Be as specific as possible about the surname(s) and area(s) you are researching.

Who knows? You might make a match!

6. You know your great-grandfather died in 1931. The State of Georgia probably maintains a central repository of vital records for that time period. By contacting the address indicated in the article, "Vital Records Office of Georgia," you may be able to obtain a death certificate for your great-grandfather. The death certificate may contain his parents' names and other information.

Each of the items listed above could provide you with that missing link that you need to carry your research one more step ahead. You will find similar collections of materials for all 50 states.

Canada

Canadian genealogists have been extremely active too. The Genealogy Forum's GFS Chuck has been instrumental in coordinating the forum's Canadian chats and in the development of the Canada area.

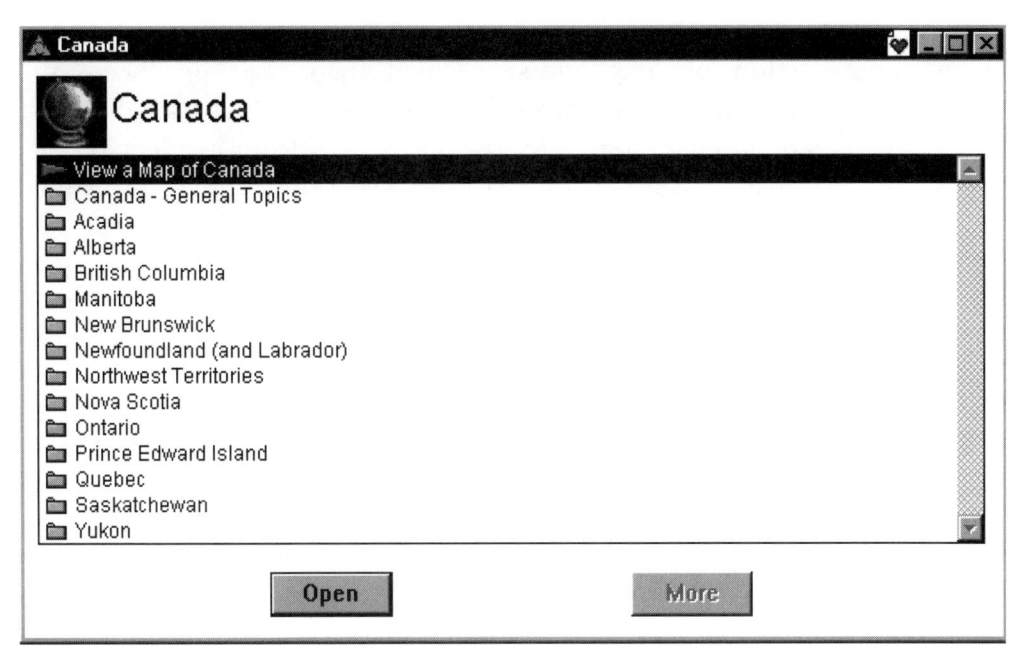

Figure 5.6

When you open the collection of information about Canada, the screen shown in Figure 5.6 is displayed. At the top of the list is a link to a full map of Canada. If you are not familiar with Canadian geography, this would be a great place to start. (You will find even more detailed maps of the provinces in their individual collections.)

The next item in this collection is called **Canada - General Topics**. This item represents a wide-ranging group of materials. Many of the available items are files containing the logs of lectures. These range from talks about the Huguenots, Scottish & Irish and Native Canadians, to discussions of Canadian cemeteries, to solutions to problems dealing with French Canadian translations. If you're looking for a great collection of Canadian Web sites, this is the place to start!

There is a huge collection of Canada Internet links available here for you to browse. They include genealogical and historical societies, census sites, libraries, government sites, and some important Canadian family sites as well.

Another important component of the Canadian area is its collection of newsletters. Team Canada has produced an online newsletter for all those interested tracing their Canadian roots. The newsletter is sent out regularly to inform readers of all of the Canadian Special Interest Group (SIG) meetings, also called chats, in the AOL Genealogy Forum. There are many interesting articles available, as well as a number of queries. All of the newsletters are in the form of easily downloadable text files, and each one has been virus-checked. Once you've downloaded a newsletter file, you can read it in any word processing application.

Within the General Topics area is available an extensive collection of material about Loyalist Canadian resources. This area, too, contains articles and another impressive collection of Web links.

The remainder of the Canadian collection is composed of intensive compilations of information about the regions of Canada.

Since the Canadian collection is so extensive, let's look at each area. (Please note that special, informal "drop-in" chat rooms are included in each of the Canada sub-collections. These take place in addition to the regularly scheduled chats discussed in the chapter about the **Chat Center**. Please be sure to read that chapter for complete information about online chats.)

Acadia — The next area is Acadia, a region of the northeastern North American continent that was a French colony until it was ceded to the British in 1713. The area then included what is now Nova Scotia, New Brunswick, Prince Edward Island, and a part of Maine. Included in the Acadia collection is an impressive set of Acadian-Cajun Web links that can take you far in your research of the people and times of Acadia. There are available several general files, as well as a small collection of Acadian Chat newsletters. More important, though, are links to the following two resources:

1. The Cajun/Acadian Message Board — Here you can read and post messages about surnames and places you are researching, as well as exchange information with other members. (Read the chapter about the **Message Board Center** to learn more about reading and posting messages.)
2. The Acadian/Cajun Chat Room — This is an area open 24 hours a day, seven days a week for you to drop in and chat with others researching Acadian and Cajun genealogy. (Read the chapter about the **Chat Center** for a full discussion of chats in the Genealogy Forum.) Since this is an unhosted chat, you are on your own to discuss any topic of interest to you and other members who choose to drop in.

Alberta — The province of Alberta is represented with a map and a set of Web links. As with Acadia, there are available links to the Alberta Message Board and the Alberta Chat Room.

British Columbia — The western-most province of British Columbia is represented with a map. The collection of Web links here contains many sites dealing with vital statistics, birth certificates, marriage licenses, death certificates, the British Columbia Wills Registry, libraries, archives, museums, genealogical and historical societies, town history sites, as well as ethnic and family resources. Links to the British Columbia Message Board and British Columbia chat room are here as well.

Manitoba — Again, you will find a province map here, as well as another collection of Web links. This group focuses on genealogical and historical resources, and includes a number of Web sites relating to the Hudson Bay Company. Other Web links to sites about the Mennonites in Manitoba will help you locate related resources and information about the contributions made by this group. There also are available links to the Manitoba Message Board and the Manitoba chat room.

New Brunswick — New Brunswick is represented on a map of the Maritime Provinces. The collection of Web sites here is impressive, containing information about every county, many of the archives and a substantial group of Web pages for various surnames. A collection of some of the Genealogy Forum's New Brunswick chat group newsletters is also included. Links also are provided to the New Brunswick Message Board and the New Brunswick chat room.

Newfoundland and Labrador — These two areas are shown together on the map included in this area. This collection contains a great deal of material, including:

- Files concerning historical timelines of the Atlantic area from 500 to 1199 A.D.
- A file regarding the Newfoundland Archives
- A file containing a list of publications about Newfoundland to help the researcher
- A file of other Newfoundland resources

- A collection of articles recollecting life in Newfoundland
- A small collection of newsletters regarding the Newfoundland chats in the Genealogy Forum
- Newfoundland and Labrador Web links (a good, balanced collection of links for both areas)
- A link to the Newfoundland Message Board
- A link to the Newfoundland chat room

Northwest Territories — This collection focuses on both the Yukon and the Northwest Territories. Contents include a modest collection of Web sites and a link to the Yukon and Northwest Territories Message Board.

Nova Scotia — Nova Scotia is represented on the map of the Maritime Provinces, but there is much more to this collection. The Web site collection here contains links to genealogical society sites, historical sites, sites related to vital records, and links to census reference resources. In addition, county Web sites are plentiful, as are library archives and museums. There are available even links to sites containing ships' passenger list references.

If you are researching specific surnames in Nova Scotia, you will definitely want to focus on the two articles available here containing literally hundreds of surnames and the Web sites associated with them.

Links to the Nova Scotia Message Board and the Nova Scotia chat room are also included in this impressive area.

Ontario — The province of Ontario is represented with its own map. Several files containing detailed resources are included in this collection. You may download any of the following:

- 1871 Ontario Census Index
- Name List Canada — Various name lists from Lanark Co. and Village Ontario, Canada, to the Church List, the Militia 1871 list, and the Voter List 1875

The Genealogy Forum on America Online — 81

- Ontario Archives Resources
- Ontario Land Records

The collection of Web links for Ontario is extensive, with well over 100 URLs listed. Links to the Ontario Message Board and the Ontario chat room are also included in this area.

Prince Edward Island — The province of Prince Edward Island is situated in the Gulf of St. Lawrence, and is represented on the map of the Maritime Provinces. There is much to be learned by browsing through the collection of Web sites here. You will find a wealth of genealogy society, library and archive sites here. There is even a site called "1768 and 1798 Island of St. John Heads of Household Censuses" that may offer help to those researching 18th century Prince Edward Islanders.

A collection of chat notes is included in this area that recaps some of the more notable of the scheduled chats in the past. Links are provided, as usual, to the Prince Edward Island Message Board and to the Prince Edward Island chat room.

Quebec — The French-speaking province of Quebec lies between Ontario and Labrador, to the north of Maine and faces two major bodies of water. In the collection of Web sites available here, you will find great Internet resources in English and/or French. With well over 100 Web sites listed, this site represents yet another impressive collection of Internet links.

Also in the Quebec area is a collection of lineage files. These include the family sheets of John Norway, James Achilles, John White, Eleazar Calkins, Edward A. Pearson, Thomas Judd, the Fritch family (in both Canada and the U.S.), and James R. Fuller. Perhaps one of these is your ancestor?

In addition, links to the Quebec Message Board and the Quebec chat room are included.

Saskatchewan — Located in the center of Canada, between Alberta and Manitoba, is the province of Saskatchewan. A map of the province is included here, as is a modest but authoritative collection of Web links. Again, here you will find links to the Saskatchewan Message Board and the Saskatchewan chat room.

Yukon — Finally, the Yukon and Northwest Territories are listed. This is essentially the same collection as discussed in the **Northwest Territories** section above. The Genealogy Forum has included the area under both listings, as resources are shared.

Mexico

The Genealogy Forum's GFS Mike has been instrumental in coordinating much of the Hispanic genealogy development in the forum. The Mexican area, like the Canadian area, is another example of great content development by an entire team.

Not only is there a map of Mexico available in the collection, but there is also available a link to a tremendous Web page, "The Hispanic Genealogy Address Book." A work obviously always under development, here you will find great resources to national and state archives, directories, literature, and a collection of civil registries by state. (Addresses, hours, telephone numbers and fees for copies of vital records are included.)

If you are researching genealogy in Mexico, this is a wonderful resource. If you have additional material to recommend to GFS Mike for inclusion on the site, please contact him by E-mail from the Web page.

British Isles

The Genealogy Forum's collection of British Isles resources provides a good starting point for the researcher. The collection opens with a map of the area, and then contains folders of materials about England, Ireland, Scotland and Wales.

England — The collection of English resources in the Genealogy Forum is small, but contains some good material. (This area is being redesigned, and additional materials are being developed.)

The article entitled "English Research" represents an authoritative discussion about locating your ancestors in specific time frames. Discussed in the article are document types such as "Feet of Fines," "Lay Subsidies" and "Inquisition Post Mortems." You probably have never heard of these but, if you are researching an ancestor prior to 1538, you must investigate the possibility that they may be of some relevance to your ancestral past. More traditional records, such as the more recent census and probate files, are also available.

Anyone researching their ancestors in England knows that church records play an important role in locating ancestors and documenting events in their lives. Another article entitled "English and Welsh Parish Registers," lists a number of books about locating and reading church records.

If you think your ancestor may have been of noble birth, you may be interested in heraldry. Another article, "Heraldry Resources & Guides," contains addresses of the foremost authorities on the subject of heraldry and coats of arms, and lists a number of good reference books on the subject.

If you are working on your English genealogy, these articles provide a starting point that can be supplemented with materials from the **File Libraries Center.**

Ireland — The Irish collection contains much more material, perhaps because family is such an integral part of Irish culture. Genealogy and lines of descent are certainly the topic of much discussion here. For a quick look at Irish History, try downloading and reviewing the file called "Irish History."

Inasmuch as language is a significant part of the Irish culture, it is appropriate that the first article in the collection concerns ancient Irish proper names. For instance, did you know that the name "Eoghan" was translated as "a young man" or "youthful warrior" in ancient Ireland? (The Anglicized versions of the name are Eugene or Owen.) Another entry in the collection is called "Irish Language (Gaelic)." This is a downloadable file containing lots of information about the language of the "Emerald Isle."

If you are interested in hiring a professional genealogist in Ireland to research your ancestry, the list of "Association of Professional Genealogists in Ireland" will provide you with ample resources.

If you would rather do the job yourself, a great place to start would be the article entitled "Genealogy Centres in the Republic of Ireland." Here you will find a listing of every county in Ireland, including contact places, names and telephone numbers. Be aware, though, that these names are always subject to change. However, if you are doing research or preliminary planning for a genealogy trip to Ireland, this is a resource that may help you.

Another extremely valuable resource is the Irish Genealogy Office. This organization provides a consulting service described in the "Irish Genealogy Office Brochure." Operated by the Genealogical Office, this consulting office employs experienced genealogists and other people familiar with Irish genealogy records. The consultant will "assess the information you already have about the earlier generations of your family. Then, based on that assessment, a course of research will be charted for you—to enable you to discover more about your ancestors, in your own time and at your own pace." Consultations can be handled by mail or in person. That means that you can do much work in advance by mail, and can visit the office in person on your arrival in Dublin.

If you are planning a trip to Ireland, there is available another resource. This is a compressed file called "Ireland (travel)" that contains a group of files about travel in Ireland. These files are compressed using a "zipping" compression utility. (Compressed files and compression utilities are often used to compact files for more rapid transmission and more efficient storage. Please see the chapter about the **File Libraries Center,** and access AOL's file tutorials described there.)

Another collection in the Ireland area is called "Irish Maps." There are over 25 maps of various counties, baronies and other areas available here, all in the form of downloadable files.

Church and parish records are always important resources in Irish genealogical research. Two articles available here, "Irish Church Records" and "Irish Parish Registers," provide insights into church history and types of information that can and cannot be found using these resources.

Links are provided to the various Irish Message Boards in the forum. Irish research is so intense in the Genealogy Forum that there are five specific boards available for the Irish genealogists: General, Northern, Southern, Eastern and Western. Depending on your area of interest and research, one or more of these message boards may be useful to you through the reading of messages and the posting of your own. (Please see the chapter about the **Message Board Center** for details about using message boards.)

Scotland — If you are researching your Scottish ancestry, you'll find a bit of help in this collection to point you to other resources. Available is information about Scottish publications, although the subscription rates may have changed. If you are interested in Scottish clan societies, there is available a file in the collection containing clan names and contact addresses. There also is available a link to another area on AOL, "The Gathering of the Clans." Chances are, however, that your best source of information for Scottish research in this forum will be through its message boards.

Wales — The Welsh researcher will revel in the contents of the Wales area. A series of more than twenty detailed and scholarly articles have been compiled that describe Welsh research in detail. Each article describes the type of record in detail, provides historical information and, in most cases, gives additional references. The topics covered here include:

- Bishop's Transcripts
- Census Returns
- Chapel Records
- Civil Registration
- Counties in Wales
- Digging Your Roots in Wales
- English, Welsh and Other Parish Records
- Poor Law Records
- Printed Records
- Private Records
- Quarter Session Records
- Tithe Maps and Apportionments
- Wales Addresses (A detailed listing of addresses of Welsh records offices, libraries, archives and other resources)
- Wales Probate Records
- Welsh Roman Catholic Records
- Welsh Lexicon for Genealogists
- Welsh Marriage Licenses
- Welsh Names
- Welsh School Records

Scandinavia

The Scandinavian area in the forum consists of Denmark, Finland, Norway and Sweden. One item in the collection, "Scandinavia — Nordic Notes," features a link to a Web site containing information on these four countries and Iceland. Another, an article called "Research Tips for Sweden, Denmark and Norway," references research aids and printed materials that may be of general help to you.

A map of each country is included in its respective collection. Individual "Research Tips" are included in the Denmark, Norway and Sweden collections, along with other miscellaneous materials. The Norwegian area's articles concerning library resources and genealogical sources may be of interest if you want to write for information.

Another important Norwegian resource can be found in the interesting article about Norwegian "Lags." (A Lag is an organization of descendants of immigrants from a particular area of Norway.) The listing included in the article is very extensive. (Be sure and maximize the article's window to cover your entire monitor screen. Otherwise, some of the formatting may be unclear.)

The Finland collection contains no materials other than a map and an announcement that the collection is under development.

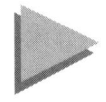

Western Europe

The Western European area of the Regions of the World is comprised of the countries of Austria, Belgium, the Channel Islands (off the coast of Normandy), France, Germany, Italy, the Netherlands, Portugal and Related Areas, Spain and Switzerland. Content in some of these areas is less impressive than you might expect. Austria, Belgium, Italy, the Netherlands and Switzerland, for instance, appear to be under construction, and feature little content other than maps.

Let's talk, however, about the content of the other countries.

Channel Islands — These islands, located off the coast of the French province of Normandy, are rich in history and tradition. In this collection is a link to the Channel Islands Web page. This site was created and is maintained by one of the Genealogy Forum staff members, GFS JohnF. It contains a wealth of information in the form of links to other Internet resources—mailing lists, Web pages for the individual islands, surname links and other sites.

France — The French collection has a limited number of resources at this writing, but is scheduled for redevelopment soon. There is available, of course, a map of France, followed by several articles of interest. The "French Resource Information" article contains some good general information and includes a timeline of important events in France between 1837 and 1871 that greatly influenced record keeping during that period.

Germany — The collection of German resources encompasses both historical and genealogical research. Of course, as a genealogist, it is important to study historical events in order to understand your ancestors' places in history and their responses to those events.

You will also find valuable information about German and Prussian history, as well as a brief history of Alsace-Lorraine. There are maps, lists of state and religious archives, information about immigrants from Russian and German migrations, and even a "how-to" article on researching Hamburg Passenger Lists.

Links are provided from the Germany collection to the forum's files of German-related newsletters, as well as to the numerous German message boards in the forum.

Portugal and Related Areas — The title of this collection is somewhat misleading. Certainly, the site features a focus on Portugal as is seen in transcriptions of the excellent online Portuguese lectures and in the collection of the Portuguese newsletters. However, there are other areas of the world populated by the Portuguese where Portuguese genealogical information is also important. These include:

- The Azores — This group of islands is located off the west coast of Portugal and is politically a part of Portugal.

- The Hawaiian Islands — Portuguese sailors and others settled in what were originally known as the Sandwich Islands. Their descendants trace their genealogy back to these ancestors. A file included in this collection lists the 27 ships on which Portuguese immigrants traveled between 1878 and 1913.
- Madeira — This group of eight islands is situated off the northwest coast of Africa, and is also politically a part of Portugal.
- Cape Verde Islands — Located off the west coast of Africa, this group of islands gained independence from Portugal in 1975.

The Portugal collection also includes links to archives and tourism information, as well as a link to LusaWeb, a Web site for Portuguese-American Communities on the Internet. This is an important and impressive resource for genealogists studying their Portuguese ancestry and that of any of the islands described above. This collection is also being enhanced in late 1998.

Spain — One significant article in the area about Spain contains information about the four national archives available there, as well as a list of other genealogical information locations. This collection is also currently under construction.

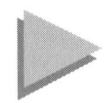

Eastern Europe

The eastern portion of Europe has been politically unsettled for a very long time. Political upheavals, racial and religious turmoil, territorial contentions and war have been all too common in this region. Over the centuries, boundaries have been drawn and redrawn many times. Capitals have shifted, place names have changed and, sometimes, towns have ceased to exist altogether.

The volatility of this area and of Southeastern Europe presents the genealogist with immense challenges. The staff of the

Genealogy Forum recognizes that it is important to have good resources available to help you in your research, and the Eastern Europe collection is full of great reference material.

Here you will find several introductory articles. The first, "About This Area," describes the Eastern Europe collection as follows:

"This area contains a collection of links to on-line resources. Some of these resources can also be found elsewhere in the Genealogy Forum, some are found in other forums, some are on the Web and some are found only here."

Another collection, entitled "Regional Background," offers an incredibly useful compilation of materials that includes:

- **Historical Maps** — Here you will find a great collection of files from the Genealogy Forum's File Libraries Center. They include a four-part set of maps of Eastern Europe maps for various time periods, including 1865-1871, 1914, 1919-1937 and 1990. In addition, there is available a link to the Web site of the Perry-Castañeda Library Map Collection. Here you will find maps of all of the countries that comprised the former Soviet Union. The importance of using the correct geopolitical map for the time you are researching cannot be stressed enough, and these maps are a valuable resource.
- **Location of Areas** — This collection contains written descriptions of the location of many place names you will encounter in your research of Eastern Europe. These include: Anhalt, Banat, Bessarabia, Bohemian Bosnia and Herzegovina, Brandenburg, Bukovina, Croatia, Dalmatia, Dobruja, East Prussia, Epirus, Galicia, Istria, Kosovo, Kurland/Courland, Livonia, Macedonia, Mecklenburg, Moldavia, Montenegro, Moravia, Pomerania, Prussia, Rumelia, Ruthenia,

Saxony, Serbia, Silesia, Slovakia, Slovenia, Sudetenland, Thuringia, Transylvania and Walachia.

Also available in the general portion of the Eastern Europe area is a collection of information about foreign language translation, including links to the AOL Foreign Languages Forum and to the Federation of East European Family History Societies (FEEFHS) database of professional translators specializing in genealogy in that part of the world.

The countries represented in the Eastern Europe collection are listed below. Each one has its own collection of materials, including a current country map. In addition, you will find research guides, Web links for individual country resources, and links to each country's message boards and file library contents in the Genealogy Forum. Special articles on topics such as historical timelines, research guides, town lists and ethnic communities in the U.S. are included in some of the collections. The countries included in the Eastern Europe collection are:

- Belarus
- Czech Republic
- Estonia
- Hungary
- Latvia
- Lithuania
- Poland
- Russia
- Slovakia
- Ukraine

If you are researching an ancestor from this region of the world, you should first determine the time frame in which you are searching. After that, a review of the maps and descriptions of locations is in order to determine the government in power at the time in question. A check of the file libraries may also help you learn more. A visit to the country's message board(s) will allow you to read messages posted by others who are researching in the same area; you can also post messages of your own, and check back later for responses. (For more information on files, see the chapter about the **File Libraries Center**; for more information about the message boards, see the chapter about the **Message Board Center**.)

If you are planning a research trip to any of these countries, it would be wise to refer to any of their research guides and Web sites for contacts and addresses. Making contact in advance can save you hours or days of wasted research time. You will have already determined what information is available at a site, the operating hours of libraries and archives, and any expenses involved. If you need to meet with people, you can set up appointments in advance. These are but a few of the resources found in this area.

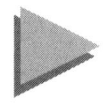

Southeastern Europe

The area of Southeastern Europe, like that of Eastern Europe discussed earlier, has experienced great turmoil and upheaval, which continues to this day. Conflict between Serbian and Croatian peoples has torn the area once known as Yugoslavia, now known as Bosnia-Herzogovina. During periods of war and unrest, records of genealogical value have often been lost or destroyed. It is necessary for genealogists to take advantage of all resources available.

Again, the Genealogy Forum's collections contain many useful materials. The same introductory materials—the "About This Area" article, the "Regional Background" collection with its compilations of maps and descriptions of research areas, and the assortment of foreign language translation resources—are present for your easy reference in the study of these areas.

The countries represented in the Southeastern Europe collection are listed below. You will note that there are listings for Yugoslavia, Macedonia and Bosnia-Herzogovina. While there may seem to be some overlap and redundancy here, there are some unique reference materials available to help you fine-tune your research.

As with the Eastern Europe area, each country has its own collection of materials, including a contemporary country map. You will find research guides in some of these collections that contain excellent contacts and addresses. Some collections even contain Web links for individual country resources, and all include links to each country message boards and/or file library contents in the Genealogy Forum. Look for special articles within each country collection on topics such as historical timelines, town lists, and ethnic communities in the U.S. The countries included in the Eastern Europe collection are:

- Albania
- Bosnia and Herzegovina
- Bulgaria
- Croatia
- Greece
- Macedonia
- Moldova
- Romania
- Slovenia
- Yugoslavia

Using these resources as described in the Eastern Europe section above can provide leads that you might otherwise not find. They also will allow you to plan any research trip more effectively, also as described above.

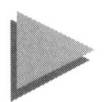

Summary About the Regions of the World

This area is constantly under development. New articles are added periodically, and new contents are being evaluated as this book is being written. Links to Web pages are rechecked on a regular basis to avoid "dead" links and to update addresses.

As you have seen, many of the areas here contain links to message boards or file libraries. In order to take full advantage of these resources, you will want to read the chapters about these facilities.

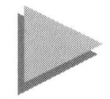

Ethnic Resources

The Genealogy Forum is well-recognized for its wealth of available ethnic resources. African American and Native American genealogists will revel in the abundance of resources to be found here. Hispanic and Jewish genealogists will also find great numbers of reference resources. And, if you are interested in the Huguenots, you too will find a plethora of materials.

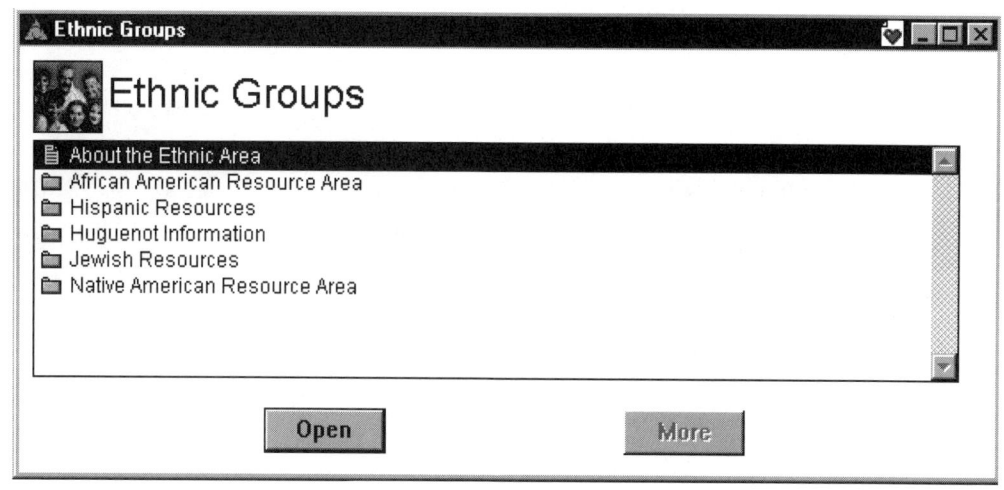

Figure 5.7

The second button on the right side of the Resource Center screen is Ethnic Groups. When you click on this button, the screen shown in Figure 5.7 is displayed. We'll discuss each of the five ethnic collections listed there.

African American Resource Area

African American, European American, and Asian American genealogists in the U.S. use the same records for research, beginning with the 1870 federal census. Before that time, however, many, but not all, blacks were enslaved, bought, sold and bartered as property. Therefore, many of the records needed to trace lineage come in the form of receipts, bills of sale, mortgages, deeds, wills, indentures, daybooks, journals and other similar documents. Records of births and deaths are sometimes found in the slave owner's financial or plantation ledgers.

The Genealogy Forum's African American genealogy team is widely recognized as the best in the country. They are dedicated to providing the best resources for the African American genealogist, and that dedication includes excellent, regularly scheduled chats and constant development of new articles and other materials for the forum.

The African American Resource Area debuted in January of 1998, representing both a complete rework of the previous African American genealogy content of the forum and a huge amount of new material. The premise of the collection is that you must study and understand history in order to properly know your ancestors and see their place in it. The content of this collection supports that foundation and builds upon it.

When you enter the African American Resource Center, the screen shown in Figure 5.8 is displayed. The first thing a new visitor should do is double-click on the "Introduce Yourself" item in the listbox. Here, you can introduce yourself to the staff who run the area and the forum. Please send an E-mail and share your thoughts and suggestions.

Next, in order to best understand what resources are available, double-click on the "Navigating in This Area" selection and

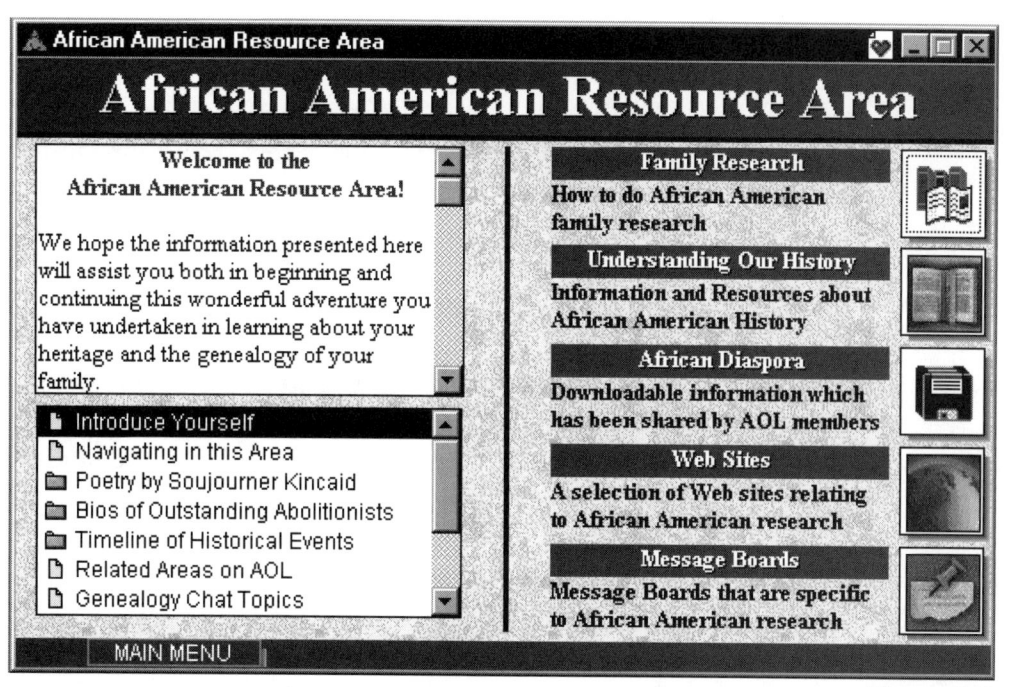

Figure 5.8

take the time to read about all the resources available.

Let's discuss each of the five buttons on the screen.

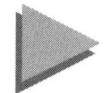

▶ Family Research

Here you will find essential research information and helpful "how-to" hints to guide you in your research planning, including an authoritative article entitled "Essential Steps for African American Research." Another, "Researching the Period of Enslavement," provides methodologies for determining slave holder(s), beginning with the 1870 census and working backwards. Finally, in this collection is an article concerning Caribbean research. It contains an historical timeline and some information about many of the Caribbean islands.

The Genealogy Forum on America Online — 97

Understanding Our History

Part of being able to successfully research your family history is understanding the times and conditions in which your ancestors lived. Click on this button for a variety of resources available to help you in your research and in your understanding of the people, places and times during which your ancestors lived. These include:

- **Timeline of Historical Events** — This extensive article is a chronology of the African American presence in the United States, beginning in 1619 with the landing of 20 black slaves at Jamestown and proceeding through 1996.
- **Bios of Outstanding Abolitionists** — This collection of over 100 abolitionist biographies is an historian's dream come true. Names, dates, occupations and biographical sketches paint the pictures of these important men and women who fought for the abomination of slavery. (**NOTE:** If you are a genealogist who may be a descendant or relative of one of the abolitionists, you will find additional reading materials listed in some of these sketches.)
- **An African American Perspective** — This document contains excerpts from a sermon delivered by the Rev. B.W. Arnett in Urbana, OH, at Thanksgiving, 1876. As an historical time capsule, it puts into perspective the position of African Americans at that time.
- **African American Church** — The church has played an important, central part in the history of African Americans. It is a place of faith, sanctuary and fellowship. Available here is a collection of Web links to more than 25 churches of many denominations. Many of these contain information of interest to genealogists, especially if you would like to write them to locate old church records.

The African Diaspora Library

"Diaspora" can be defined as any group that is dispersed outside its original or traditional homeland.

The African Diaspora Library contains downloadable information which has been shared by members of AOL in the form of computer files. Explore the numerous holdings of the Library and download whatever you find to be of value in your area of research. You are invited and encouraged to share any information you might have that may be helpful to other researchers by uploading it to the library.

For detailed information about downloading and using files, and about uploading your files, please see the chapter about the **File Libraries Center**.

Web Sites

There is a tremendous amount of African American genealogical information on the Internet these days. The Genealogy Forum's African American Resource Area has compiled over 130 intensive and informative sites for you, which include libraries and archives with large holdings about African American history and genealogy. Available are databases, online newsletters, sites about slavery and reconstruction, sites about African American history and a wide array of others. This is an impressive collection.

Message Boards

For the genealogist, networking is an essential skill. You have to reach out and communicate with others by posting queries and responding to those posted by others. To help you with this, the Genealogy Forum has several message boards available specific to African American research. These can be accessed by a click on this button. The screen shown in figure 5.9 will be displayed.

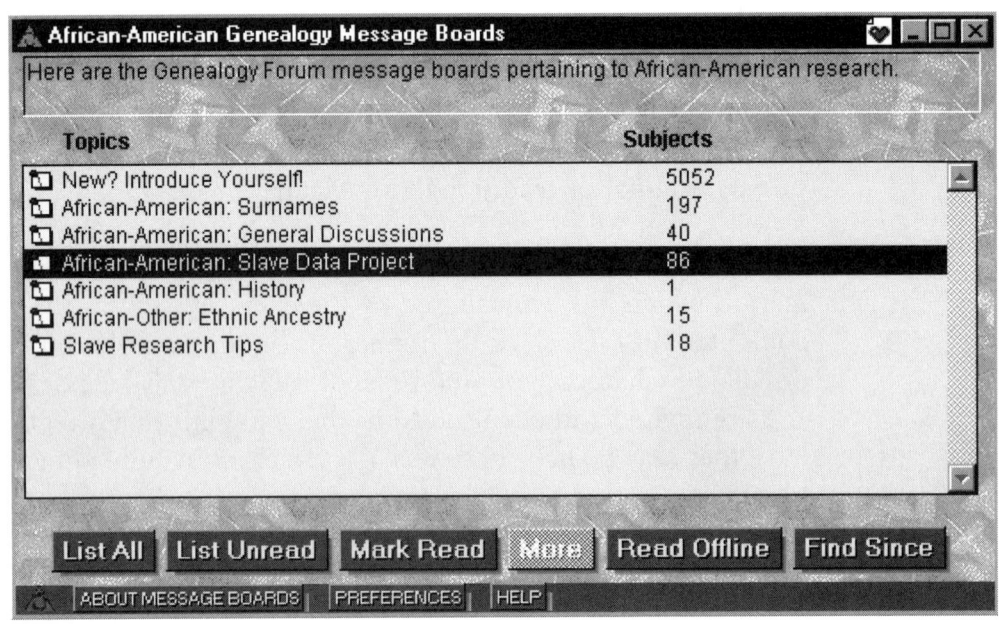

Figure 5.9

As you can see, the message board topics available include:

- **New? Introduce Yourself** — This is a message board you can use to let others know the surnames you are researching and the areas in which you are interested.
- **Surnames** — Exchange information here on specific surnames you are researching. Post messages yourself and respond to those posted by others. This is the place to make connections!
- **General Discussions** — This board is used for messages on almost any topic that is of interest to African American genealogists.
- **Slave Data** — This board is used to communicate information about documents created and kept by slave owners that mention slaves. This includes wills, deeds, bills of sale, day books, ledgers and other documents. The information gathered here will become part of a master reference collection to be housed at the Anniston, AL, Public Library.

- **History** — This area is used to post messages regarding African American history and events.
- **Ethnic Ancestry** — This board is used to discuss ancestors of mixed African and other ethnic group ancestry.
- **Slave Research Tips** — This area is used to exchange information and research techniques for locating records about slaves.

In order to take full advantage of the message board facilities, please see the chapter about the **Message Board Center**.

Other areas of interest in the African American Resource Area are listed in the listbox, and include:

- **Poems by Sojourner Kincaid** — As a tribute to African American genealogy, famous American poet Sojourner Kincaid Rolle agreed to contribute two of her original poems to this area. Be sure to take a few minutes to read her insightful verse.
- **Related Areas on AOL** — Links to several other AOL forums are included here that complement the African American Resource Area.
- **Genealogy Chat Topics** — The full schedule of chats in the Genealogy Forum is linked here so that you can locate scheduled African American chats.

The African American Resource Area is constantly growing. The African American team that runs the chats is working to develop new content for this area, so be sure to check back often for new materials.

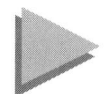

Hispanic Resources

The Hispanic Genealogy Group is an informal, and constantly growing, association of online genealogists who meet regularly in the Genealogy Forum to promote and discuss all aspects of Hispanic genealogy. Since mid-1996, the group has had its own Web site, the AOL Hispanic Genealogy Group Home Page. The Web site serves as an external focal point, outside the forum, for Hispanic genealogy-related activities and resources collected from all over the Hispanic world. A link to this Web page is a focal point of the Hispanic Resources collection.

Once at the Web site, explore the resources there. However, don't fail to connect with the Crossroads link, another important part of this Web site. Here you will find the Hispanic Genealogy Address Book, a compilation of many important resources. Featured are resources for most of the Central American, South American and Caribbean countries. The entire Hispanic Genealogy Group Home Page, however, is a growing concern. Be certain to check back often for additional content.

You will find resources for Cuba, Puerto Rico and Spain here. The Puerto Rico collection also contains a set of files with information from the Hispanic Genealogy Society of New York (HGSNY).

Another collection concerns the Society of Hispanic Historical and Ancestral Research (SHHAR). SHHAR is a non-profit volunteer organization with the specific goal of helping all Hispanics (Spanish language heritage) research their family history. You will find a link to forty files concerning Hispanic heritage in this collection. In addition, some of the files here are included in the collection as text articles.

Finally, the Hispanic Resources area contains a link to Hispanic Online, another forum on AOL (Keyword: **latino**) devoted to Latin culture and events. You may want to use the message boards there to search for additional genealogical connections.

Jewish Resources

The search for your Jewish roots can be a difficult journey, especially when you are researching in Europe. Jewish genealogists are heavily dependent on networking with individuals and organizations, and are looking for alternative record types in many cases. Recognizing this, the Genealogy Forum's Jewish Resources collection contains several strong resource materials for your reference.

There is available a link to AOL's Jewish Community Forum (Keyword: **jewish**). Here, you can exchange information with other people, especially on the message board for Family and Personal Matters where there is a category for genealogy.

Next, there is a list of Jewish Genealogical Societies. You will find these helpful in determining what records are available and where they may be located. These societies may provide extremely helpful advice and counsel for your genealogical quest.

A file called "Jewish Genealogy FAQ" may be downloaded from here. It contains the answers to many commonly asked questions about how to begin researching your Jewish genealogy.

Finally, there is available an extensive bibliography that contains many Jewish and general reference books and other publications. Please note, however, that there may be newer editions of some of the books listed. Be sure and check "Books in Print" at your library or ask your local bookseller for help in determining most recent editions.

The Genealogy Forum has begun to revise its Jewish collection in order to build something similar to the African American and Native American collections. Check back regularly to see their progress.

Native American Resource Area

There is a growing interest on the part of Native Americans in genealogy. In addition to personal genealogical research, there is a growing interest in the histories, tribal tradition and the many languages of Native Americans. Fortunately, many records have been preserved that make such inquiries possible.

The Genealogy Forum introduced the **Native American Resource Area** in late-March of 1998. This large collection contains many of the materials previously available in the forum, plus a vast amount of new content. Here you will find resource techniques, historical information, access to files in the libraries, a rich collection of Native American-related Web sites, links to forum message boards and even an impressive collection of Native American art that was created specifically for the collection. It is possible that this is the most complete collection of online Native American genealogy research materials available.

When you double-click on the selection for the Native American Resource Area, the screen shown in Figure 5.10 is displayed. It looks much like many of the other "Center" screens in the forum. The screen can be said to be divided into three sections: the introductory text in the upper left quadrant, the listbox in the lower left quadrant, and the five buttons on the right half of the screen that represent the major content of the Native American Resource Area.

The first thing a new visitor should do is double-click on the item in the listbox called "Meet the Staff." Here you will learn about the many knowledgeable and talented people who serve Native American members in the forum. Also in the listbox is the Native American Art Gallery. Don't miss the artwork created by artist Jak Bowen specifically for the Native American Resource Area.

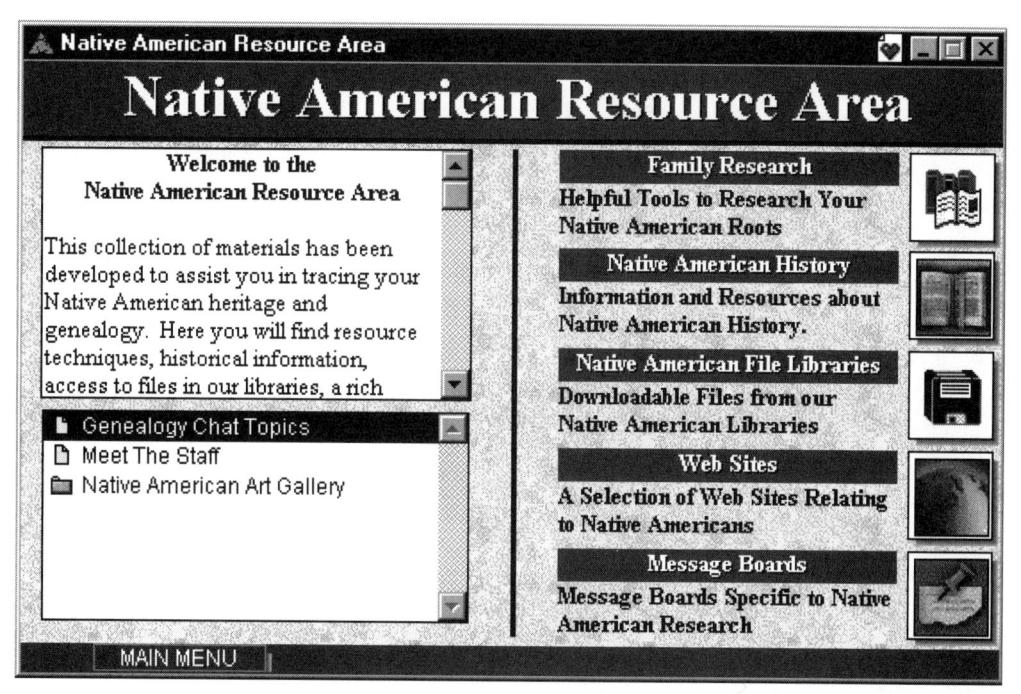

Figure 5.10

Let's move to the five buttons on the screen and discuss each one in detail.

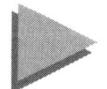

Family Research

As you begin your search for your Native American roots, you will need some starting point. This area contains an article, "5 Steps to Native American Genealogy." The 5-step research model in the **Beginners' Center** provides a good, basic technical approach for the beginning genealogist. The Native American researcher, however, deals in many cases with additional, different records from other genealogists, and may therefore wish to use this article as a starting point.

Native American History

This collection is truly remarkable. The Genealogy Forum has compiled information and reference resources for all of the major Native American tribes. Let's discuss each of the groups of materials here:

- **Lectures** — Included here are transcripts of several lectures from regularly scheduled Native American chats.
- **Genealogy of Pocohontas** — This fascinating article discusses the truths and the myths surrounding this larger-than-life historical figure.
- **Indian Schools** — Here you will find the story of Indian children being forcibly removed from their families and placed in boarding schools in order to "assimilate" them into Western society. If you are looking for information about these schools and the children who were placed there, this article contains Web links and a list of the National Archives and Records Administration's (NARA) microfilm publications covering these "Indian" schools.
- **Melungeons** — The Melungeons are a group of Native American people whose origins are somewhat uncertain. Some say they are descended from the settlers of the famous "Lost Colony" of Roanoke Island. Others say that they are descended from the Portuguese. A link to an excellent Melungeons Web site is included here.
- **Canadian Tribes** — In this collection you will find a list of all the tribes and sub-tribes of Canada, grouped by province and area.
- **Southeastern United States** — This collection includes a list, by state, of all the tribes and sub-tribes settled there. More important, however, are the collections of materials about the following tribes:
  - **Cherokee** — This group of materials contains a history of the Cherokee nation and a list of Cherokee tribes and villages. Detailed information is included about the Cherokee Rolls and all of the

NARA microfilm records available for research.
- **Choctaw** — This group includes a list of all the Choctaw records available from NARA on microfilm, as well as a substantial number of contacts, books and other resources.
- **Creek** — This area contains a list of NARA microfilm records for the Creek Rolls.
- **Chickasaw** — This area contains a list of NARA microfilm records for the Chickasaw Rolls.
- **Seminole** — This group contains a list of NARA microfilm records related to the Seminoles, as well as a list of helpful Web sites and an extensive bibliography of printed Seminole resources.
- **Northeastern United States** — This collection includes a list, by state, of all the tribes and sub-tribes settled there. Tribal collections are included for the following:
  - **Delaware** — A list of the Delaware Rolls resources is listed here.
  - **Ottawa** — Microfilm resources from NARA, the LDS Church and the American Genealogical Lending Library (AGLL) are listed, along with a number of Web links and a substantial bibliography.
- **Northwestern United States** — This collection includes a list, by state, of all the tribes and sub-tribes settled there, as well as information about NARA microfilm for the Flathead Rolls.
- **Southwestern United States** — This collection includes a list, by state, of all the tribes and sub-tribes settled there.
- **Mid-Western United States** — This collection includes a list, by state, of all the tribes and sub-tribes settled there.
- **Plains States** — This collection includes a list, by state, of all the tribes and sub-tribes settled there, as well as

information about NARA microfilm holdings and a bibliography about the Comanche tribe.
- **California Region of the United States** — This collection includes a list of all the tribes and sub-tribes settled in the California area.
- **Other regions** — This collection includes a list of Native American tribes and sub-tribes settled in Hawaii, Mexico and Central America.

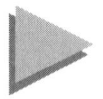

How do I Use This Information?

As a Native American, you will appreciate the information in the collections described above. You can determine the tribe and any sub-tribe you need to research. Then, if you are descended from a tribe, such as the Cherokee, for which there are detailed materials included, you can obtain books from the library to learn more. You can also obtain microfilm records from NARA to research your ancestors.

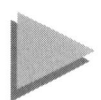

Native American File Libraries

The Genealogy Forum maintains two libraries of Native American materials. The first contains files of treaty information, and the second contains a wonderful collection of Native American stories. This latter group is especially significant, in that it allows members to access the stories online and perpetuate them. You can contribute to this important collection of Indian lore by writing a story and uploading it to the file libraries.

For details about downloading and uploading files, please see the chapter about the **File Libraries Center**.

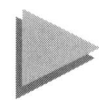

Web Sites

If you are looking for Web sites relating to Native Americans and genealogical research, you have come to the right place. There are over 100 Web sites included in the Native American collection. These include tribe-related Web pages, government and business council sites, and links to Web pages created by, and for, Native American researchers.

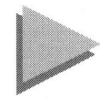

Native American Message Boards

There are six message boards in the forum specifically devoted to Native American topics. They are:

- Native American History
- The 5 Civilized Tribes
- The Eastern Tribes
- The Plains Tribes
- The Western Tribes
- Melungeons & Other Mixed Races

The message boards provide places for you to post queries and exchange information with others researching the same tribes, places and names as you. Remember, networking is important—and the message boards can help. Please see the chapter about the **Message Board Center**.

Finally, the last thing to note in the Native American Resource Center is the Genealogy Chat Topics document located in the listbox. You have seen this in other collections before. It contains the schedule for all chats in the Genealogy Forum. We will discuss chats in detail in the chapter about the **Chat Center**, but suffice it to say there are several Native American chats held each week. Check the schedule and plan to attend.

The Native American Resource Area is constantly growing. The Native American team that run the chats is also working to develop new content for this area. As more Native American materials become available through NARA, and as more Web sites are identified, information will be added to this collection. Be sure and check back often for new materials.

Huguenots

The Huguenots were French Protestants of the 16th and 17th centuries. They suffered much religious persecution, and many began a migration from France to seek religious freedom.

The Genealogy Forum recognizes the Huguenots as an ethnic group that, having originated in France, was forced to disperse in the cause of religious freedom. The Huguenot resources here consist of a collection of files, each of which contains the text of an informative lecture delivered in the Genealogy Forum. If you are interested in Huguenot history and research, these lectures will provide a good foundation for your further investigation.

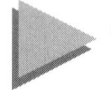

Vital Records/Other Records

The next area of the Resource Center to explore is the **Vital Records/Other Records** collection. You started in the **Beginners' Center** and learned research techniques and the types of forms to use to record information, but were not told where to get most of that information or what to look for.

The Vital Records/Other Records collection contains groups of articles describing various types of records resources. Most of the articles here are written by genealogists just like you who have used a particular resource and have written an article to explain to others how to use it. What better way to share your expertise and make a difference in someone else's genealogical research?

The types of records included here are:

- Adoption Records
- Birth Certificates
- Cemetery Records
- Census Records
- Church Records

- Death Records
- Funeral Home Records
- Land/Deed Records
- Maps and Genealogy
- Marriage/Divorce Records
- Military Records
- Naturalization Records (a Web link)
- Probate Records
- Railroad Retirement Board
- Social Security Records

Settle down for a little reading on the record types above. If you have some knowledge and expertise you would like to share, please contact George Ferguson via E-mail at gflgeorge@aol.com to discuss submitting an article for inclusion here.

Addresses

Genealogists are great letter-writers, because letters are the medium by which they obtain copies of most of their vital records. Genealogists know that a courteous letter, containing specific details that the recipient can use to locate the specific records, can bring many rewards. Of course, a SASE helps too.

The Genealogy Forum has compiled lists of many important addresses for you. These addresses cannot replace good genealogy address books available in bookstores. However, this collection is impressive and offers a great starting point to contact the organizations discussed below.

- **American Legion National Headquarters** — The American Legion is a society of American veterans of World War I. Originally formed in 1919, it later grew to encompass military veterans of all successive wars.
- **Government Facilities** — This collection includes contact information for the National Archives and

Records Administration (NARA) and all of its locations. The NARA Web site is included, as is information about how to order NARA inquiry forms and publications via E-mail. An introductory article about the Library of Congress is also included here.

- **Genealogical Societies** — One of the greatest strengths of this Addresses area lies in this collection of genealogical society addresses. Here you will find addresses of genealogical societies in all 50 states, plus all the Jewish genealogical societies across the country. If you are researching a specific area, that region's local genealogical society can help you. They can point you in the direction of libraries, archives and other resources in their area. They also may have unpublished information in their files that they will share with you for the cost of copies and postage. In addition, genealogical societies offer reasonably priced memberships that usually include a subscription to a newsletter or journal. These materials can provide you with invaluable insight into local history, inform you about conferences and other events, and may allow you to post queries for your surnames.

- **Historical Societies** — As a complement to the list of genealogical societies, the collection of addresses for historical societies can be a great resource. Here you will find addresses for the historical societies of all 50 states. Sometimes you will find that genealogical and historical societies are combined into a single organization. If they are separate, however, you should make use of both entities to help further your research.

- **Libraries and Archives** — You will find an impressive collection of addresses here. The Genealogy Forum has compiled, for each of the 50 states, a collection of the most important libraries and archives' addresses. In addition, you will find the DAR Library and others listed.

▶ Other Resources

Behind the button marked **Other Resources** in the Resource Center is a miscellany of materials. Let's talk about the most important items found here.

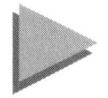

▶ Ancestral Seasonings

Do you remember your grandmother's cakes and breads? Did your aunt make unusually good pickles? Is there a special family recipe that has been passed down from generation to generation? Those are exactly the types of recipes that can found in the **Ancestral Seasonings** collection.

Take a look at the screen shown in Figure 5.11. In the Ancestral Seasonings collection, members like yourself have shared

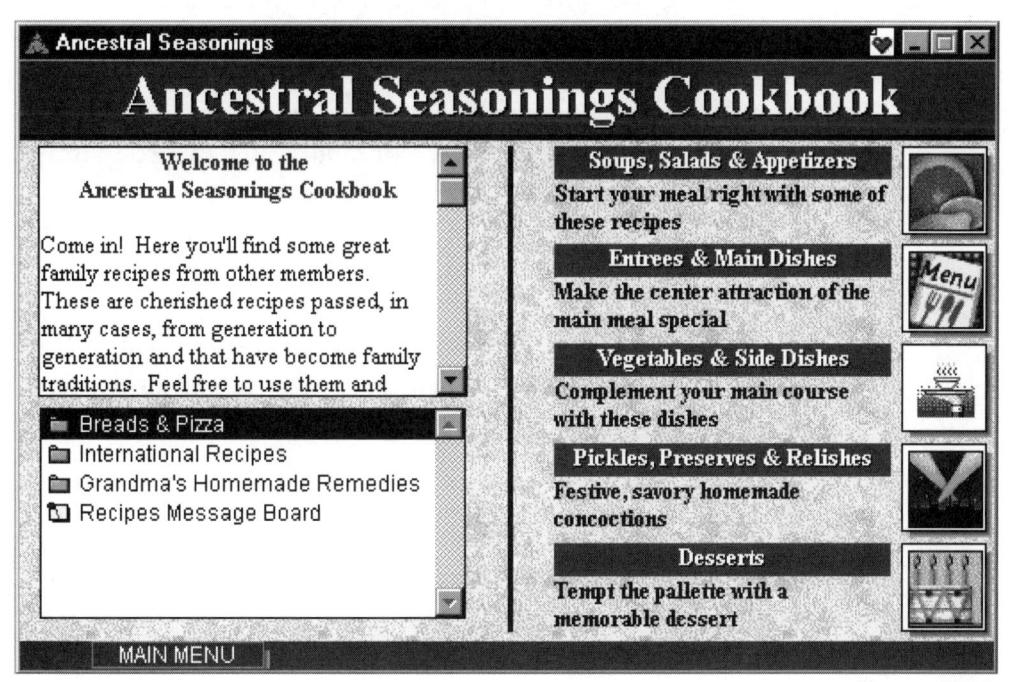

Figure 5.11

The Genealogy Forum on America Online — 113

their famous (and infamous) family recipes. Grouped into categories, you can browse for a new recipe for dinner tonight or for your next special family occasion. Feel free to share recipes from your family by posting them on the Recipes Message Board.

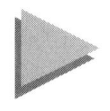

Perpetual Calendar

Did you ever wonder what day of the week your mother was born? Well, if you know she was born on July 10, 1911, and you use this link, you'll soon learn that she was born on a Monday. You'll find this Web-based perpetual calendar useful in your genealogy research, as well as in other areas of your life. Make this one a Favorite Place!

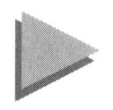

Other Items of Interest in the Resource Center

There are several other items located in the listbox on the Resource Center screen that you will find of interest. At the top of the listbox is a link to another forum on AOL, called "**Tell Us Your Story**," which concerns the American Immigration Experience. Not only can you share your own story, but you can also search the family stories database. You never know what connection you may make, not to mention the fact that there are some terrific tales available here!

The **Genealogy Conferences & Events** collection lists important conferences, seminars, lectures, meetings and other events. You can learn a great deal at one of these events, so be sure to check for upcoming events near you.

In the **Genealogy Forum Newsletters** collection, you will find copies of online newsletters produced by various groups in the forum. You will remember from the chapter about the **Main Screen** that the forum produces its own monthly "Genealogy Forum News." In this collection in the Resource Center, you will find links to all the back issues of the "News." In addition, there are available newsletters published by the Canadian, German, Hispanic, Irish & Scot, New England, Publishing and Surname groups.

▶ Summary

The Genealogy Forum's Resource Center is a wonderful source of information. As you can see, the **Regions of the World** offers a wealth of information to help further your research across many areas of the globe. **Ethnic Resources** contains tremendous material in the form of specific master collections for the African American and Native American genealogist. There are also good reference materials for Hispanic and Jewish researchers, as well as for people researching the Huguenots. The **Vital Records/Other Records** collection offers informative written material to help educate you in using specific record types. The **Addresses** area is full of excellent contacts and reference resources. And, the **Other Resources** area offers a group of miscellaneous reference tools and information that you may find useful.

The Resource Center continues to grow, with new material added frequently. You will find yourself returning here again and again for important reference tools, as well as to learn or remind yourself how to properly research specific areas. Simply stated, this area is a true treasure trove!

6 ▶ The Message Board Center

IN PREVIOUS CHAPTERS, THERE WERE MANY REFERENCES MADE TO THE **MESSAGE BOARD CENTER.** You will find yourself spending many hours here. It is the most frequently visited area of the Genealogy Forum because people make connections and get results here. It is not unusual for a member to make a connection with a long-lost cousin through the message boards. More frequently, members connect with others working on the same lines and begin to share information and documents, often becoming fast friends and collaborative partners.

Think of a message board as an electronic bulletin board. You will type a message, or notice, and post it for others to read. Likewise, you will read other postings. Messages remain on the message boards for over two years from the date of posting. If you find information of interest in a posting, you have the options of: 1) posting a reply for all other readers to see, 2) sending a reply via private E-mail to the person who posted the original message, or 3) doing both simultaneously.

Message boards are not unique to the Genealogy Forum. They are used in many of the forums in the AOL Channels area. They provide a convenient and timely way for members to share information, and to reach many people at once. Usually, you will be communicating with people you don't know or with whom you have never communicated, which is to say that you probably have never exchanged E-mail or IMs with them before. Message boards are like newspaper advertisements. They allow you to reach many people at once. People may read your posting and decide whether to respond, depending on their interest.

The Genealogy Forum's **Message Board Center** and its companion, the **Surname Center**, are the places where you will make the most contacts with others researching the same surnames and regions as you. This is where you post queries – notices of who and what you are seeking. And, like thousands of others, you have available here an excellent opportunity to make contact with distant and/or long-lost relatives.

In order to get the most out of the message boards, it is very important for you to learn how to use them. This includes learning how to:

- Set your personal preferences so that you can manage your message traffic.
- *Properly* create a subject line so that people can easily find your messages.
- Create an effective query for posting on the message board.
- Respond to other people's messages.

Let's look at The Message Board Center's main screen, then discuss the organization of the area and its many message boards, as well as the proper format and etiquette for posting messages. We'll also share some practical examples of how you can use message boards to make connections with other people.

The Genealogy Forum on America Online — 117

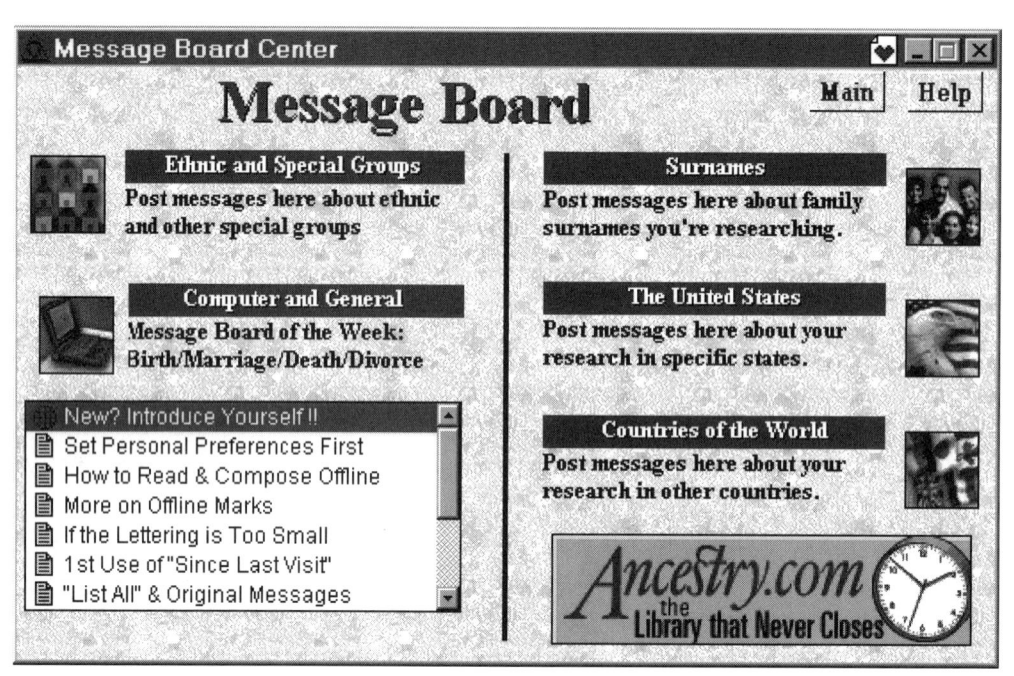

Figure 6.1

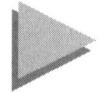

The Message Board Center Screen

As you have seen in previous chapters, you can get to the Message Board Center from many locations in the Genealogy Forum. Certainly, you can start on the forum's main screen and click on the button labeled "Messages" to get to the Message Board Center. There are also links from many of the other "centers" to the message boards—including the Beginners' Center, the Resource Center main screen and most of the collections in the Regions of the World and the Ethnic Resources areas, as well as other places in the forum.

When you arrive at the Message Board Center, the screen shown in Figure 6.1 will be displayed. Like the other centers you have seen, there is a consistent look and feel to the screen. There are displayed the five buttons on the screen that will connect you to five distinct groups of message boards. In addition, you will find the listbox containing a huge amount of "how-to" information, as well as answers to the most frequently asked questions about the message boards.

The first thing you should do is read the article in the text box in the upper left quadrant of the screen, followed by the article in the listbox titled, "Set Personal Preferences First." Here, you will learn about the options you can use to make the message boards work best for you. It is a good idea to print this article so that you have it at your fingertips when setting up your personal preferences.

Setting Your Personal Preferences

The first time you enter any of the message boards, you will see a small button at the bottom of the window labeled "PREFERENCES." Click on that button and the Global Preferences window shown in Figure 6.2 will be displayed. This is where you control your message board set-up. The preferences you set here will apply to all message boards you read on AOL.

You should first set up a signature block. The information you include here is appended to every message you post, as well as to every private reply you send to someone else's posting. You should certainly include your real name. You may choose whether to include more personal information. You should also certainly include a list of the surnames you are researching. It's a good idea to list surnames in capital letters in everything you write. This makes them easy to locate in the body of the message.

The inclusion of other surnames in your signature block will help people reading your postings to determine if the information in your message really applies to them. For instance, if a member sees your posting about John T. Smith and also sees other surnames, such as McGee and Presley, that member may be able to infer that your John Smith is the John T. Smith that he or she has been researching.

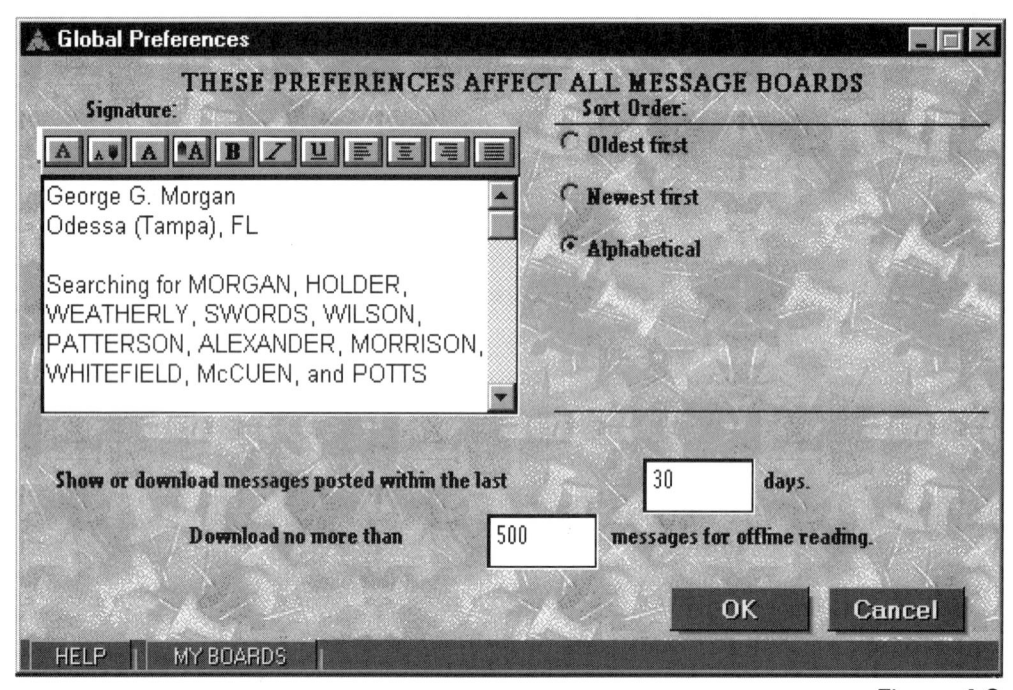

Figure 6.2

Next, you will want to specify the Sort Order of the messages. It is here that you decide the sequence in which you want your messages presented to you. You can choose to have them ordered in the following ways:

- **Alphabetical** — Messages will be sequenced alphabetically by subject.
- **Newest first** — Messages will be listed by date, with the newest messages at the top of the list and the oldest messages at the bottom.
- **Oldest first** — Messages will be listed by date, with the oldest messages at the top of the list and the newest messages at the bottom.

If you're looking for specific surnames, you will probably want to opt for the alphabetical sort option.

You can also specify the number of days' worth of messages

that you want to view at a time. On each message board, you will be able to indicate how many days back you wish to view. The forum staff suggests that you set the number at 999. However, if this number is overwhelming the few times that you try to read the messages, you can set it at a lower number, such as 30 days, and work your way up.

The final option allows you to set the maximum number of messages that will be downloaded for off-line reading. At the writing of this book, only AOL Windows users could download and read message board postings off-line. Please read the article in the listbox on the Message Board Center Titled "How To Read & Compose Off-line" for more information about how to use this function.

Organization of the Message Boards

The message boards are organized into logical groups, and are accessed by using the buttons on the Message Board Center's main screen. Let's talk about each group of message boards:

Surnames — This is the most popular group of message boards. It is here that members post messages called "queries" about the surnames they are researching. (Please see the section later in this chapter that describes how to properly and most effectively formulate, create and post a query.)

You will find the surnames organized in several ways to provide you with a flexibility of access.

- Surname Message Board — Complete lists all messages for all surnames, arranged in groups A-K, L-Z, the collection of Mayflower surnames and the collection of the top 1,000 surnames in the United States.
- Top 100 Surnames in the USA—a compilation of the

top surnames as defined through the U.S. Census Bureau. Messages are posted here specifically for those surnames.

- Surnames by Letter of the Alphabet — Provides easy access, with the alphabet broken down into ranges and all the top 1,000 U.S. Surnames, beginning with the letter "A." For example, the letter "A" contains ranges for names beginning with AA-AF, AG-AM, and AN-AZ, followed by the top "A" surnames.

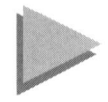

The United States

The second most popular group of message boards is that for the 50 states. People post messages here about specific places in a given state, as well as queries related to individuals who lived in those states. Here are two examples:

- A member posted a message asking for help and information in determining the current name of a specific town in North Carolina called Leaksville. Several members responded that the current name is Eden. This information will help the researcher determine where to search for records of ancestors who lived in Leaksville.
- A member posted a query asking for any information about a certain William WHITFIELD or WHITEFIELD who lived in Caswell County, North Carolina, in the early- to mid-1800s. Another member posted a response with some genealogical information. The two members subsequently made contact and exchanged additional materials. Both benefited from the exchange of information and extended their research.

The United States area is initially divided into two alphabetically arranged groups: Alabama to Nevada, and New Hampshire to Wyoming. Within these groups, each state is a stand-alone message board with topics and postings specific unto itself.

Countries of the World

This collection contains individual message boards for all countries other than the United States. The collection is broken into three geographic groups:

- Eastern Europe/Asia/Australia
- North and South America
- Western Europe and Africa

Some countries' message boards, such as those for Canada, are very heavily used. Others, such as Azerbijam, have relatively little activity. Regardless of the activity level, the old saying, "Nothing ventured, nothing gained," most certainly applies here. Don't make the assumption that nobody is checking and reading a particular message board. You should post messages and see what responses you get.

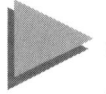

Ethnic and Special Groups

This group of message boards is perhaps the most complex of the collections to describe. The Genealogy Forum has dubbed it "People, Places and Times" because there is such a diverse group of materials here. The major content areas that you will find here include:

- Ethnic and Religious Groups
- African American message boards on a variety of topics
- Asian Americans
- Cajun/Acadians
- Greek Americans
- Huguenots
- Irish Americans
- Italian Americans

- Jewish genealogy topics
- Melungeons
- Molly McGuires
- Mormons
- Native American tribes and other topics
- Palatines
- Pennsylvania Dutch
- Quakers and Mennonites
- Scot Americans
- Scot/Irish Americans
- Spanish Americans
- History and Historical Information
- Time periods
- Events, such as the Revolutionary War, the War of 1812, the battle at the Alamo, the Gold Rush, the U.S. Civil War and the Holocaust
- Specific Time Periods and Events
- Colonial times
- Salem Witch Trials
- Epidemics and their influences on society
- Criminals and crimes
- Pioneers and their travels across the North American continent

As you can see, this is a very diverse group of topics. You, too, can start new subjects for discussion on the message boards, as well as participate and contribute to discussions in ongoing topics.

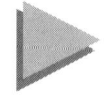

Computer and General

This collection contains two very important groups of message boards. Let's talk about each.

Computer Tools and Techniques message boards are the places where you can learn more about genealogy and computers.

Here you will find discussions of all the major genealogy database programs. You can read what others have to say about the features and functions of the products, their strengths and weaknesses, and their good and bad points. Feel free to post your own questions. You can be sure that someone will answer you.

Also on these message boards, you will find discussions of the best genealogy Web sites for specific research problems. You will see inquires from members who are looking for Internet resources, not to mention recommendations by other members of what they feel are great resources.

The other collection under the **Computer and General** button is **General Genealogy**. This is one of the most important of all the message boards in the Genealogy Forum. It contains a tremendous wealth of topical message discussions. You will find discussions about:

- Vital records
- Genealogical and historical societies and organizations
- Genealogy products and services
- Heraldry
- Libraries
- Maps
- Railroads
- Scams
- Seminars and conferences
- Educational opportunities

Don't overlook this important area of the Message Board Center.

Also in this collection is a category titled "Complete Genealogy Message Boards," which is a one-stop listing of every message board in the Genealogy Forum. If you get lost and/or can't locate the message board you're looking for, this is a good place to look. You may want to add this specific message board to your Favorite Places.

Working With List Messages

When you go to one of the message boards, you will see a list of topics displayed. Figure 6.3 shows an example of the WHITFIELD/WHITEFIELD surname message board listing the topics. You will notice that a description of the message board appears at the top.

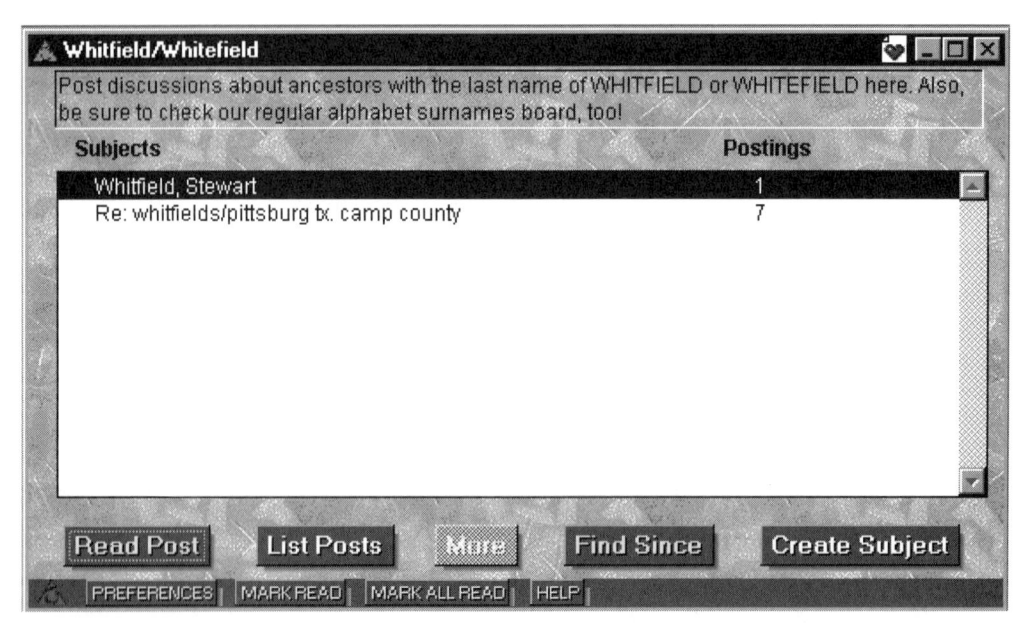

Figure 6.3

In the example displayed in Figure 6.3, there are two subjects listed. The first shows that there is one posting; the second shows that there are seven postings. The two subjects listed there appear because they and their contents have not been read.

A subject and all of its replies is referred to as a thread. Think of it as a "thread of conversation." It allows you to read the first message and follow the progression through the entire discussion. In so doing, you are "following the thread."

At this point, you have several options available, each

represented by a button on the bottom of the message window. These options are:

- **Read Post** — Click here to read the posting that is highlighted on the list. If there are multiple postings, clicking on this button will open the first one in the sequence.
- **List Posts** — Click here to display a listing of information about all the postings in the item highlighted on the list. For instance, when I highlighted the item with seven postings, and clicked List Posts, the window shown in Figure 6.4 was displayed. The author's screen name, the size of the posting and the date and time of the posting are all listed. This is a useful feature if you are expecting or looking for

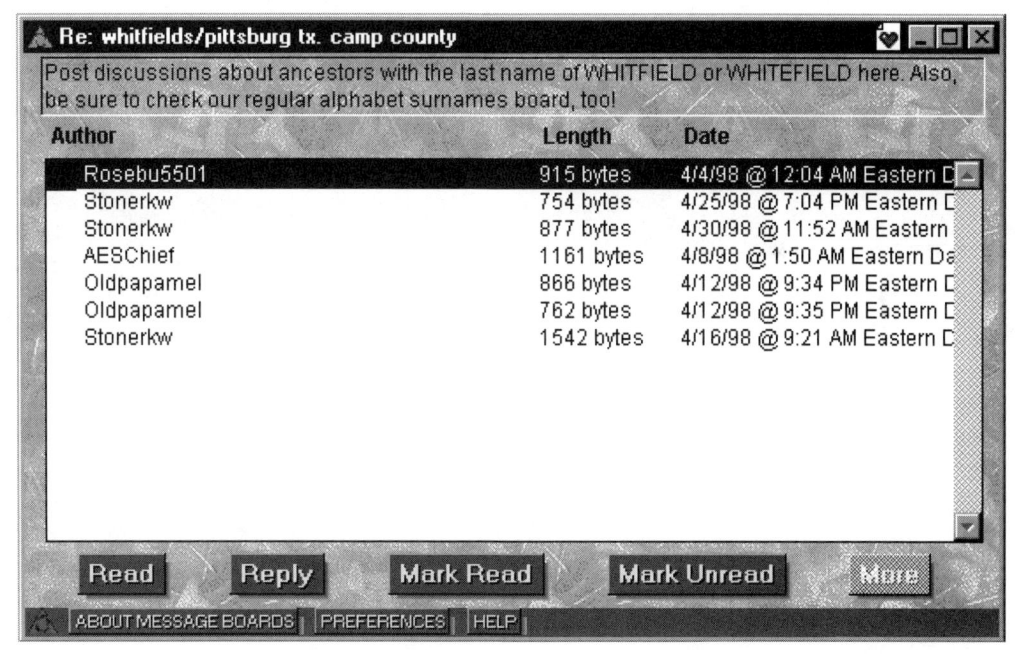

Figure 6.4

responses from any particular individual.

- **Find Since** — This is the most useful of the function buttons in this area. Here you can specify what

The Genealogy Forum on America Online — 127

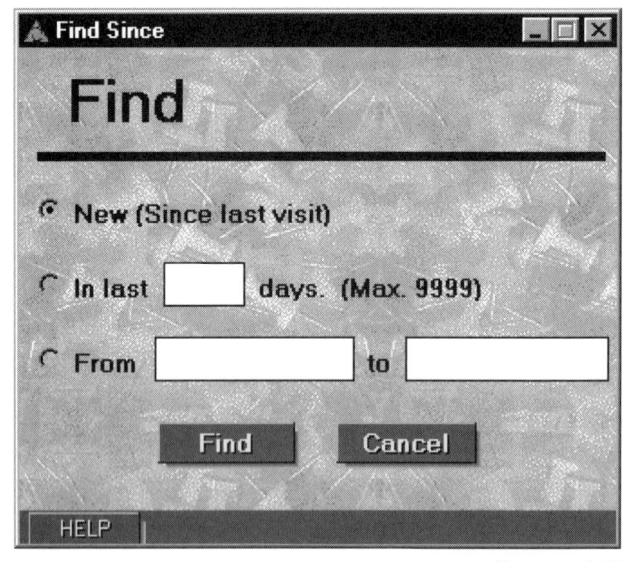

Figure 6.5

messages you want to see. You should know that once you have opened a message, it will be marked as having been read. After that, the message will no longer appear on your list. To view older messages that you have already read, click on the Find Since button. The window shown in Figure 6.5 will be displayed. The default setting (indicated by the black dot in the radio button) is set to display "New" messages —those that have been posted since your last visit to the message board. You can, however, click on the second radio button and enter a number representing the number of messages to display. If you want to view messages posted only during a particular range of days, click on the third radio button and specify the dates. (You must use the mm/dd/yy format.) In the WHITFIELD/WHITEFIELD example above, the default displayed only the two subjects that had not been read. However, by using the Find Since option and specifying display of messages posted in the last 120 days, the list shown in Figure 6.6 was displayed. Now there are six subjects listed.

- **Create Subject** — Clicking on this button will present you with a new message screen where you can start a new subject thread. The posting will be made only to the message board where you are currently located. (Details about creating a properly formatted and effective posting will be covered later in this chapter.)
- **Preferences** — The first button along the bottom of the window. As discussed earlier in the chapter, you

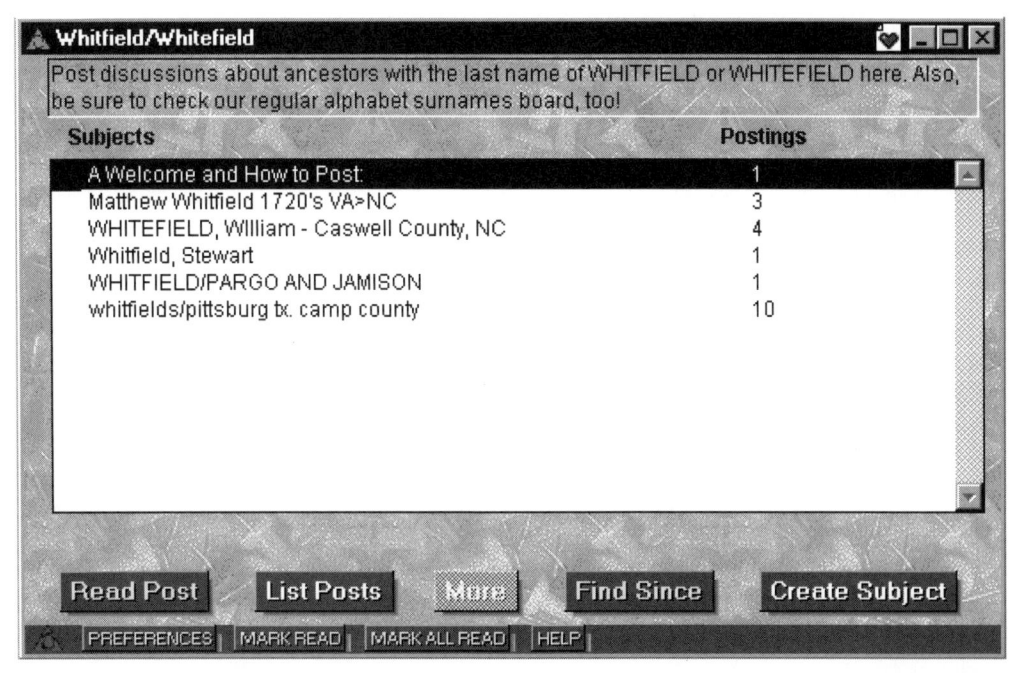

Figure 6.6

can set your preferences for how messages are displayed for you. You can also create or modify your personal signature block — the information that appears at the bottom of every posting and/or E-mail reply.

- **Mark Read** — You don't have to read all the message board postings. If there is a subject that you would like to ignore, simply highlight it and click on the Mark Read button. A small confirmation box will be displayed indicating that the thread has been marked as read.

- **Mark All Read** — Perhaps you decide you're not interested in reading any of the subjects. If this is the case, simply click the Mark All Read button. A small confirmation box will be displayed indicating that the message board has been marked as read.

- **Help** — The Help button on the message screen provides a small amount of descriptive information.

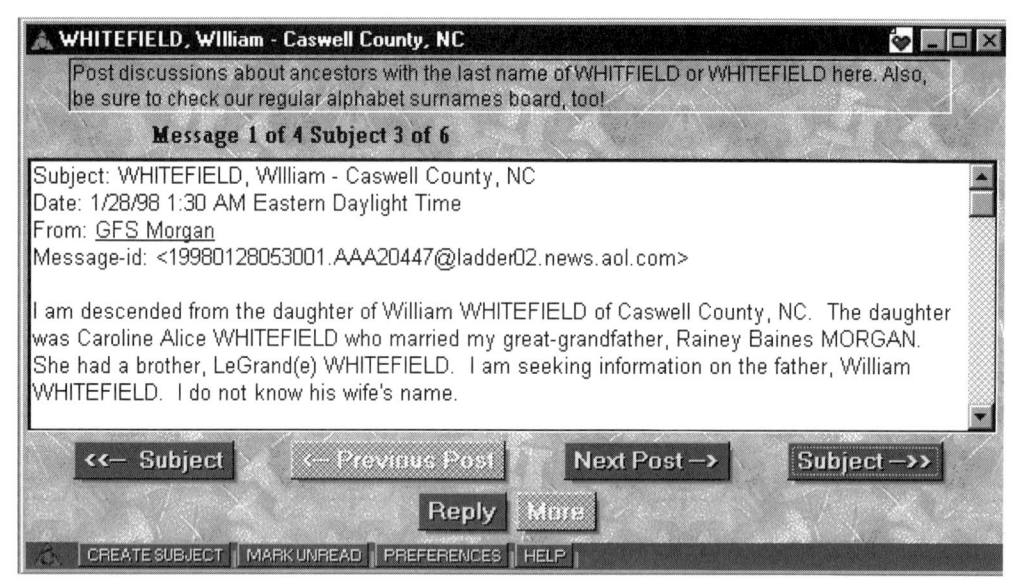

Figure 6.7

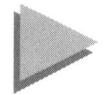

Reading Messages

Let's now look at an existing message posted by another member. When you opened the WHITFIELD/WHITEFIELD message board, there were subjects displayed. When you used the Find Since option, older messages that you had already read were displayed. Let's select the one titled "WHITEFIELD, William - Caswell County, NC" and click on the Read Post button. The window shown in Figure 6.7 will be displayed.

(**Note:** Some users will find the message window too wide for the screen. If that is the case, follow these instructions: Click on the blue title bar at the top of the window with your left mouse button, hold your mouse button down and drag the window to the left on the screen until the right side of the window can be seen. Release the mouse button. Move the mouse pointer to the right side of the screen and place it over the right edge of the window until a black, double-headed arrow appears. Then, press and hold your left mouse button and drag it to the left. This will change the width of the window. Release the mouse button and the width of the message has now been changed. Now, move your mouse pointer back to the blue title bar. Click and drag the window back to the center of your screen for easy viewing.)

You can now read the message posted by another member. You will notice a number of buttons at the bottom of the window. If a button is gray, that function is not available to you at the moment. Let's discuss each button:

1. **<<— Subject** moves you to the previous subject on the message board.

2. **Subject—>>** moves you to the next subject on the message board.

3. **<— Previous Post** moves you to the previous message posted within this subject.

4. **Next Post —>** moves you to the next message posted within this subject.

5. **Reply** presents you with the window shown in Figure 6.8. The reply will be discussed shortly in this chapter.

6. **CREATE SUBJECT** is the first of several buttons at the very bottom of the window. Here you can create a new subject within the message board in which you are located.

7. **MARK UNREAD** is used if you are reading a message and, if when you leave it, you want it to remain unread.

8. **PREFERENCES** allows you to set your preferences for how messages are displayed. You can also create or modify your personal signature block—the

information that appears at the bottom of every posting and/or E-mail reply.

9. **HELP** The Help button on the message screen provides a small amount of descriptive information.

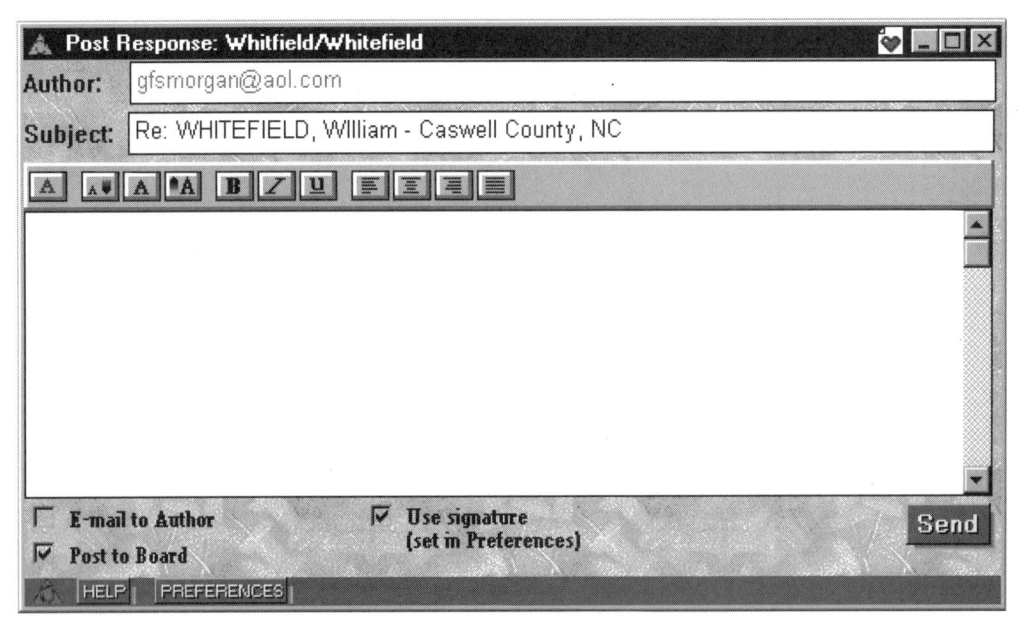

Figure 6.8

Replying to Messages

When you decide to reply to a posted message and you click on the Reply button, a window such as the one shown in Figure 6.8 will be displayed. The author's/sender's E-mail address and Subject boxes are completed for you. The Subject is the same as that in the message to which you are responding, with the addition of "RE:" at the beginning of the subject line. It is important to leave this pre-filled subject line as it is if you want your reply to be included in the thread.

Under the Subject box are a number of small buttons. These can be used to format the content of your message and are similar to some of the tool bars found in popular word processors. For more information about how to use these, please visit the AOL Keyword: **mail extras** for details about changing text.

Type your response in the large white area. Remember, you are responding to someone else's message. You will want to provide useful information and not waste their time. It is customary among genealogists to place surnames in all capital letters. This makes it easy for the reader to scan a written document and locate specific surnames of interest.

Here are some essential tips for any message board posting:

- Don't type in all uppercase. It is difficult to read and signifies shouting.
- Use uppercase for surnames. This makes them easier to pick out of a written document.
- If what you want to communicate is of a personal or private nature, send your reply only by E-mail.
- If what you want to communicate is of interest to a wide audience, send your reply both as a posting to the message board and as an E-mail response to the original message's author. This will ensure that he/she receives the information quickly.

Beneath the message area are three check boxes. The default when you send your reply is to post it to the message board. Your reply will then become part of the thread. You may also choose to send your reply to the original author. It is recommended that you send your replies to both the message board and the author.

In addition, the default is set to send the signature information you defined in your preferences at the end of you reply. If you don't want to send your signature information, simply click on the checkbox to de-select the option. (**NOTE:** You can access and change your preferences from the button at the bottom of the window.)

When you are ready to post your reply, simply click on the Send button.

Creating a Properly Formatted and Effective New Subject

This is the moment of truth. You are ready to post your first query to one of the message boards. Let's say that you want to learn if anyone else has information about your great-grandmother from Georgia. What are the steps you must take to post the message? Let's run through them.

- Locate the right message board on which to post the message. Many people make the mistake of posting a message in the wrong place. (A surname posting on the Computer message board is unlikely to get any responses.) Consequently, the message gets far less exposure than it should, resulting in few, if any, responses. In the example above, it would not be improper to post a message on both the Surnames and Georgia message boards. That way, you double the chances that someone looking for that surname or someone researching in Georgia will see the message.

- Create a thoughtful and meaningful Subject. Don't create a subject line that reads, "HELP!" Nobody will look at it because they have no idea what it is about. It is always a good idea to begin a subject line with the surname. That way, your message will be sorted alphabetically in surname order, and the chances of people finding your message will be increased. Surnames should be typed in uppercase. Additional descriptive information, such as location and time period, may also help other members quickly locate your material.

A proper subject line for a surname query might read:

"SWORDS, Penelope - Floyd Co., GA - 1866 to 1914"

A proper subject line for a geographic query might read:

"Sheva, NC - Seeking Original Name of This Town"

- The body of your message should contain as much information as possible in order to help readers determine whether they can help you. This information would include:

  1. Placing surnames in upper case.
  2. Using complete first, middle and last names, if you know them.
  3. Indicating geographic regions where you are searching. If you are seeking the origin of an individual, provide a backward path if possible. **Example**: Seeking origin of Robert Andrew WOODS who lived in Hillsborough (Orange) NC from 1830-1877. He was in Staunton (Augusta) VA in 1826-1827. Earlier in Cecil Co., MD in 1825. Seeking prior residence and think it is Girvan, Scotland.
  4. Include name of spouse and/or children.
  5. Include every shred of information that might be useful.
  6. Be specific about what you need. "Seeking any information" is fine if you are just starting a difficult tracing. However, "Seeking proof of marriage of Frederick James Williams and Roxanne Jane Omburg in Charlotte (Mecklenburg) NC in 1901" certainly informs readers of precisely what they can do to help you.

When you're satisfied that the message is ready to be posted, decide whether you want to include the signature block that you set up in your personal preferences. When you are ready to post the message, click on the Send button. Your message will be posted to the message board and will remain there for more than two years. Check back regularly to see what replies are posted.

If you would like to reply to a posting, simply click on the Reply button. A reply form like the one shown in Figure 6.3 will be displayed. Here you can type a response to the posting. When you are finished, look at the options in the lower left corner of the form. You may choose to post your response as another posting on the message board, to send your response as a private E-mail to the person to whom you are responding, or to do both simultaneously. Check the appropriate option(s) and click on the Send button.

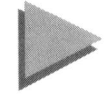

▶ Examples of How to Use the Message Boards

Here are examples of a few of the message boards in the Genealogy Forum and how you can use them:

- Surname Message Boards
    1. Make connections with other people doing research on the same surnames as you, and exchange copies of evidentiary documents you both have located.
    2. Learn about family associations that have compiled information and perhaps publish a newsletter.
    3. Make a connection with a cousin or other relative who may also be working on the family genealogy.

- State Message Boards
    1. Obtain addresses of state agencies where you can obtain records.
    2. Learn about state, county and local genealogical societies.
    3. Make contact with people willing do free courthouse look-ups for you.
    4. Share information with other members about

research problems specific to a particular state.
5. Make contact with others researching in the same geographical area as you.
6. Make contact with distant relatives.
7. Make contact with people who know your family history.

- Ethnic Message Boards
  1. Share information on difficult research problems in particular ethnic groups, including:
     - Doing Jewish research in Europe.
     - Locating original slave owners names in African American research.
     - Tracing family information for Native American ancestors who were forced to relocate.
     - Learning about the origins of Acadian, Cajun and Melungeon ancestors.
  2. Learn about upcoming chats in the Genealogy Forum.
  3. Learn about the historical periods in which your ancestors lived and the events that influenced their lives.
  4. Make contact with other people researching the same areas and lines as you.
  5. Connect with distant relatives.

- Computer Topics
  1. Learn about the strengths and weaknesses of genealogy database software from using the products before you buy.
  2. Learn about new genealogy-related Internet Web sites.

- Ships Passenger Lists
  1. Locate resources for locating ship arrival records.

    2. Obtain addresses and strategies for locating ships records from other members who have had success.
    3. Learn about passenger arrivals at Ellis Island and its predecessor, Castle Garden, in New York.

- Recipes Message Board
    1. Obtain old family recipes from other members.
    2. Share some of the recipes passed down through your family.
    3. Learn about old cooking and baking techniques.
    4. Get answers about how to translate directions for "a hot oven" into modern oven temperature settings

▶ Summary

Whatever your genealogical interest, you will find message boards that will provide you with stimulating information. Message boards can be an intensely effective genealogical research vehicle, if you use them properly.

7 ▶ The File Libraries Center

GENEALOGISTS ARE GREAT AT SHARING INFORMATION WITH ONE ANOTHER. In the last chapter, you learned about the **Message Board Center**, where you and other AOL members can post messages and queries allowing you to share information with one another. But messages are simply that—small text messages that are usually typed manually. While you certainly *could* type a long message of up to 32,000 characters in length, you probably don't want to. Other members would certainly not read through it.

When you want to exchange larger amounts of information, you will usually want to save it as a computer file and then send the file. This is especially true with data you extract from your computerized genealogy database or other programs. You may want to send a copy of a file to another person as a file attachment to an E-mail message. Better yet, you may want to make the file generally available to many genealogists at once.

The Genealogy Forum makes it possible to share your files with many people simultaneously through its **File Libraries Center**.

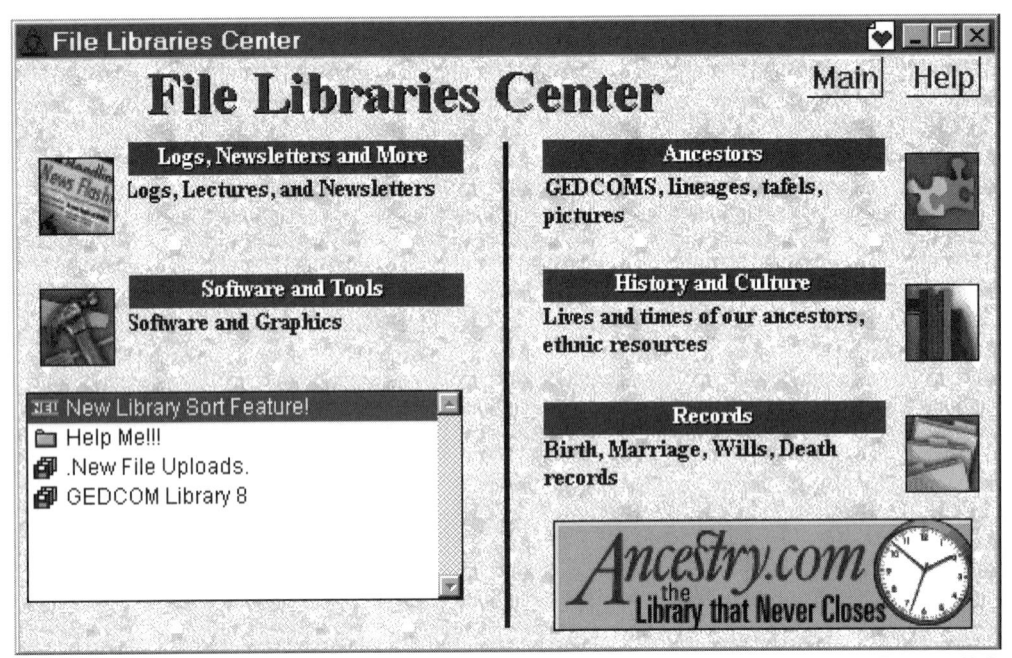

Figure 7.1

In the File Libraries Center you will find thousands of files available that have been uploaded by other AOL members and by Genealogy Forum staff. The files are arranged in categories to help you easily find what you are looking for. You can download files of interest to you that may help with your research. You also can upload your files to become part of the library.

To access the File Libraries Center from the Genealogy Forum's main screen, simply click on the button labeled, "Files." The screen shown in Figure 7.1 will be displayed. As with all the other centers, the screen can be said to have two groups:

- There are five main topic areas, each with its own buttons and descriptive text. These are the larger, logical groupings of files. We will discuss each of these areas and their contents in detail later.
- The listbox in the lower left hand quadrant contains a collection of informative "how to" articles and links to the two "New File Uploads" libraries.

▶ Organization of Material in This Chapter

Each of the file areas and the types of files they contain will be discussed in this chapter. Before we talk about them, however, let's talk about how files get into the libraries. That done, we'll talk about the logistics of uploading files. Finally, we'll discuss how to download files.

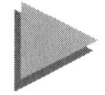

▶ How Do Files Get Into the Libraries?

The files in the File Libraries Center are of various types. There are files from genealogy databases, newsletters, historical files, maps, archives of logs from online lectures and chats in the forum, recipes, tips, genealogy forms, photographs, software, and more. They have all been uploaded by AOL members or Genealogy Forum staff from their computers to the Genealogy Forum on AOL. Ultimately, each file goes into a permanent library. In the meantime, however, the process goes through the following steps:

1. A file is uploaded to the Genealogy Forum's "New File Uploads" area. (Full uploading instructions appear later in this chapter.)
2. The file arrives in a file holding area.
3. One of the file librarians reviews the files in the holding area.
4. Each file is downloaded by the librarian and checked for viruses, using the most current version of a virus detection software package.
   - If the file contains a virus, it is rejected.
   - If the file is virus-free, the process continues.
5. Depending on the content of the file, it is then placed in one of two "New File Uploads" libraries as follows:
   - If the file contains family tree information in the GEDCOM file format, it is placed in the "New File

Uploads GEDCOM" library. (GEDCOMs are a standard file format, usually extracted from a genealogy database program. These will be discussed later in this chapter.)
- All other files are placed in the "New File Uploads" library.
6. Files remain in these two libraries as follows:
   - GEDCOM files remain in the same library until the library area is filled. A new library is then opened and new files are added there until that library is filled.
   - All other files remain in their library for about a month. The forum's file librarians then move each file to its most logical category, depending on the file description. For example, a file described as containing information about the Civil War would be moved to the "1620 - Present - Modern History" library. A file containing transcribed obituaries for some locale would be moved to the "Death Records, Obits and Wills" library.

The "New File Uploads" libraries are shown in the listbox in the lower left hand quadrant of the File Libraries Center screen. You and other members can access the files once they are made available in these libraries, as well as after they are moved to their permanent locations. By placing newly arrived files in the "New File Uploads" libraries, the Genealogy Forum makes it easy for you to quickly identify the new items you have not reviewed.

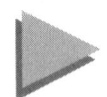

Why Do I Want to Upload Files?

The Genealogy Forum welcomes genealogy-related files that you might like to upload. You will want to upload your genealogy database file, no matter where you are in the research process. Many people think that because their work isn't complete, they should wait and upload their file later. Nothing could be less beneficial. By uploading your genealogy database files, you accomplish two things:

1. You share your information with other researchers. The information in your file may provide someone else with the "missing link" they were seeking.
2. You increase the chances that someone else researching the same lines will see your file and contact you to share their information.

Other files containing things such as graphical images of maps, written accounts of battles, transcribed obituaries or wills, and many, many more subjects are wonderful contributions to the body of online knowledge. You don't have to be the best writer in the world to submit written information; you just need to be accurate and write in a format that other people can read.

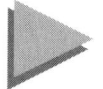

How to Upload a File

Uploading a file from your computer to the Genealogy Forum is a simple process. Simply follow the steps below and refer to the screen images. If you get lost, start again.

Before you upload a file, please read the "Guidelines for Uploading Files" section in this chapter.

1. From the listbox in the lower left hand quadrant of the File Libraries Center screen, select and open the "New Files Uploads" item. A screen like the one shown in Figure 7.2 will be displayed.
2. Click on the button at the bottom of the screen labeled, "Upload File." The screen shown in Figure 7.3 will be displayed. This is the template you will use to describe your file.
3. In the SUBJECT box, type the title of the file. It is important that this be a meaningful description. This

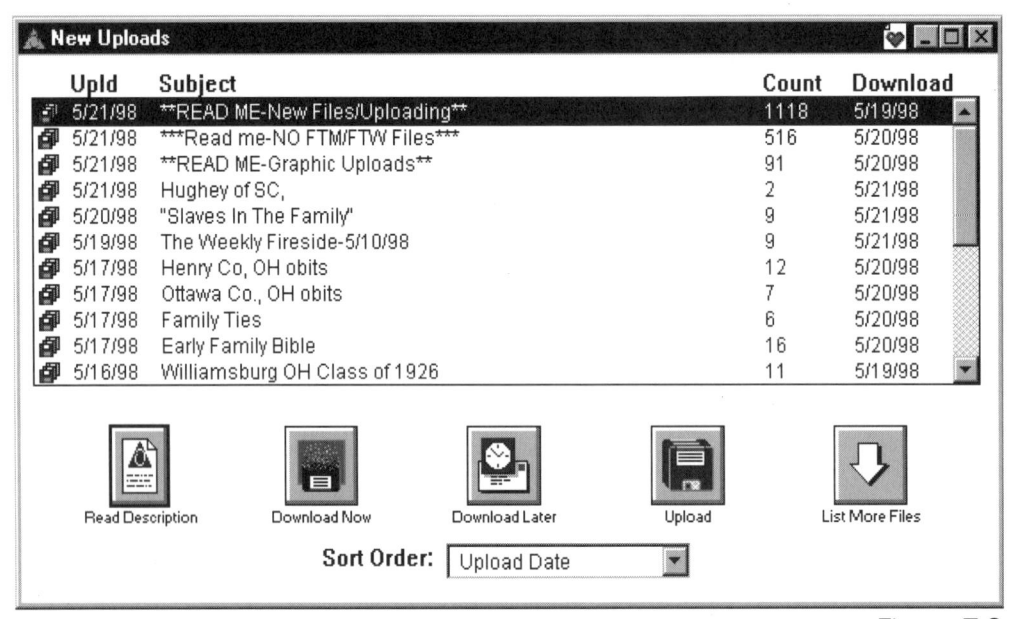

Figure 7.2

Figure 7.3

144 — The Genealogy Forum on America Online

will be the file description that people will see in the library list. Figure 7.2 shows you how such a list appears. By providing a good description, you ensure that people will be able to tell what is inside your file just by looking at the title.

- Family files should read:
  SURNAME IN UPPERCASE - Dates - Location
  Example: ALEXANDER - 1725-1946 - MD & NC
- Other files should read:
  Description - Any appropriate dates - Any location
  Example 1: Lee's Surrender - 1865 - Appomattox, VA
  Example 2: Map of Sweden - 1900

4. In the AUTHOR box, provide the name of the author of the file. This is generally the name you are using as the person submitting the file. You can also add your E-mail address, if you would like.

5. Leave the EQUIPMENT box blank.

6. In the NEEDS box, please specify text reader. If the file is larger than 24K and you have compressed (zipped) the file, please specify the decompression (unzipping) utility as one of the needs.

7. In the DESCRIPTION box, please provide a good description of your file. This is an important part of your file upload, because other members use the description when trying to decide whether to download your file. For example, if your file contains information from a family Bible, please give details of the names in the Bible, and the time period.

8. The Language at the bottom of the screen can be left marked as English.

9. Next, you must select the file to be uploaded. To do so, click on the button labeled, "Select File." A window like the one shown in Figure 7.4 will be displayed. To select the file you wish to upload, follow the instructions below. (**NOTE**: The window shown in Figure 7.4 is from Windows 95. Your window may be different, if

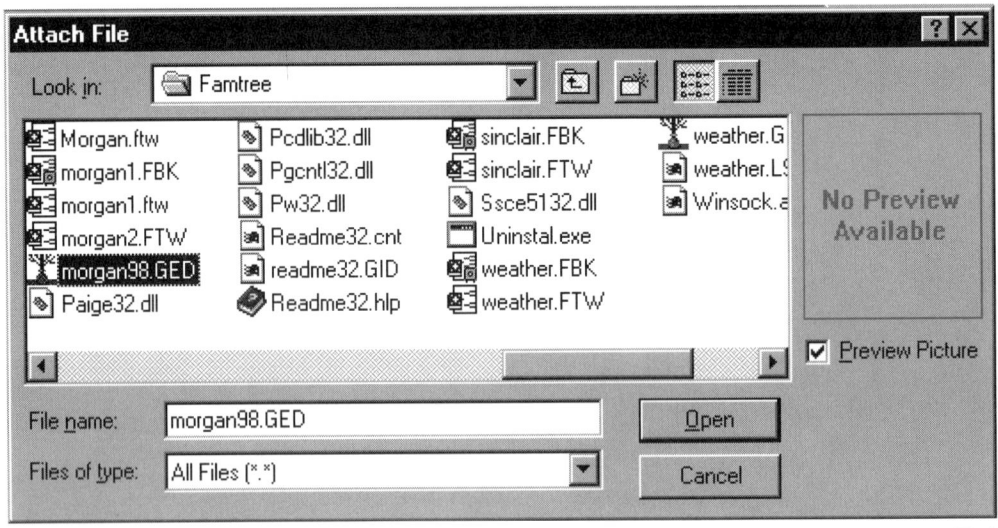

Figure 7.4

you are using another computer operating system. The process for selecting and attaching your file may also vary. Please check the user manual for your operating system for more information.)

- In the box labeled "Look in:" at the top of the window, click on the down arrowhead on the right. Locate the system drive, directory (and any sub-directories) where the file is located.

- In the large window below, locate the file and highlight it by clicking on it once with your mouse. (In this example, the filed named morgan.GED is highlighted.) The file name will be placed in the box below labeled "File name."

- Click on the button labeled "Open."
- The "Attach File" window you were just working in will close, and the file name and its path will have been inserted into the box in the upload screen.

10. At this point, your upload description screen should be complete. Your screen should now look something like the one shown in Figure 7.5. Take a few moments to review your information. Check for spelling errors and make sure you have attached the *correct* file.

Figure 7.5

[New Uploads window showing:
- Subject: MORGAN Family - 1735-1998 - NC
- Author: George Morgan gfsmorgan@aol.com
- Equipment:
- Needs: Text reader or GEDCOM reader
- File: C:\FAMTREE\MORGAN98.GED
- Description: This file contains the genealogy of the MORGAN family in NC from the arrival of Goodloe Warren MORGAN from England in 1735 to June of 1998.

The file contains the following major surnames:

MORGAN, WILSON, ALEXANDER, POTTS, WHITFIELD/WHITEFIELD, HOUSTON, DAVIDSON, PATTERSON, BALL, HOLDER, & WEATHERLY
- Language: ENGLISH]

11. When you have finished the editing, you are ready to upload the file. Simply click on the "Send" button. AOL will begin the upload, and you will see a File Transfer window like the one shown in Figure 7.6. The slide rule bar will move from left to right, representing the percent of transfer completed, until it is done. At

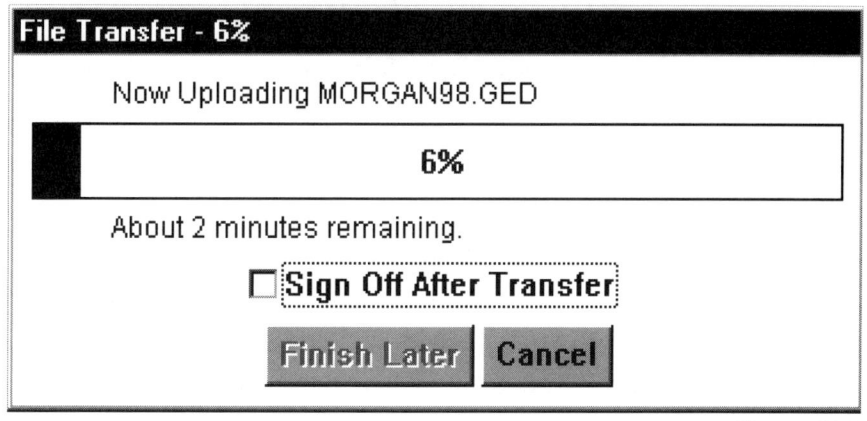

[File Transfer - 6%
Now Uploading MORGAN98.GED
6%
About 2 minutes remaining.
☐ Sign Off After Transfer
Finish Later   Cancel]

Figure 7.6

The Genealogy Forum on America Online — 147

the conclusion of the transfer, a small window will be displayed that reads, "Your file has been submitted and will be reviewed." If your computer supports sound, a voice will say, "File's done." Click on the OK button.

12. If your file is formatted correctly, it should be released within 72 hours into a "New File Uploads" library. You will not get a notification; you should check the "New File Uploads" area yourself.

You have now completed your first file upload. Congratulations!!!

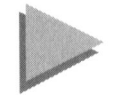

Guidelines for Uploading Files

There are some guidelines you should follow when you plan to upload files to the File Libraries Center.

- First of all, you should never upload copyrighted files, unless you are the copyright holder or unless you have written permission from the copyright holder. In that case, you should provide the Library Administrator, GFA Beth, with a copy of a written release for that specific file. For more information, please send an E-mail inquiry to GFA Beth on AOL.

- Upload items in ASCII (plain text) format, unless they are computer platform-specific.

- Please supply a reasonable file description that details the contents of your file. This helps the library administrators and other users, and makes it easier to assign the file to its appropriate library.

- Please try to cite your sources in your files. Other genealogists are eager to read and use your file. By citing the sources of your information, you make it easier for others to locate the same informational resources. And, while you may be a wonderful genealogist, other people still will want to verify and corroborate your material.

- Do not use any characters such as ""*, -, &, =, +, -, @" or others in the subject line of your file description when uploading. These could prevent the file from being properly sorted. The library staff will remove these characters before releasing the file into a library.

- Please do not upload duplications of the same file to different libraries by giving them different names. This causes extra work for the staff, and may result in your file not being released.

- Any uploads which violate the above rules, or which contain a computer virus, will be rejected. In such cases, the person who uploaded the file will be asked to rectify the problem and re-upload. If there is a problem with your file, you will receive an E-mail from a member of the library staff.

- The Genealogy Forum reserves the right to refuse any file it receives that, in its opinion, may be found to be unsuitable for the Genealogy Forum. Likewise, any files previously uploaded that are found to be of an unsuitable nature will be deleted.

The Genealogy Forum library staff is responsible for all the libraries. They check the "New File Uploads" area frequently for new files. Usually, but not always, your file will be released within 72 hours of the time you upload it.

Other newly uploaded files may not appear in the "New File Uploads" library. Some, such as meeting (chat) logs and message board archives, are immediately placed in their respective libraries. You will need to check those libraries as well, if you want to see those new files.

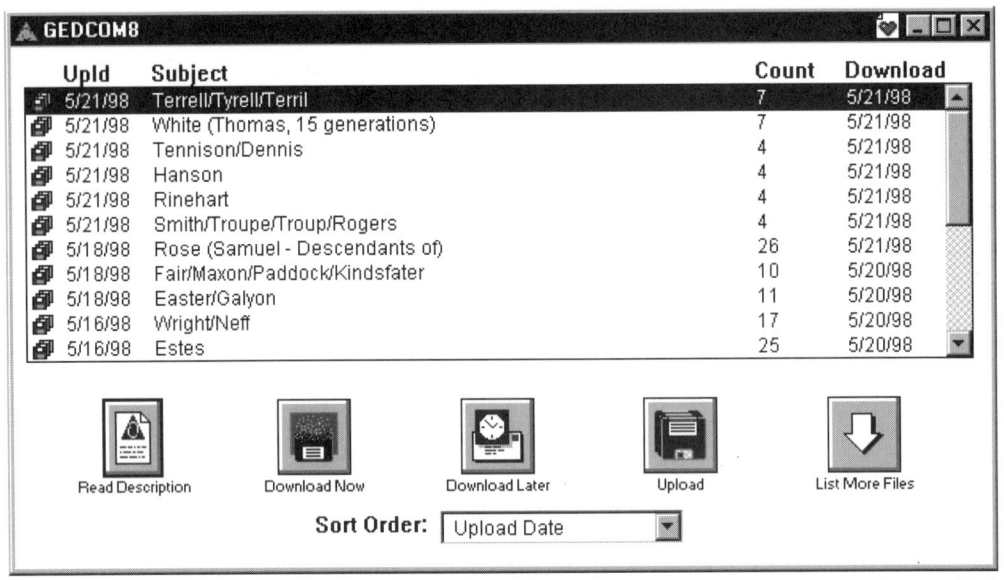

UpId	Subject	Count	Download
5/21/98	Terrell/Tyrell/Terril	7	5/21/98
5/21/98	White (Thomas, 15 generations)	7	5/21/98
5/21/98	Tennison/Dennis	4	5/21/98
5/21/98	Hanson	4	5/21/98
5/21/98	Rinehart	4	5/21/98
5/21/98	Smith/Troupe/Troup/Rogers	4	5/21/98
5/18/98	Rose (Samuel - Descendants of)	26	5/21/98
5/18/98	Fair/Maxon/Paddock/Kindsfater	10	5/20/98
5/18/98	Easter/Galyon	11	5/20/98
5/16/98	Wright/Neff	17	5/20/98
5/16/98	Estes	25	5/20/98

Figure 7.7

How Do I Locate Files to Download?

Let's talk first about the typical file library screen. When you enter a library, a screen such as the one shown in Figure 7.7 is displayed. In the large window, you will see a list of the file descriptions. You will remember this from the upload discussion earlier in this chapter. Hopefully, the author provided a meaningful description to help you understand what might be inside the file.

At the left of the file description is the date on which the file was uploaded. This tells you how current the file may be. To the right are columns labeled, "Count" and "Download." The "count" figure represents the number of times each particular file has been downloaded. The "download" date indicates the last time the file was downloaded.

▶ *Important!*

The most important thing for you to know about file libraries is that America Online has not yet provided a search facility for them. In other words, there is no way for you to open a library and search for a specific word or phrase. The Genealogy Forum staff have, however, indexed all the GEDCOM files—extracts from a genealogy database program. These are searchable from the "Search the Forum" facility discussed in a later chapter.

In the meantime, however, there is a file sorting facility available that can help you locate files. At the bottom of the screen is a window labeled, "Sort Order." To change the order in which the files are sorted, click on the down arrowhead button on the right side of the Sort Order window. A pop-up window will be displayed with the following four options:

- **Upload Date** — The list can be sorted by the date of upload. This is helpful if you are looking to see what has been added since the last time you visited the library.
- **Subject** — The list can be sorted alphabetically by subject. This is helpful, for example, if you are looking for a specific surname in a long list.
- **Download Count** - The list can be sorted based on the total number of downloads of all the files in the list. This list is sorted with the most downloaded files located at the top, and the least downloaded located at the bottom.
- **Download Date** — The list can be sorted based on the download date. The most recently downloaded files appear at the top of the lists, and the least most recently downloaded files at the bottom.

NOTE: Once you have listed all the files for a library, one particularly helpful feature is the "Find in Top Window" facility. To locate a word, such as a surname, simply click on the Edit menu at the top of the AOL window and select "Find in Top Window." A small window will be displayed. Type the word you are seeking and press the Find button. Repeat this process to find other occurrences. This is especially helpful in a GEDCOM or Lineage library, where you may have sorted by subject, with the result that the surname you are seeking is not the first one in the title. For example, let's say you were seeking the surname SZYMANSKI, and the name appeared in the following title:

WEST/SZYMANSKI/JOHNSON - 1810-1948 - NJ/VA

You would never find the name in the Sort By subject. By using "Find in Top Window," you could quickly locate a file with this surname in a large library that you might otherwise have had to read all the way through.

There are five buttons across the bottom of the screen shown in Figure 7.7. Let's discuss each:

- **Read Description** — When we discussed uploading files earlier in this chapter, you learned how to complete the upload form. Besides the subject line, you added information about the type of file and a description of the contents. This included the surnames in the file or other descriptive information. When you click on the Read Description button, you will be able to read the descriptive information provided by the person who uploaded the file. You can decide here whether you want to download a copy of the file for yourself.

- **Download Now** — When you click on this button, you indicate to AOL that you wish to immediately down load the file that is currently highlighted in the list. At that time, a window on your computer is opened that is similar to the one shown in Figure 7-8. The name "Download Manager" appears at the top of the window. By default, the system is set up to download the file to

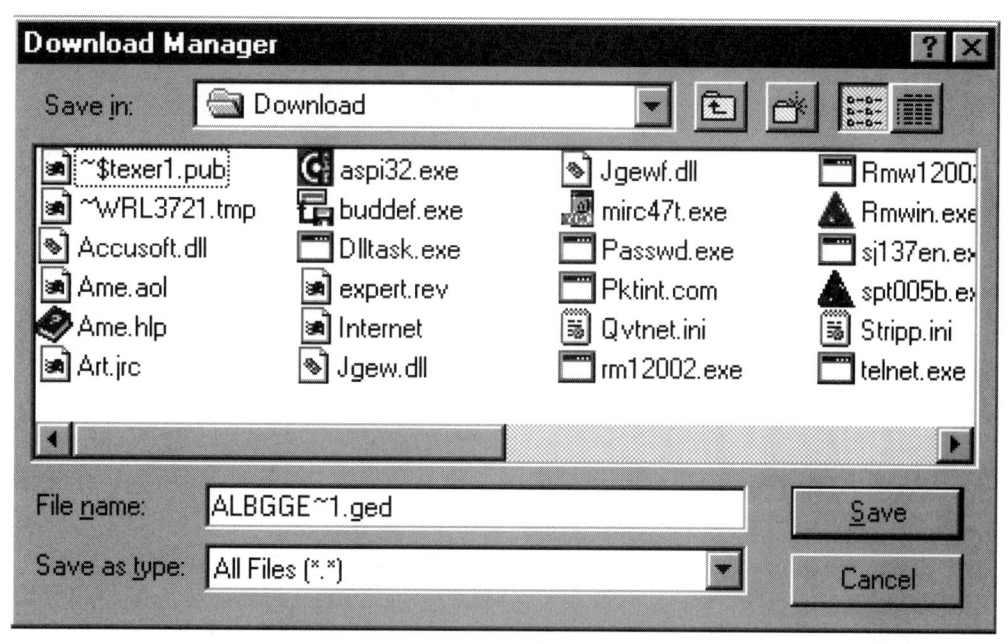

Figure 7.8

your AOL Download directory. Follow these steps to download:

1. You may change the default by clicking the down arrowhead on the right side of the "Save in" window, and then by selecting the disk drive, directory and any sub-directory to which you would like to save the file.
2. You will notice that the file name is already placed in the "File name" window. You can rename the file before it is saved to your computer.
3. When you are ready to save the file to disk, simply click the Save button.
4. A File Transfer window will appear. It will show the progress of the download. If you do nothing at this point, the file will be saved to disk. If you change your mind and decide you don't want the file after all, click on the Cancel button in the File Transfer window. If you start the transfer and

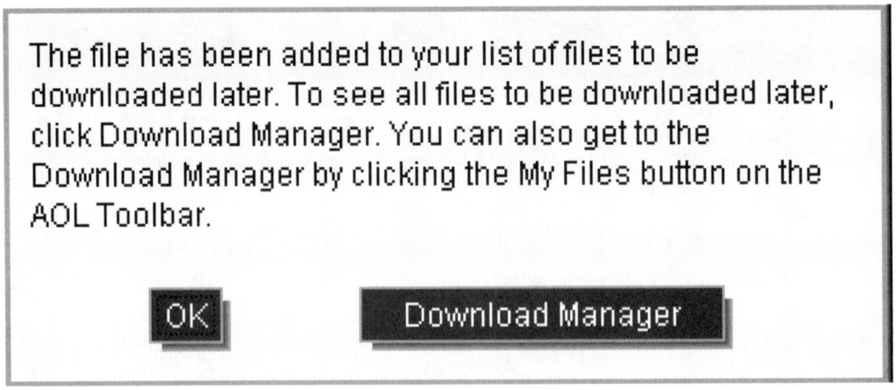

> The file has been added to your list of files to be downloaded later. To see all files to be downloaded later, click Download Manager. You can also get to the Download Manager by clicking the My Files button on the AOL Toolbar.
>
> [OK]   [Download Manager]

Figure 7.9

decide you want to interrupt it, you can resume it later. Simply click on the Finish Later button and the transfer will stop. You can resume it later by coming back, highlighting the file again, and then by clicking on the Download Now button again. If you don't want to wait and watch the file transfer, click on the box labeled, "Sign Off After Transfer."

- **Download Later** — This button allows you to select a number of files as you review them and specify them to be downloaded at a later time. This is convenient if you want to identify several files and then set them up to download after you've finished working at your computer. You can simply start the download by indicating that the computer should log off of AOL when the transfers are complete. You can then leave your terminal.

Follow these steps each time you locate a file you want to download:

1. Double click on the file name in the list.
2. Click on the Download Now button. The confirmation window shown in Figure 7.9 is displayed. To confirm you want this file, click on

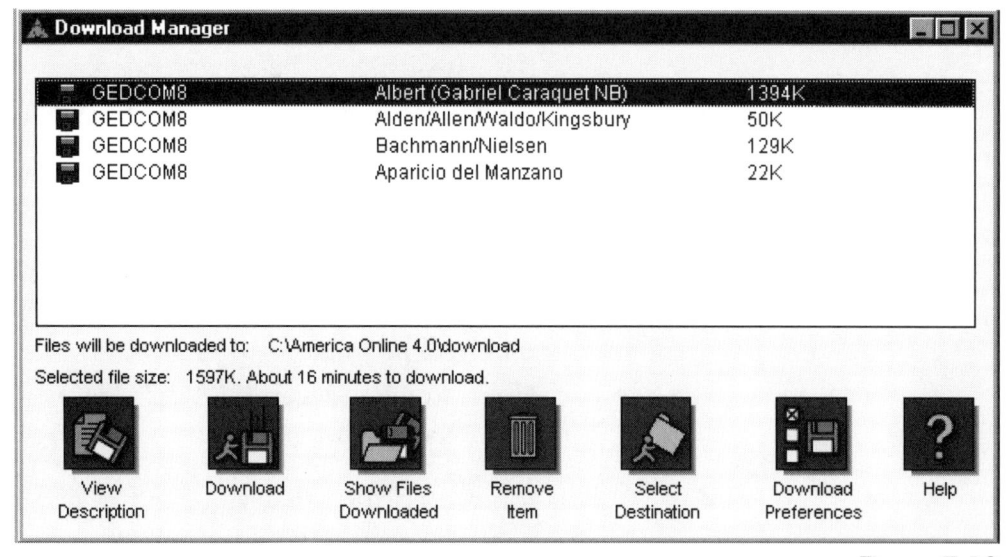

Figure 7.10

the OK button. If you want to review the files you have selected, click on the Download Manager button.

Follow these steps when you have selected your last file and are ready to download the files:

1. Select the Download Manager. The Download Manager window shown in Figure 7.10 will be displayed, along with the list of the files you selected for downloading.
2. Review the list.
3. There are six buttons at the bottom of the Download Manager window:

    - **View Description** allows you to read the file description.
    - **Download** begins the download process as described above under Download Now.
    - **Show Files Downloaded** shows you information about the files you have most recently downloaded.

- **Remove Item** allows you to delete a file from the list of files to be downloaded.
- **Select Destination** allows you to specify where on your computer you wish the files to be downloaded and stored.
- **Download Preferences** allows you to customize how you want downloaded files to be handled and to which default directory they will be loaded.
- **Help** provides access to AOL's Help documentation.

4. When you are satisfied that you want to download all the files in the list, click on the Download button. The file transfer process will begin. Each file will be separately transferred to the place you indicated on your computer.

   Once the transfer is complete, you can review the files transferred in the Download Manager. Simply click on the Show Files Downloaded button. In the window that appears, in addition to some of the options already discussed, you can view the description and check the status of any file that transferred to your computer. You can also decompress files that may have been made smaller by the person who uploaded them. For more information on these options, please refer to the Help documentation on AOL.

- **Upload** — This is the button used to begin the upload process discussed earlier in this chapter.
- **List More Files** - Only a limited number of file names are loaded into the list window at a time. In order to keep adding groups to the list, click on the List More Files button. When there are no more files to be listed, the button will turn gray.

Decompressing Files

Large files are sometimes compressed in the interest of conserving disk storage space or reducing file transfer time. It is the person who uploads the file, not the forum librarians, who compresses the file. He or she will use a file utility program to compress the file. If a file has been compressed, it will usually be noted in the file description window. Another way to recognize compressed files is by checking their file extensions. Common compression file extensions are .zip and .gz.

A common compression utility is a "zipping/unzipping" program. You may choose to use one of these programs when working with your files. To obtain a copy of a compression program, check in the Software and Tools file libraries described later.

Whew! Now that you know how to upload and download files, you need to know what there is available in the File Libraries Center. You already know about the "New File Uploads" and the "New File Uploads GEDCOM" in the listbox. Let's now discuss the five buttons on the right side of the File Libraries Center screen and the organization of the materials there.

All About the Libraries

The file libraries are collections of related files arranged into logical groups. The five buttons on the center's screen represent major categories. Within each category are sub-categories. Let's discuss each major category.

Ancestors

The Ancestors collection contains a number of different types of files. They are:

- *Ahnentafel* **Library** — Ahnentafel is a German word meaning "ancestor table" or "pedigree." An *Ahnentafel* file is usually formatted in such a way that it can be read by a genealogy database program that supports *Ahnentafel* formatted data. The file is of a text type that can be easily read. This format is much less common than in previous years. Generally speaking, GEDCOM files (below) are much more common. Files found in the Ahnentafel Library, however, may provide you with some information not otherwise available.
- **GEDCOM Libraries** — Most genealogy database software programs provide the facility to extract files to allow people to share their data with one another. The intent is that the recipient can import data into his or her program and not have to re-key it. In order to facilitate this, a common format called GEDCOM (short for GEnealogy Data COMmunication) was developed. Names, dates, places and other information in data fields are formatted in such a way that it can all be read from program to program.

    You will find many GEDCOM libraries in the File Libraries Center. The files in them have been compiled over time from submissions by other AOL members. Once a library is filled, another one is begun. Therefore, if you are searching for information about your surname, you should check each library. (**NOTE**: Be sure to use the List More Files button to list every file title. Use the Sort Order option, and then use the Find in Top Window facility to locate surnames that are part of the file title, but are not at the beginning of the title.)

- **Surnames Archives** — The contents of the Surnames Message Boards from previous years have been archived in this area of the File Libraries Center. While these messages are generally several years old, there may be information in them that may be of help. Please note, however, that members who posted these messages and their E-mail addresses may no longer be on America Online. Contacting the author may be impossible. Still, you may find some information that can further your research.

- **Tafel Libraries** — The "Tiny Tafel" is a variation of the *Ahnentafel*. These files tend to be smaller and contain only surnames, date ranges and locations. Since these files tend to be smaller than *Ahnentafel* and GEDCOM files, they often will be listed as simple text documents. Some, however, are quite large. It therefore makes sense to store them as files. The format of the "Tiny Tafel" is explained in detail in Chapter 8.
- **Photographs** — In years past, the Genealogy Forum conducted photo contests. In the Ancestors library group, there are available libraries of photographs from those contests. Subjects include baby pictures, wedding pictures, school pictures, pet pictures and others.

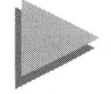

History and Culture

The History and Culture collection contains a wide variety of files. If you are looking for information about specific historical periods, you can be sure to find something here. If you are researching ancestors of a particular ethnic group, there is a wealth of files available here too. And, if you're just looking for a new recipe to try out on family or friends, you may have just hit the mother lode. Let's discuss the contents here:

- **Histories of Specific Times** — There are available here files of historical information from pre-500 A.D. to present.
- **History Lectures and Meeting Logs** — These files contain the proceedings from online meetings and lectures conducted by the History group in the Genealogy Forum. Much of this material relates

specifically to the U.S. Civil War and events of that era.

- **African Diaspora** — Here, African American researchers will find biographical files, census record transcriptions, wills, obituaries, marriage information, slave records, plantation record information, etc. There is a wide diversity of information to be found here, and the African American researcher would do well to cull through all of the materials presented in this library area.
- **Civil War** — These Civil War file libraries contain histories of many units, files describing battles, photographs of the Civil War era, recent reenactments and much more.
- **Hispanic** — There are two libraries for Hispanic researchers available here. One is the Hispanic library; the other is the SHHAR library. The latter contains materials uploaded by, or related to, the Society of Hispanic Historical and Ancestral Research.
- **Jewish** — There is a small library of Jewish resources available in this forum, which is comprised primarily of JewishGen Digests from some time back.
- **Regional & Ethnic Archives** — This is perhaps the most diverse collection of files in this area. These files are comprised of archived messages from a wide range of message boards—from Native American to Molly McGuires, from Southern Asia to the Caribbean, from U.S. Presidents to the DAR/SAR, from Ships' Passenger Lists to the Pennsylvania Dutch, etc. Look here for archived messages from several years back for information on many topics.
- **European Message Archives** — As with the regional and Ethnic Archives, you will find here archived message board content for the countries of Europe.
- **Maps** — There is an impressive collection of map files available in this library. Not only are there many U.S. maps featured, but there is also a vast collection of Irish

county and parish maps, as well as maps of a number of European countries and cities. Civil War, WWI and WWII maps may also be found here.
- **Recipes** — Members have generously shared some of their old family recipes in the form of files in this library. Like the Ancestral Seasonings collection in the Resource Center and the Recipes message board, this is yet another place to find a new dish for your next special dinner. It could also be that you have a special family recipe that you would like to share.

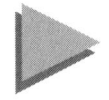

Records

The next major collection is the Records libraries. The fact that members have shared sometimes massive files of local and regional information in file format is impressive. There are libraries for each of the following types of records:

- **Bible, Birth and Marriage Records** — You will be impressed with the scope of many of the files here. Marriage records from many counties have apparently been transcribed and uploaded to the library. In a few cases, there appear to be state records available as well. Transcriptions of many individuals' Bible records are also abundant. Don't forget to use the Find in Top Window facility here to locate specific surnames.
- **Death Records, Obits and Wills** — This library contains individual obituaries, death record information and transcriptions of huge quantities of obituaries from specific newspapers and counties. In addition, you will find that members have uploaded files containing the text of wills, estate inventories and estate settlements for specific individuals. There are also cemetery headstone inscriptions available here. You never know what you will find in these libraries!
- **Genealogical Records** — This library contains another

potpourri of files. Ship passenger lists, tax rolls, oaths of allegiance, census indexes, probate record indexes, rosters of soldiers, veteran lists, pensioner lists, Scottish clans, family records, land lottery lists, etc.

- **National Archives Library** — For the most part, the content of this library is comprised of indexes. This library is by no means complete. However, some AOL members have taken the time to compile and copy various census indexes for some counties and states. There are also files available containing indexes to the National Archives catalog of microfilm information regarding Ship Passenger Lists.

- **Research Tips and Resources** — This is another collection of vast diversity. Do you want to know how to read Soundex codes? Do you want tips about how to write a family history manuscript? Did you want to find a bibliography to help you with your Huguenot research? What about Frequently Asked Questions (FAQs) on Jewish or North American genealogy research? Where do you get free genealogy forms? This is but a tiny list of subjects you will find in this collection. There are plenty of "how-to" files and reference files available here. You need only look through the list, read the descriptions and download the interesting resources available here.

- **U.S. State Message Archives** — Here you will find archived older messages from the message boards for each state. Some of these files contain messages going as far back as 1995. You may find some valuable information by downloading and searching through the files. However, be aware that many of the people may no longer be on AOL. Contacting them for more information may be impossible.

Logs, Newsletters, and More

One of the major attractions of the Genealogy Forum is the chats. Regularly scheduled online meetings on specific subjects draw a huge number of members. Whether discussing Irish genealogy, how to use the Internet for genealogy, New England ancestry, Native American forced migrations, Portuguese research, historical societies in Newfoundland, or any of scores of other geographical or ethnic topics—people love the Genealogy Forum chats. Some of the chats occasionally include lectures as well. As a result, logs containing the content of some of the more important chats and lectures are filed in the File Libraries Center. You will find the log files of these chats and lectures in the following libraries:

- **Genealogy Meeting Logs** — These are files from many different group meetings across the forum.
- **History Meeting Logs** — These files relate to the U.S. Civil War History group.
- **Genealogy Lectures** — There are multiple libraries available in this forum that contain the logs of all the important lecture topics.
- **History Lectures** — There are available files in this library relating primarily to the U.S. Civil War. Other historical lectures are included here as well.

Some of the more active Genealogy Forum staff and volunteer members produce newsletters to help extend the knowledge of people with similar interests. Many of these are archived in this library. Among the most prominent are:

- **The Genealogy Forum Newsletter** — This prolific newsletter is published once a month for all members of the forum. It contains informative articles, stories and recollections shared by members and staff, as well as news about events in the forum and in the world of genealogy. Each newsletter is archived here for reference.

- **Portuguese SIG Newsletter** — This newsletter is produced by the staff who run the Portuguese Special Interest Group (SIG) and who also host the Portuguese chats.
- **The I & S Newsletter** — This newsletter is intended for people researching their Irish and Scottish roots, and contains surnames and research tips.
- **BOBO Roots Cellar** — This newsletter is produced by one of the forum staff for persons researching the BOBO surname.

In addition, there are available specific family newsletters, as well as older newsletters from some other areas of the forum. These newsletters can be a tremendous source of information. Check to see which ones might be of interest to you.

Finally in this collection, there is available a library of Ancestor Photos and Graphics. Included in this library are several hundred images. They include such things as:

- Family photographs from as far back as the mid-1800s to recent family reunions
- Pictures of homes and homesteads
- Photographs of tombstones
- Photographs of towns and cities
- Photographs of rural landmarks and rustic scenes
- Images of coats of arms and other heraldic symbols
- Graphic images of old documents
- Other graphics that might be used in producing genealogy-related publications

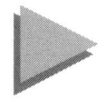

Software and Tools

This collection contains a number of library collections. If you are looking for software that might interface with your existing genealogy database program, you might find it here. Some of the available software may be dated; you will have to be selective and perhaps run some comparisons. There are libraries available for both PC and Macintosh users, and there still are DOS programs available in the archive.

In addition, two of the libraries we discussed earlier are linked in this collection. These are the Genealogy Tips and Resources library, and the Ancestor Photos and Graphics library.

How You Can Get the Most from the Libraries

The File Libraries Center contains thousands of files, and offers a vast wealth of information and resources. The Genealogy Forum library staff, led by GFA Beth, does an incredible job making sure that every file is free of viruses. You can download any file with the assurance that it is not infected.

It is unfortunate that America Online has not yet provided a file search facility. Such a facility would be a tremendous boon to genealogy researchers in the Genealogy Forum. All the same, the forum staff has done a creditable job with its libraries. Materials in the libraries are well-organized and easy to access.

In order to get the most from the File Libraries Center, you need to invest the time in reviewing the contents of each of the major areas. While Genealogy Forum librarians can organize major collections and group like materials together, there are unique topics and materials available that don't merit their own libraries. They must be filed among other materials.

Consequently, it is important that you investigate the libraries. Learn what is available. Look for new files periodically. A possible methodology for investigating the library contents might be to:

1. Enter a major category, such as Ancestors.
2. Select a library, such as GEDCOM 3.

3. Specify Subject as the Sort Order.
4. Continue to click on the List More Files button until no more files can be listed. (Remember, the button turns gray.)
5. Scroll down and look for the surname you are researching or use the Find in Top Window facility.
6. Select the file and click on the Read Description to determine if the file is of interest to you. If so, click on either the Download Now button (to immediately download the file) or the Download Later button (to save the file to the Download Manager for later downloading).
7. Continue looking through the library.
8. Repeat the process as necessary.

If you download a GEDCOM file that you would like to view in your genealogy database software program, please be sure to refer the software's user manual for instructions on how to import and read these files.

Take the time, also, to peruse the New File Uploads libraries. After you have gone through them once, you can go back the next time and use the Upload Date option in the Sort Order window. You will see the new files that have been uploaded since your last review.

As you can see, the File Libraries Center offers a great deal for the active genealogist. All you have to do is learn what it is you're looking for, and then look for it!

8 ▶ The Surname Center

THE KEY TO TRACING YOUR FAMILY TREE IS TO FOLLOW YOUR SURNAMES THROUGH THE MAZE OF RECORDS YOU COME ACROSS, AS WELL AS THROUGH THE STORIES YOU HEAR FROM YOUR FAMILY. Beginning with yourself and working backward through your parents, grandparents, great-grandparents and beyond, your goal is to trace every surname and locate every piece of information possible.

In Chapter 6, you learned about the **Message Board Center**, and how to post effective messages to make contact with others researching your surnames. In Chapter 7, you learned about the **File Libraries Center**, and about uploading and downloading GEDCOMs and other files.

One of the most important tools the Genealogy Forum offers is the **Surname Center**. Here you will find a consolidation of all the information about specific surnames in the Genealogy Forum. The Surname Center combines the resources of the surname message boards and the file libraries, and adds Internet Web page resources and addresses of family associations. The result is an ever-growing central location where you can find almost everything that exists in

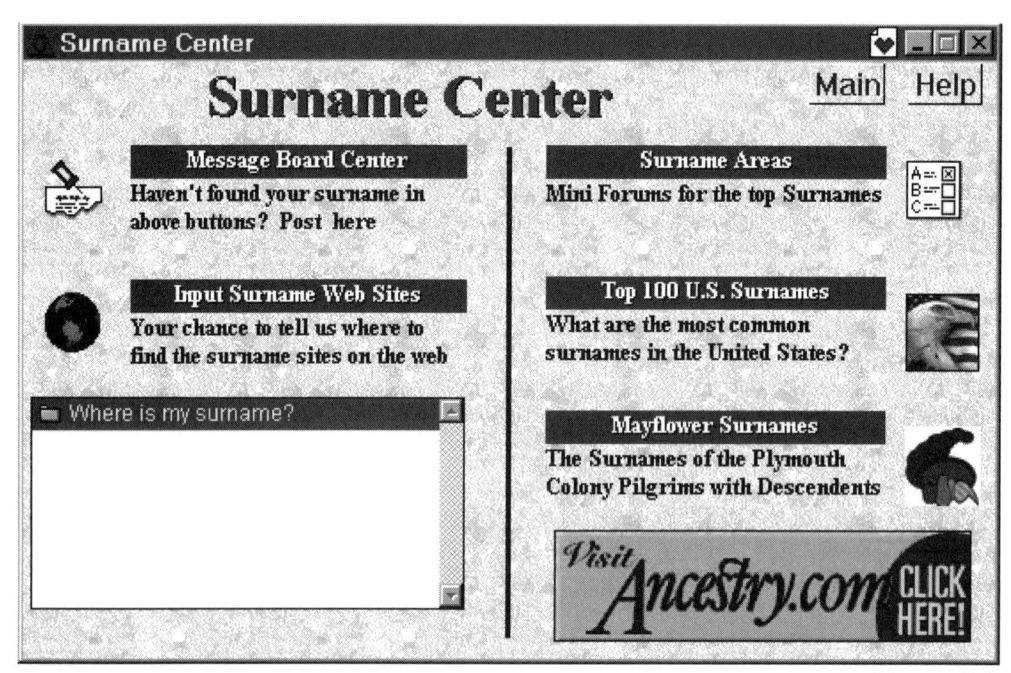

Figure 8.1

the forum about a given surname.

From the Genealogy Forum's main screen, click on the button labeled "Surnames." The Surname Center screen shown in Figure 8.1 will be displayed. This materials on this screen, like all the other Genealogy Forum centers, can be said to be divided into two groups:

- Five main topic areas with buttons and descriptive text that contain major collections of logically organized materials. We'll discuss each of these collections in detail.
- A listbox in the lower left corner containing additional information for your reference.

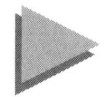

Surname Center

Clicking on the Surname Areas button takes you to an alphabetized collection of surname resources. Here you will find information

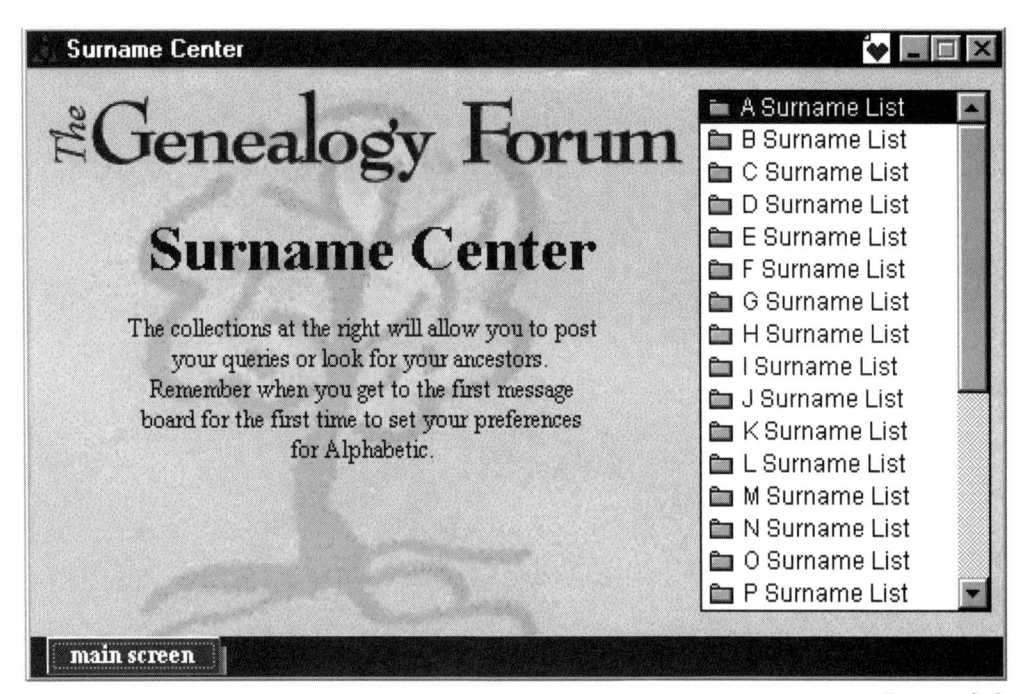

Figure 8.2

about the top 1,000 surnames in the United States, as determined by the U.S. Census Bureau in the 1990 Federal census. See figure 8.2.

Let's select the letter B from the alphabet and click on the "B Surname List." The small window shown in Figure 8.3 is displayed.

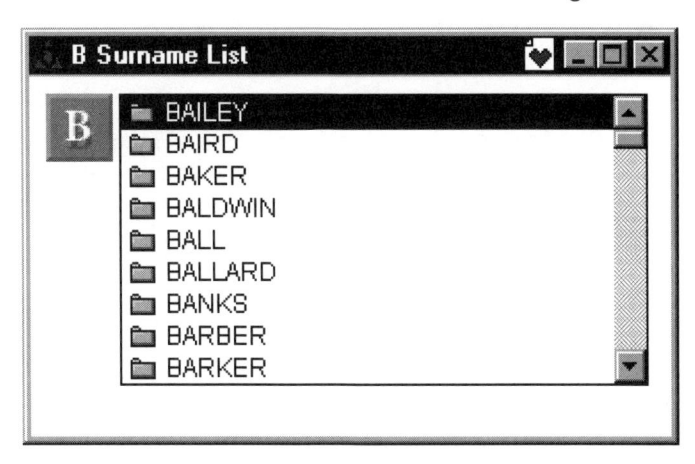

Figure 8.3

The Genealogy Forum on America Online — 169

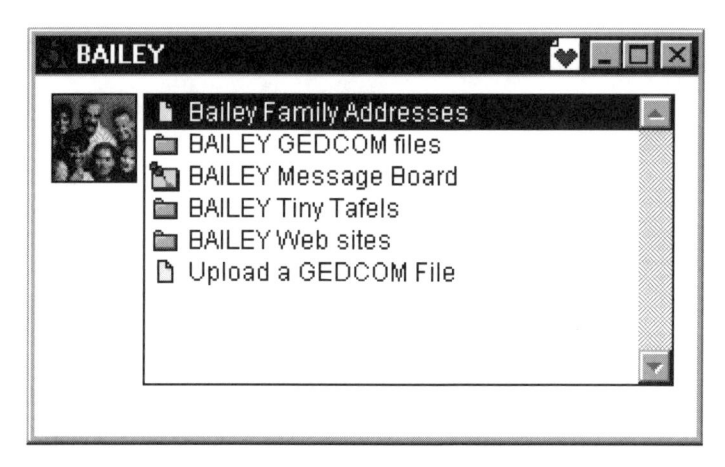

Figure 8.4

It contains all the surnames beginning with the letter B that are part of the top 1,000 list.

If you want to see the contents of the BAILEY surname collection, place your mouse pointer over the name BAILEY and double-click. The window shown in figure 8.4 will be displayed.

Depending on the surname, the contents of the surname collection may vary. In the BAILEY surname collection shown in Figure 8.4, there are six items from which you can select. Let's discuss each of the BAILEY collection contents so that you can have a sense of what materials are available to you.

Bailey Family Addresses (Family Associations)

There are family associations across the world that focus on compiling and documenting information about specific surnames. Some of these groups compile databases and share data with others, either for free or for a small fee. Other groups publish newsletters, soliciting and sharing information in their publications. Still others act as organizers for surname reunions.

The Genealogy Forum is constantly compiling information about family organizations and adding contact information to the

Surname Center. At this writing, the BAILEY collection contained a half-dozen family organization addresses.

If you're looking for more information about ancestors with a specific surname, you certainly should not miss the opportunity to make contact with family associations with your surnames. The minimal time spent writing a letter and the low price of a stamp may bring you that "missing link" information you have been seeking. In addition, some groups who publish newsletters charge a small fee to defray expenses. However, don't hesitate to ask for a free copy so that you can evaluate whether you'd like to subscribe.

▶ Bailey GED-COM Files

As discussed in Chapter 7 about the **File Libraries Center**, GEDCOM files contain data extracted from genealogy database software programs. These files contain names, dates, places and a myriad of other bits of information that you, the genealogical researcher, have compiled and entered into your database.

AOL Members who use the Genealogy Forum are generous in sharing their research. That is what makes the forum such a great place. And, while your research is never completely done, by extracting a GEDCOM file and uploading it to AOL, you accomplish two things:

1. You share your research with others and help them with their research.
2. You significantly increase the chances that others who find connections in your GEDCOM file will contact you and will share their research.

This is a wonderful resource in the world of genealogy, and the Genealogy Forum has thousands of these GEDCOM files in its libraries.

If you are interested in viewing the list of BAILEY GEDCOM

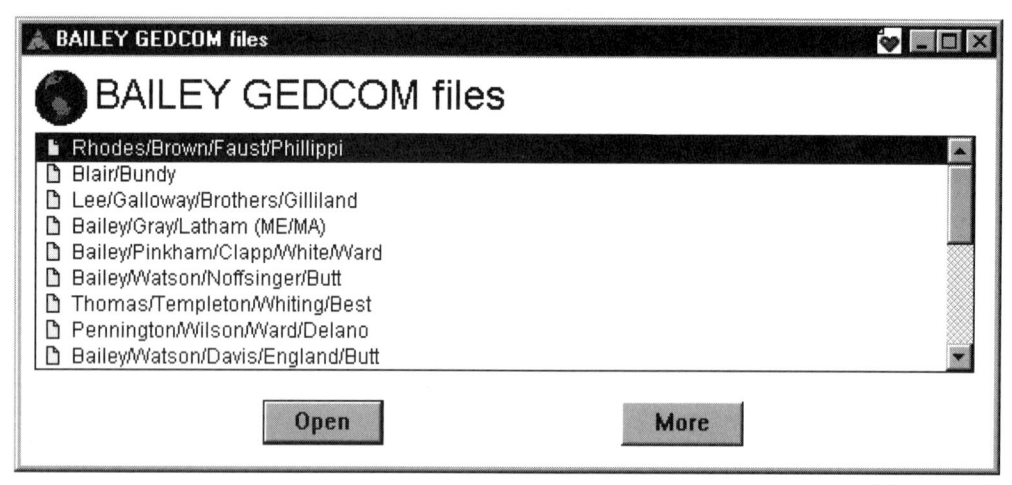

Figure 8.5

files, simply double-click on that item in the window shown in Figure 8.4, and the window shown in Figure 8.5 will be displayed. You will find a collection of GEDCOM files in the forum with the surname BAILEY in them. How is that determined? It is determined by the file's descriptive information, which was provided by the

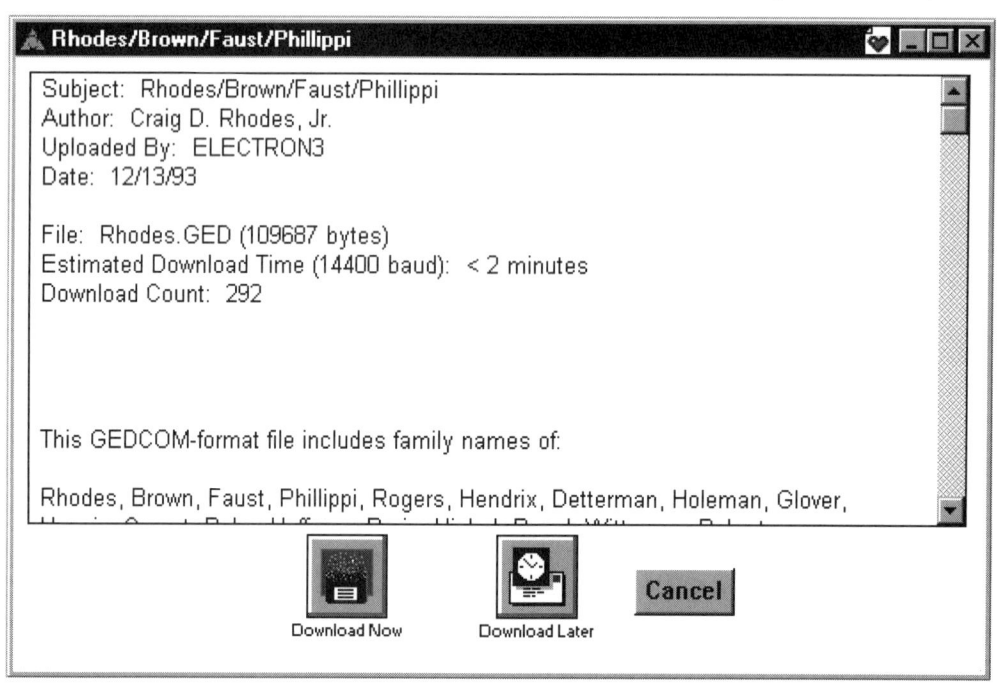

Figure 8.6

172 — *The Genealogy Forum on America Online*

member when the file was uploaded.

There are two buttons on the bottom of this window. The Open button will display another window for you that contains details about the file in the list you have highlighted. (You may also open the window by pressing the Enter key on your computer keyboard, or by double-clicking on the selection with your mouse.)

When you open the new window, it will look something like the one in Figure 8.6. You will notice that the BAILEY surname is not included in either the title bar or the Subject line. If you were to scroll down in the window to view the full description, you would see that the author listed the BAILEY surname as one that is included in the GEDCOM file.

You have the choice of downloading the file now or later. Please see Chapter 7 about the **File Libraries Center** to learn more about downloading files.

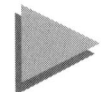

BAILEY Message Board

This option provides you access to the message board specific to your selected surname. For information about how to use the message boards, and about how to create effective query messages, please see Chapter 6 about the **Message Board Center.**

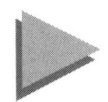

BAILEY Tiny Tafels

"Tiny Tafels" are text files containing abbreviated genealogical information. ("Tiny Tafel" is a shortened form of the German word, *Ahnentafel*, which means genealogical tree or table. "Tiny Tafels" are shortened versions of the larger *Ahnentafel* files.) Whereas a GEDCOM file contains full names, dates, detailed locations and a wide variety of other information, a "Tiny Tafel" contains only a sketch of information. A Tiny Tafel is useful in locating other people who are researching the same surnames in the same places, and from the same time period.

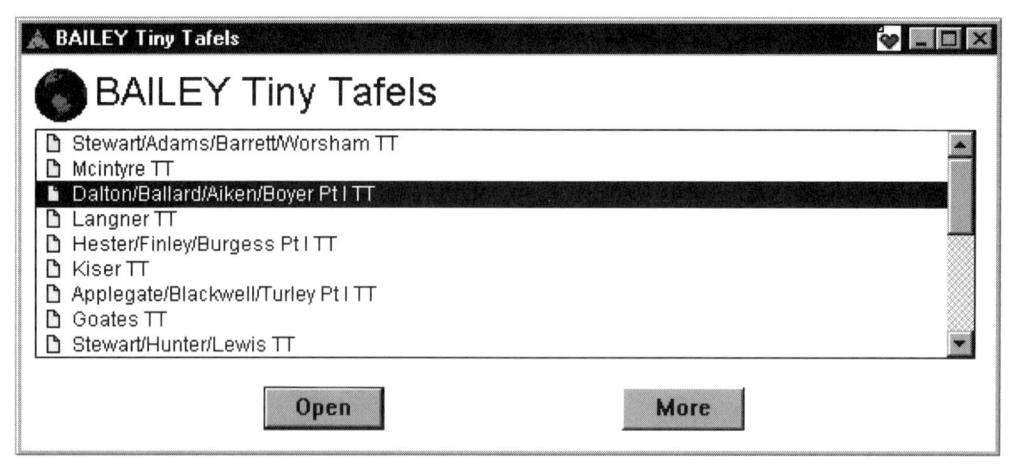

Figure 8.7

You will find many "Tiny Tafels" in the File Libraries Center featured as files, and many others as text file format only. The latter have been placed in the Surname Center. Some "Tiny Tafels" exist in both areas, and in both formats.

To view the list of "Tiny Tafels" in the Surname Center, double-click on the BAILEY Tiny Tafels option in the window shown in Figure 8.4. The window shown in Figure 8.7 will be displayed. Let's look at the one called "Bailey/Blanton/Carr/Nolan TT" by double-clicking on it (or by highlighting it and clicking on the Open button).

When you open the "Tiny Tafel," you will see the window displayed in Figure 8.8. At the top of the file, you will see the following records, or lines of information:

N John Doe
A 1234 Maple Street
A Odessa, FL,33556
A jdoe12@aol.com
T 813-555-1212
D /IBM/
F Brother's Keeper 5.2
Z 54 Brother's Keeper MP

174 — The Genealogy Forum on America Online

In the information above, the name of the person who submitted the information is shown in the "N" record. This person's address is shown in the first two lines of the "A" record, with their E-mail address shown in the third "A" record. The telephone number is shown in the "T" record. The "D" record indicates what type of data processing equipment (computer) this person used (IBM or Macintosh or other). The "F" record indicates what genealogy software program was used. The "Z" record usually includes the number of surname lines in the file, and perhaps some other information.

```
Bailey/Blanton/Carr/Nolan TT

N Jack Banks
A 3076 Allen's Fork Road
A Burlington, Kentucky
A JBanks@AOL.COM
T 606-586-9229
D /IBM/
F Brother's Keeper 5.2
Z 54 Brother's Keeper  MP
B400 1620:1856 BAILEY\Gloucestershire, England/Leslie County, Kentucky
B520 1765:1981 BANKS\Nebraska
B453 1849:1849 BLANTON
B655 1615:1884 BROWNING\England/
C514 1830:1830 CAMPBELL
C600 1660:1660 CARR
C450 1782:1782 CLEM
C512 1733:1759 COMBS\Virginia/Virginia
```

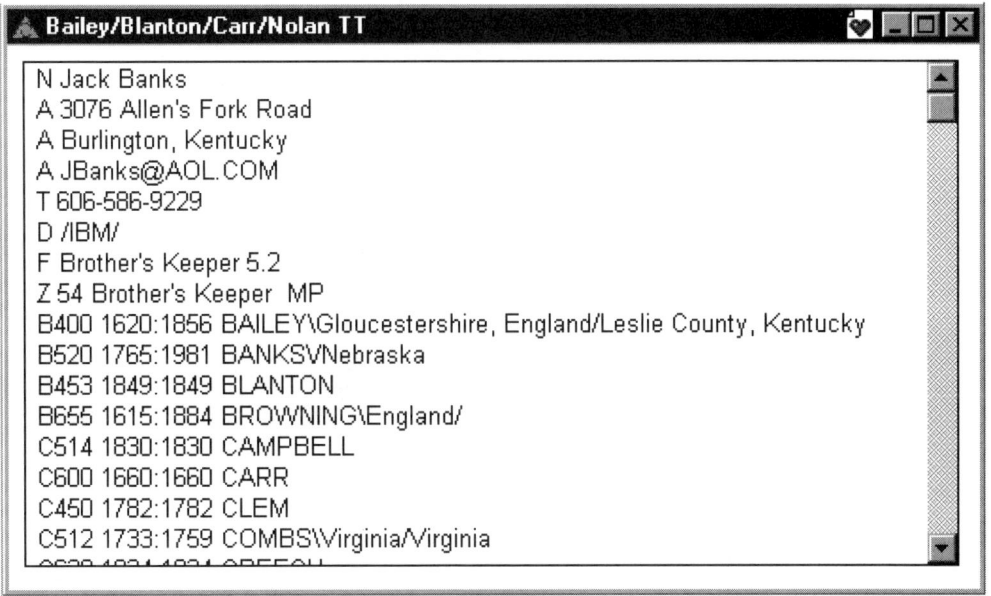

Figure 8.8

The next records look like the following:

B400 1620:1856 BAILEY\Gloucestershire, England/Leslie County, Kentucky
B655 1615:1884 BROWNING\England/
C514 1830:1830 CAMPBELL

The B400 is the Soundex code for the surname BAILEY being listed on this line. (Please refer to the article about Soundex in the

Resource Center on America Online.) The next numbers, 1620:1856, represent a range of years. The surname, BAILEY, is shown next, in uppercase, and is followed by a backward slash and the name of a place—in this case, Gloucestershire, England. This is followed by a forward slash and the name of another place—Leslie County, Kentucky.

What the above tells you is that this person, John Doe, has the surname BAILEY in his genealogy database. The information this person has on the BAILEY surname begins in the year 1620 in Gloucestershire, England, and ends in 1856 in Leslie County, Kentucky.

In the second example above (BROWNING), the Soundex code for the name is B655. This person has information beginning in 1615 in England and ending in 1884, with no place listed.

In the third example (CAMPBELL), the Soundex code is C514, and this person has information available for someone of that surname in 1830 only.

In some cases, you will see question marks listed in the date and/or place fields. Either the software program the person is using or the person has entered these. They indicate that the information is unknown, or is in question.

At the bottom of a "Tiny Tafel" file is a line that looks like this:

W 24 Aug 1998

This indicates the date that the "Tiny Tafel" file was created.

When you are in a "Tiny Tafel" file in the Surname Center, you can easily search for a specific surname within a large file. To do this, click your mouse on the Edit option on the menu bar at the top of the AOL screen and select the Find in Top Window option. You will be presented with the window shown in Figure 8.9. Enter

Figure 8.9

the surname you are seeking, click on the Find button, and the surname will be highlighted.

Once you have located a surname or group of surnames that match the one(s) you are researching, the contact information in the "Tiny Tafel" can help you make connections with others researching the same lines. Please note, however, that the Genealogy Forum maintains these "Tiny Tafels" for several years. Contact information (address, E-mail address and telephone number) may have changed. The originator may no longer be an AOL member, may no longer be at the address included in the file, and/or may have changed telephone numbers.

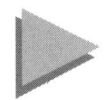

BAILEY Web Sites

With the introduction of the Internet as a venue for genealogical research, more people have begun publishing their family trees on Web pages. Recognizing the need for a centralized collection of Web pages by surname, the Genealogy Forum added a surname Web page facility to the Surname Center. (You will learn later in this chapter how you can have your own surname Web page added to the Genealogy Forum.)

When you open this option, a window such as the BAILEY Web sites shown in Figure 8.10 will be displayed. Here you will find links to all the Web pages submitted by other AOL members who

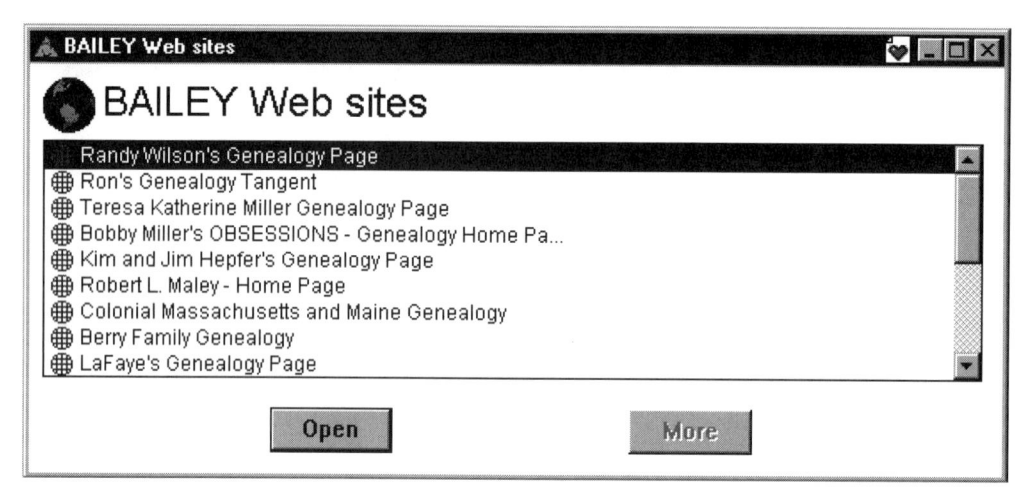

Figure 8.10

use the Genealogy Forum. You can access their Web pages by highlighting an item in the list and clicking on the Open button. (You may also open it by double-clicking on the item.) The Web page will be opened using the AOL Internet browser.

In checking some of the Web pages, you may not easily find the surnames you are seeking. Certainly, you can use the "Find in Top Window" function discussed earlier in this chapter. However, please be aware that the Genealogy Forum accepts the Web page links without verifying the content, and you may have to browse through multiple levels of member Web pages to locate the surname content you want.

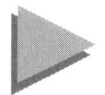

Upload a GEDCOM File

As discussed earlier, sharing your own GEDCOM files can help other researchers, and can increase your chances of connecting with others who can share information with you. If you have created a GEDCOM file from your genealogy software program, you can upload it while you are in the File Libraries Center, or you can upload it from here.

Initially, your file will be placed in a New Uploads area. Eventually, your file will be moved to a library where members can search and locate the file. When you upload your GEDCOM, it is important that you include a detailed description of your file. Be sure to list all the major surnames in the file. The "Search the Forum" facility discussed in a later chapter can be used to locate items by keyword. This facility also allows you to enter a surname and locate all the items in the Forum that include that surname, including files whose descriptions contain the surname.

▶ Top 100 U.S. Surnames

The information found in the Top 100 U.S. Surnames area can also be found in the Surname Areas button, under the top 1,000 surnames listing. The Top 100 U.S. Surnames is a subset of the larger collection. In fact, it was the beginning point for the larger collection. The Genealogy Forum has continued to maintain this collection because members have requested it. It provides a smaller area to navigate. Therefore, if you find your surname in the Top 100 U.S. Surnames collection, you can simply go here instead of to the larger collection.

▶ Mayflower Surnames

If one of your ancestors came from England on the *Mayflower*, survived the voyage, and lived to produce children, their surname will be included in this collection. In addition, anyone else with the same surname will be included here as well.

If your surname is one of the top 100 or top 1,000 (such as SMITH), you will find your surname collection in the Surname Areas collection, in the Top 100 U.S. Surnames collection and in this one. The information is all the same; the collection is simply linked in all three areas.

If your surname is BREWSTER, however, your surname is not one of the top 100 or 1,000 surnames. A BREWSTER was, however, on the Mayflower. Therefore, the only place you will find the BREWSTER collection is under the Mayflower Surnames collection.

Therefore, look in all three places the first time you go searching for your surname.

▶ Message Board Center

This button in the Surname Center connects you to the Message Board Center discussed in Chapter 6. If you have not found your surname in the Surname Center so far, you should go back to the Message Board Center. Look for messages posted by others researching your surname(s), and post messages of your own.

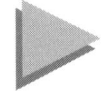

▶ Input Surname Web Sites

Earlier, when discussing the Surname Areas and when looking at the BAILEY surname example, you saw Web sites for specific surnames. The Input Surname Web Sites button allow you to submit your own Web page for addition to the Top 1,000 surnames collections.

If your Web site contains one or more of the top 1,000 surnames, you can submit the Web page address (URL) and the Genealogy Forum will add it as a resource for others to access. You should also check back here often to see what new Web sites other people submit. You never know where that next lead will come from!

To submit your Web site, click on the Input Surname Web Sites button. Read the introductory screen describing the project, and then click on the "Top 1,000 Web Sites" button. The screen shown in Figure 8.11 will be displayed.

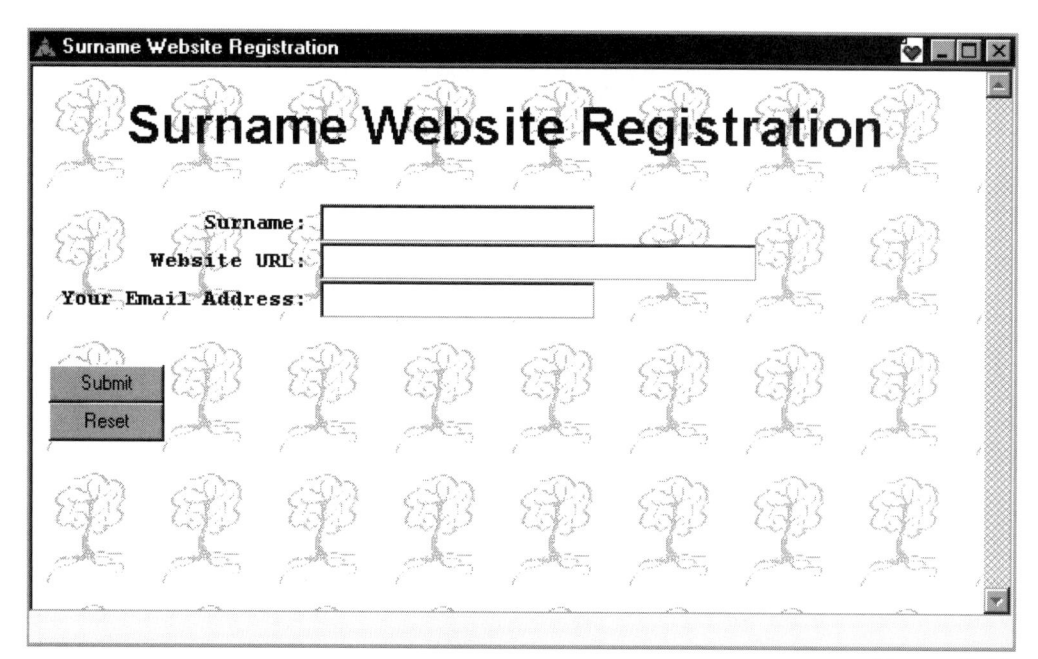

Figure 8.11

Enter all of the surnames that are referenced on your Web page into the "Surname" box. The information you enter here will be used to create an entry in the Genealogy Forum. It is therefore recommended that you enter this information in uppercase. The box will accept many characters, so type in your surnames until you can type no more.

Enter the Web address of your Web page in the "Website URL:" box. Please include the full address, as in this example:

http://members.aol.com/jdoe12/myfamily.html

Finally, you should include your own E-mail address. This will provide a way for the Genealogy Forum staff to contact you in the event that there are questions about the Web page.

There are two buttons on the screen labeled "Submit" and "Reset." If you make a mistake and want to start over, click the Reset button. It will clear the form and let you begin again. When you are ready to send the information to the Genealogy Forum, click on the Submit button. Your Web site will be added to each of the applicable top 1,000 surnames within two weeks, usually less.

Summary

The Surname Center is a tremendous resource for you. If you are researching one of the top 1,000 U.S. surnames, you will find family association contacts, GEDCOM files to help your research, "Tiny Tafels" to provide you with contacts to others doing similar research, links to Web sites created by people researching the same names, and links to the surname message boards. This single, consolidated site is the most popular place in the Genealogy Forum, and with good reason. Don't overlook this terrific resource.

9 ▶ The Chat Center

CHAT ROOMS ON AMERICA ONLINE PROVIDE A WAY FOR PEOPLE WHO SHARE A COMMON INTEREST TO GET TOGETHER "LIVE" IN A VIRTUAL CONFERENCE ROOM FOR DISCUSSIONS. There are many chat room facilities, available as part of the various forums on AOL, and as part of the People Connection.

The Genealogy Forum uses a number of permanent chat rooms, also known as "conference rooms," which are grouped together in the **Chat Center**. The Genealogy Forum uses chats for educational and social purposes. These chats include:

1. Regularly scheduled chats called **SIGs** (Special Interest Groups) meet to discuss such topics as how to research in every state in the U.S., how to research in almost every geographical area overseas, how to research specific ethnic groups, how to use the Internet for genealogical research, and how to compare genealogy software programs. There are even discussions available of historical eras, primarily the U.S. Civil War period. SIGs are hosted by Genealogy Forum staff members

who have knowledge, experience and expertise in each respective area.

2. Some chats in the SIGs may take the form of lectures, wherein a specific educational topic is presented, and then followed by a question-and-answer period. Most of these lectures are presented by the hosts.

3. Scheduled chats called **DIHs** (Drop-In Hours) also meet regularly, just like the SIGs. The difference is that these chats are unhosted. Members meet and share information with one another in a casual forum during a DIH.

4. There is even a conference room available in the **Reunion Center** specifically for use in discussing and holding online family reunions.

While there will be at least one chat every week that you will find of interest, there will likely be more. All you have to do is check the schedule and then attend.

Let's look at the Chat Center's screen, talk about the conference room structure and then discuss how to get the most out of the Genealogy Forum's chats.

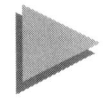

The Chat Center Screen

The Chat Center screen is accessible from the Genealogy Forum's main screen. Simply click on the button labeled "Chats," and the screen shown in Figure 9.1 will be displayed.

The Chat Center screen can be said to be divided into two groups of materials. They are:

- Buttons and descriptions for five chat rooms

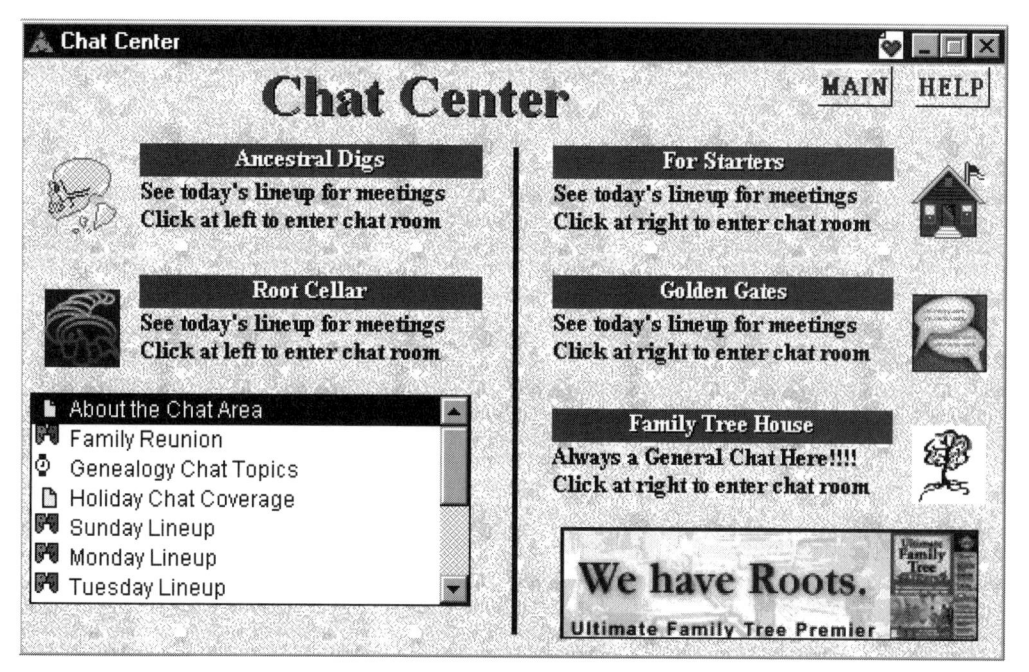

Figure 9.1

- A listbox containing information about the Chat Center and schedules of every event to be held during the week.

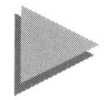

Check the Schedule

The first thing you want to do is check the schedule for upcoming chats that may be of interest to you. You will see in the listbox an item labeled, "Genealogy Chat Topics." This is the full list of every chat—SIG or DIH—scheduled in the forum, and is always up-to-date. Double click on this item in the listbox to open it. (NOTE: This is a rather large document and requires a short amount of time to completely load and format on your computer. If you open the document and scroll through it before the loading is completed, you may encounter some strange formatting. If this happens, simply close the document and reopen it again. Allow it to load completely this time.)

When the document has loaded, and you begin scrolling

Genealogy Chat Schedule

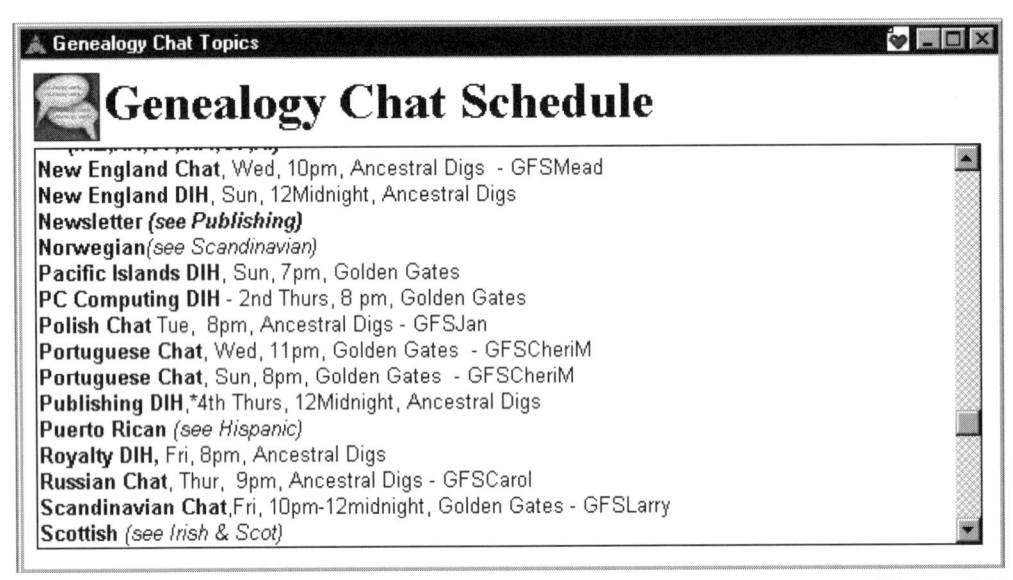

```
New England Chat, Wed, 10pm, Ancestral Digs - GFSMead
New England DIH, Sun, 12Midnight, Ancestral Digs
Newsletter (see Publishing)
Norwegian (see Scandinavian)
Pacific Islands DIH, Sun, 7pm, Golden Gates
PC Computing DIH - 2nd Thurs, 8 pm, Golden Gates
Polish Chat Tue, 8pm, Ancestral Digs - GFSJan
Portuguese Chat, Wed, 11pm, Golden Gates - GFSCheriM
Portuguese Chat, Sun, 8pm, Golden Gates - GFSCheriM
Publishing DIH,*4th Thurs, 12Midnight, Ancestral Digs
Puerto Rican (see Hispanic)
Royalty DIH, Fri, 8pm, Ancestral Digs
Russian Chat, Thur, 9pm, Ancestral Digs - GFSCarol
Scandinavian Chat,Fri, 10pm-12midnight, Golden Gates - GFSLarry
Scottish (see Irish & Scot)
```

Figure 9.2

through the schedule, you will find every scheduled chat listed alphabetically by name. Figure 9.2 shows a section of the chat schedule. The day of the week, the time and the chat/conference room locations are listed. All times shown are U.S. Eastern Time (ET). (**NOTE**: Daylight Savings Time is observed in the Genealogy Forum. If your area does not observe Daylight Savings Time, you should calculate the time for your area.)

If the chat is one of the hosted SIGs, the primary host's name will be listed in the schedule. If the chat is one of the unhosted DIHs, there will be no host name shown. The chat hosts are given certain holidays to spend with their families. Consequently, don't expect to see forum staff hosting the chats on the days following, although some of the die-hard hosts may show up anyway:

- New Year's Day
- Good Friday
- Easter
- Passover
- Memorial Day

- Independence Day
- Labor Day
- Rosh Hashanah
- Yom Kippur
- Thanksgiving Day
- Chanukah
- Christmas Day
- New Year's Eve

In addition to the complete Genealogy Forum chat schedule, you will find a schedule in the listbox for each day of the week. These schedules list, hour by hour, the chats planned for the day. (To determine whether the chat is a hosted SIG or an unhosted DIH, refer to the full chat schedule.) Blue, underlined hypertext links are included to make it easy for you to join a chat in progress. Simply click on the hypertext link and you will enter the chat/conference room.

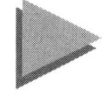

Inside a Chat Room

You can enter a chat room by:

1. Clicking on a button on the right side of the Chat Center screen.
2. Clicking on a blue hypertext link to the chat rooms at the top of the complete "Genealogy Chat Topics" schedule.
3. Clicking on a blue hypertext link to each of the chat listings in the daily "Lineup" schedules.

If you click on one of the buttons on the Chat Center screen, an intermediate screen will be displayed describing the room. This allows you to go to the schedule to check events or you can proceed directly into the chat room.

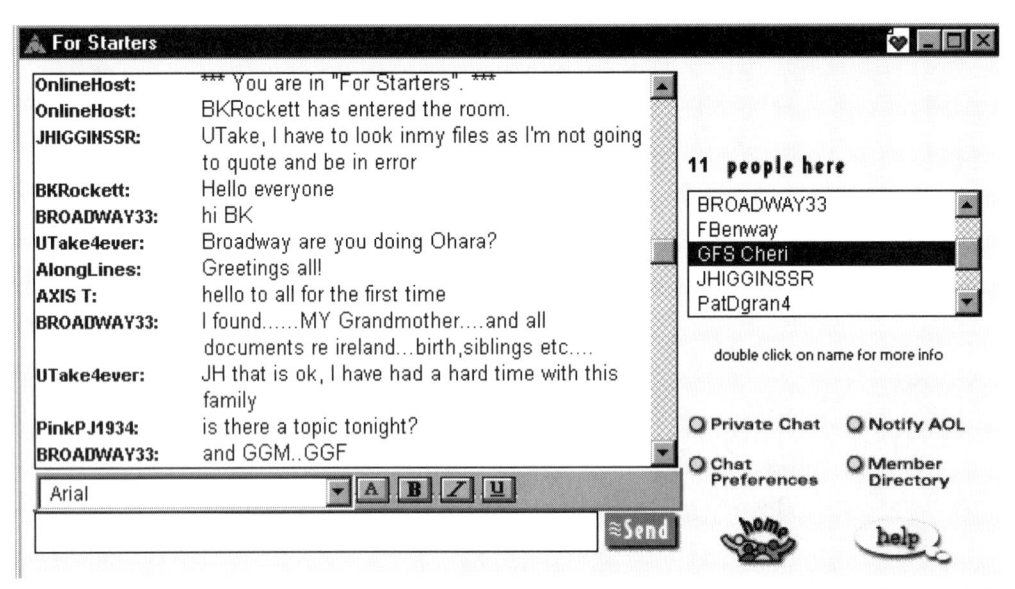

Figure 9.3

When you enter a chat room, a screen similar to the one shown in Figure 9.3 will be displayed. This example shows the "For Starters" conference room, which is usually used for beginning genealogy chats.

(**NOTE**: This example was created using the AOL software for Windows, Version 4.0. If you are using another version for the PC or Macintosh, your screen may look different, and all the functions may not be available to you.)

You will see the discussion taking place between the people in the room in the large box on the left with the scroll bar. Their screen names appear at the left, followed by a colon. Their comments appear as text.

At the bottom of the screen under the text area is a white box. A button labeled "Send" is positioned to the right of it. The white box is where you type your comments. When you want to participate in a conversation, click on this small, white box, type your comment and then send it. To send, you can either click on the Send button or press the Enter key on your keyboard.

In the area between the text area and above the small, white box where you type your text, you will see a collection of controls. These are shown in Figure 9.3.

Here, you can change the typeface of your comments. To do so, click on the down arrowhead at the right side of the typeface window. A pop-up menu will appear. Scroll down to a typeface you like and click on it. The pop-up menu will close and the new typeface's name will appear in the box.

The next control button is labeled with a blue "A." Click on this button and a color palette window will be displayed. Click on a color to select it and then click on the OK button. The text you type will now appear in that color. Click again to select another color.

The next control button is labeled with a bold, black "B." Click on this button and your text will appear in bold face. Click again to reverse this effect.

The next control button is labeled with a slanted letter "I." Click on this button and your text will appear in italics. Click again to reverse this effect.

The next control button is labeled with an underlined letter "U." Click on this button and your text will be underlined. Click again to reverse this effect.

(**NOTE:** Only other members who have a version of the AOL software that supports different fonts, colors, bold, italics and underline in chat rooms will be able to see your special formatting.)

On the right side of the screen is a smaller scroll box showing the screen names of the members in the chat room. If you are attending a hosted chat, or SIG, you can easily identify the hosts. Their names begin with GFS, followed by some other name, or with GFH, followed by some other name. For instance, GFS Drew is the

The Genealogy Forum on America Online — 189

lead host in the Internet chat on Sunday evenings. He shares the responsibility for managing the event with GFS JohnF, GFS Byron and GFS TomS. Hosts whose names begin with the letters GFH are in training as hosts. Once they complete their training, they can select their own GFS name.

At the top of the box containing the attendees' screen names is a count of the number of people currently in the room. The capacity of these five primary chat rooms in the Genealogy Forum is 47 people, including hosts. (There are other chat rooms used for special events whose capacity is larger.)

While you are in the chat room, you can double-click on a member's screen name in the box at any time. This will display a small window like the one shown in Figure 9.4. From here, you have three choices:

Figure 9.4

1. **Ignore Member** — If there is a member whose chat you do not wish to see, click on the small box to add a check mark. When you close the window, that member's subsequent chat will no longer be visible to you. This is useful if someone enters the chat room and begins disruptive behavior.
2. **Send Message** — Click on the button or text of this selection to send an Instant Message (IM) to the member. This is useful when you want to exchange information privately with another member in the room.
3. **Get Profile** — Click on this button to display the member's profile, assuming they have created one.

Below the scroll box containing the members' screen names

are four more buttons and two icons. Let's discuss each:

- **Private Chat** — Click on this button to create a private chat room where you and other members can meet. You will leave the first chat room and go to a private room. Be sure to note the screen names of the other user(s) you would like to meet. Once in the private room, you can send them an IM to invite them to join you. Private chat rooms are of great value when you have met someone researching the same material as you and want to discuss things in more detail. A private room is, in many cases, superior to IMs or E-mail, especially when there are more than two people involved in the discussion.
- **Notify AOL** — Occasionally a member will enter a Genealogy Forum chat room and exhibit objectionable behavior. Such behavior includes foul language, written abuse or attacks on people in the room, repetitive cut-and-pastes, or other, similar activities. You may report this objectionable behavior to AOL authorities. AOL may then choose to warn the member and/or cancel the member's account. Click on this button and a window will be displayed that allows you to report the member's offensive behavior.
- **Chat Preferences** — Click on this button to customize your preferences for chat rooms. These include:
  - Notification via a small text message when new members arrive in the room.
  - Notification via a small text message when members leave the room.
  - Double-spaced text on the screen. (This can make busy chat room text easier to read and follow.)
  - Alphabetize the list of members' screen names in the small scroll box.
  - Enable chat room sounds.
- **Member Directory** — Click on this button to search the

AOL Member Directory. (Please see the chapter, Introduction to America Online, for more details about how to use the Member Directory in your genealogical research.)

- **Home** — Click on the "Home" icon and you will be connected with AOL's "People Connection" area. This is the central location for chat rooms that are not affiliated with any specific forum.
- **Help** — Click on this button for a brief description of chat rooms and conference rooms. For detailed Help about chat rooms, you should refer to the Help facilities available at the menu bar at the top of the AOL screen.

Now that you know what the screen looks like and all of the features that you can use there, let's discuss how to make the most of the Chat Center.

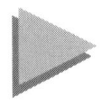

How a Chat Works

Genealogy Forum chats are scheduled events. As discussed earlier, you can check the chat schedules shown in the listbox on the Chat Center's main screen. Check for the topic, day of the week, time (always shown in Eastern time) and chat room location. The five chat rooms in the Chat Center are:

- For Starters
- Ancestral Digs
- Family Treehouse
- Golden Gates
- Root Cellar

In addition, there is another chat room in the **Reunion Center** called the Family Reunion conference room. Other small conference rooms are available in the **Resource Center** in the Regions of the World/Canada area, as well.

To attend a chat, all you need to do is enter the room. Sometimes, there are more people than spaces available in a chat room. At those times, you may find yourself in another holding area. If this is the case, keep trying to enter the chat room. The chances are good that you will soon be able to enter.

If you are attending a hosted chat, or SIG, one of the GFS or GFH hosts will usually greet and welcome you. The hosts have many responsibilities, and each host receives special training in how to host a chat. First and foremost, a host is supposed to make sure you have an enjoyable experience. One of a host's jobs is to facilitate the chat. Hosts are chosen for a chat because of their knowledge or expertise in the topic area. As part of their hosting responsibilities, the chat host will try to answer members questions about the topic of the chat and/or point to other resources in the Genealogy Forum that might be of help. Chat hosts are also trained to maintain order and minimize disruptions.

Lecture Chats and Use of "Protocol"

Specially prepared lectures are sometimes presented in some chats. In these cases, one or more of the hosts may present the material, or a host may act as an emcee to introduce a special guest lecturer.

Members are asked to remain "silent" during the lecture, which means that members should not type in any comments. Keep in mind that there will always be a Q&A period at the conclusion of the lecture. Also, the hosts may ask you to use "protocol" in lecture chats.

Protocol is a method of managing questions and comments from members attending the lecture/chat. In this scheme, members are asked to hold all questions and comments until the end of the lecture. At that time, you can "hold up your hand" as follows:

- To ask a question, type a question mark and press the Send button.

- To make a comment, type an exclamation point and press the Send button.

One of the hosts will maintain a list of the people whose questions or comments are "in queue." Each person's question or comment will be addressed in the order in which it was received. This is done as follows:

- Your **?** or **!** is noted and logged by the host keeping track of the queue.
- When your screen name is called, you type your question or comment.
- When you have finished typing what you have to say, type **/ga**. This means "Go ahead."
- Questions will be fielded by hosts or, if appropriate, opened up for comments and discussion by the members present. (Protocol will continue to be used.)
- The queue list will be handled until all questions or comments are completed, or until the allotted time for the SIG expires.

The use of protocol makes it easier for a lecture to be presented, and provides a fair and orderly way for member questions and comments to be presented.

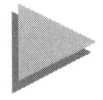

▶ *Chat Etiquette*

There are certain rules of etiquette that you should observe when attending a chat. These make it a more efficient and effective experience for everyone who attends.

1. Take responsibility to know the subject of the chat before entering a chat room. Nothing wastes more of a host's time and the time of other members in the chat room than the host having to repeat the subject of a chat to a new arrival.

2. Stay on subject. For example, if the chat topic is Irish research, don't start asking questions about New Hampshire research.
3. If there is a lecture in progress, please comply with the use of protocol. It is considered extremely rude to interrupt a lecturer.
4. Don't start asking about specific surnames until, or unless, the host asks for "surname roll call."
5. Be polite to other members, and don't ridicule anyone else's questions. There are no stupid questions. The only stupid question is the one left unasked. The purpose of the chats is to share information and educate.
6. If you want to exchange information of a private nature with another member in the chat room, please communicate via IM or E-mail. If there are more than two people who want to talk on the subject, you might want to arrange to meet later in a private chat room.
7. Please don't type all of your text in all upper case. This implies shouting, and is difficult to read.
8. Please type surnames in uppercase. This makes them easier to spot.
9. Please don't use, or play, sounds while in a chat room.
10. Please use the Notify AOL button in the lower right corner of the chat room screen to report disruptive behavior in the chat room.

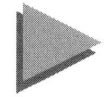

Logging a Chat

There are times when you will wish you had a copy of a chat you just attended. Perhaps a great lecture was presented. Maybe there were some interesting research tips presented. Or perhaps the chat proceeded at such a quick pace that you want to reread the text at a more leisurely rate. Fortunately, there is way for you to capture the full content of a chat. It is called the **Chat Log**.

(**NOTE**: The following instructions are applicable in AOL for Windows version 4.0. They may vary from platform to platform and version to version. Please check the AOL Help facility for your version of the software for specific instructions.)

To record a chat using the chat log, first enter the chat room. Once you are inside, click on the icon on the toolbar labeled, "My Files." Select the option listed as "Log Manager." A window similar to the one shown in Figure 9.5 will be displayed.

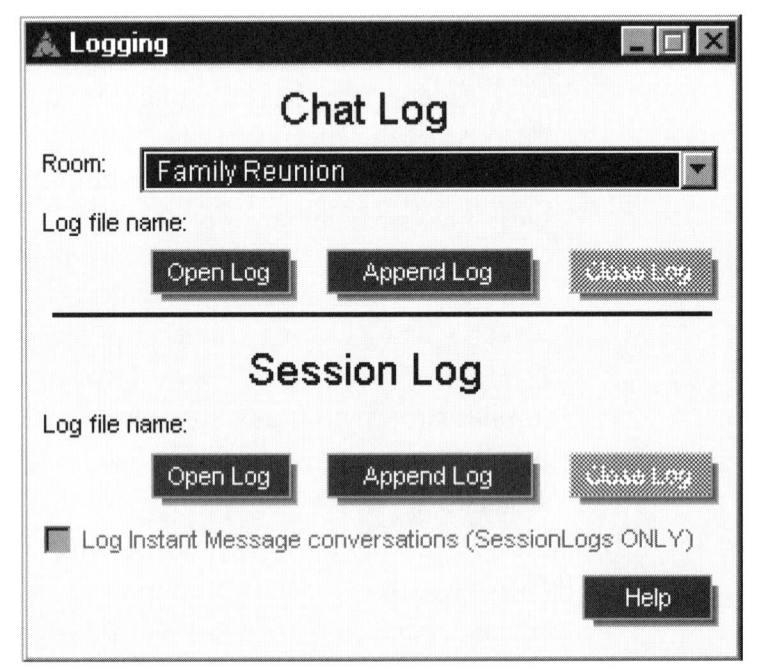

Figure 9.5

The name of the chat room is displayed in the Room box. To begin capturing a log of the chat, simply click on the Open Log button. A window will be opened that allows you to assign a name to the log file and designate where it will be stored. Once that is accomplished, you can close the Log Manager window. The logging has begun. All activity will be preserved in the log file.

When you have finished logging the chat, open the Log

Manager again and click on the Close Log button. Logging is now stopped. If you decide to add material to the log later, you can click on the Append Log button and additional proceedings will be logged. Stop the appending by clicking on the Close Log button again.

Once you have logged the chat, you will want to read it. You can open the log with any text file reader, such as a word processor. You can also locate the file, wherever you chose to store it on your computer, and open it while using AOL. Simply go to the AOL menu bar and select File and the Open option, locate the file and double-click on the file name. You can now read the log of the entire chat proceedings at your leisure. You may also elect to print the file.

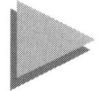

Making the Most of the Chats

You can learn a great deal by participating in chats. You should consult the schedule and decide on a chat you want to attend. Make a note of the day, time, conference room location *and topic*. Please remember that all times on the schedule are Eastern, and that you may have to convert the schedule's time to your local time. For starters, select topics covering such topics as:

- Beginning genealogy
- A state in which one of your ancestors lived
- A country from which an ancestor came
- How to use the Internet in genealogy research
- The U.S. Civil War
- How to use a Family History Center (FHC)
- Computing chats (for PC or Mac)

You will certainly find topics of interest to you and you will learn from the talented and knowledgeable staff members who host the chats. As with the message boards, participating in a chat may help you make contact with a long lost relative, or with someone working on the same surnames that you are researching. Try attending a few chats. You'll be hooked!

10 ▶ The Internet Center

NOTHING HAS REVOLUTIONIZED THE WAY WE COMMUNICATE AND SHARE INFORMATION LIKE THE INTERNET. Although the Internet originated almost 30 years ago, it wasn't until the early 1990s that it came into widespread use. The World Wide Web was introduced in 1993, with graphical Web browsers following shortly afterwards. Browsers—the software programs running on your computer that allow you to jump from Web site to Web site—provide you with the ability to view text and graphics. Today, in mere seconds, we have access to Web sites all over the world.

For the genealogist, the Internet is a rapidly growing resource for secondary records. Private individuals are publishing their genealogies on personal Web pages. Other people, such as the incredibly prolific Cyndi Howells, continuously compile links to genealogy-related Web sites and other resources. (See Cyndi's Web site at http://www.cyndislist.com) Non-profit volunteer organizations, such as the USGenWeb Project, are working together to provide Internet Web sites for genealogical research in every county and every state of the United States. Regional, state, county and local genealogical and historical societies are publishing materials on their Web sites. Libraries are placing information about their genealogical collections and access to their online catalogs on their Web pages. Government entities, such as the National Archives and Records Administration (NARA), provide vast amounts of online information to genealogists. And commercial entities such as Ancestry, Inc., and Family Tree Maker are providing subscription databases in which you can locate pointers to primary record sources.

You also can subscribe to E-mail mailing lists on a variety of genealogy-related topics. Mailing lists are made up of people who share an interest in the same topic, and who exchange E-mail communications with all the other members of the list. From genealogy research tips to surnames, from ship passenger lists to national, state and regional genealogy, from ethnic groups to historical events—there are literally hundreds of mailing lists to which you can subscribe.

In addition, there are genealogy-related Usenet Newsgroups available. Operating much like the Genealogy Forum's Message Board Center, the Usenet consists of electronic bulletin boards on the Internet where people can post or read messages and respond to the entire newsgroup, or to a specific author.

These Internet resources can teach you genealogy, give you research tips, supply you with leads, help you fill informational gaps or provide the "missing link" you've been seeking. While these are all resources, you must remember that they are secondary sources—pointers to the original sources. Everything you find on the Internet must be as thoroughly researched as if you were starting from scratch. You must confirm the existence of every record yourself. You must view the original or obtain a copy for your review. Then, verify the information and corroborate it with other sources. And, always document your sources so that you and successive genealogical researchers can verify *your* work.

The Genealogy Forum has created its **Internet Center** as a focal point for its members' genealogical research. Here, you will find a vast collection of the best available Internet sites. New sites are added all the time, making this a tremendously valuable resource for your genealogical research.

Please be aware that Web pages seem to come and go. Even those that have enjoyed some longevity occasionally disappear. Consequently, you may occasionally encounter "dead" links. In those cases, please send an E-mail to GFS Byron to alert him to check the sites.

There's a lot to see and learn about in the Internet Center, so let's discuss the area in detail.

The Internet Center Screen

The Internet Center is accessed from the Genealogy Forum main screen. When you click on the button labeled "Internet," the screen shown in Figure 10.1 is displayed. The Internet Center screen, like the other forum centers, consists of two groups of information:

- There are five major groups of materials available in the Internet Center. They are represented by the five buttons and descriptive text on the screen. We'll discuss each of these areas in more detail.
- The lower left hand quadrant contains a listbox of a number of important features that will help you find your way around this center, or which will link you to other helpful areas.

Please notice the blue, underlined items under some of the button titles. These are hypertext links to weekly choice picks in these categories. The Internet Center staff are constantly looking for new and exceptional genealogy resources. New highlights are

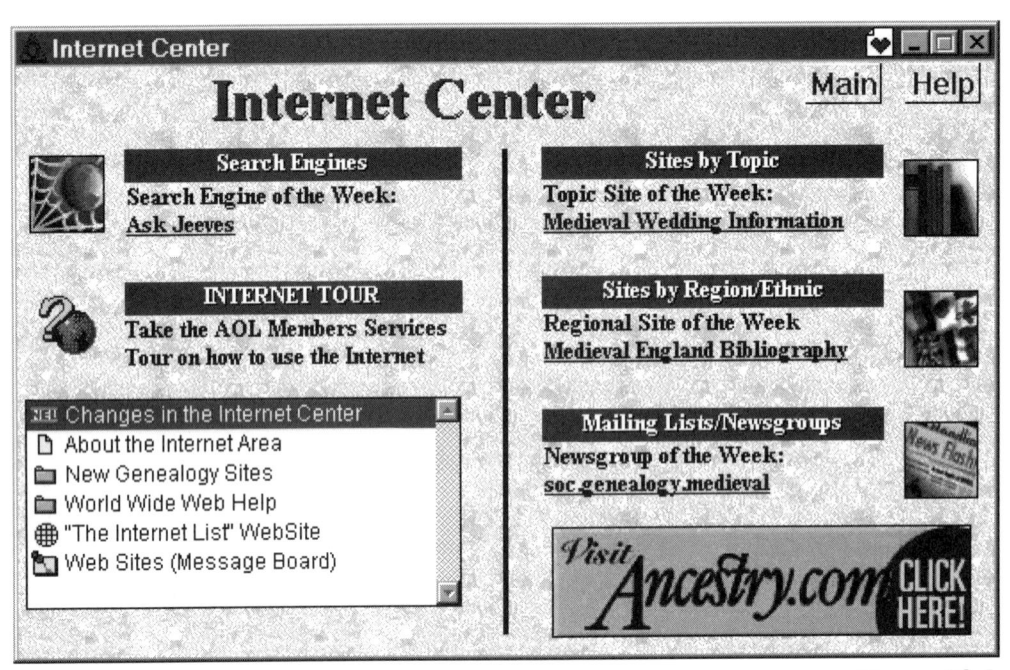

Figure 10.1

placed here on a regular basis to help keep you informed. You will want to check these out. To visit one of these items, simply click on the blue hyperlink.

For a brief overview of what you will find here, click on the article in the "About the Internet Area" listbox. Each category behind the five buttons on the right side of the screen is described here. Next, let's work through each of the five buttons.

Sites By Topic

This collection of resources is impressive indeed! The forum has collected a wealth of Internet links, and categorized them into logical groups that make it easy for you to locate what you are looking for. Let's discuss them:

- **Courses on the Internet** — The forum's **Beginners' Center** offers a wealth of "how-to" information for people just starting their genealogical adventure. A number of these are listed here. However, if you are interested in something more formal in the way of instruction, you can locate plenty of resources here. There are Internet-based, self-study courses available, offered by colleges, universities and others. There are also several courses taught online for which you must register to attend at specific times. Don't overlook the link to the Genealogy Forum's chat schedule because these, too, are educational offerings.

- **Events** — If you are looking for genealogy conferences and other events to attend, you will find two collections of events here. The first is a link to an Internet site, and the second is a link to the forum's conference collection. Both sites provide up-to-date schedules of meetings, lectures, conferences and reunions.

- **General Genealogy Internet Sites** — This collection contains the créme de la créme of the Internet sites. The most impressive and comprehensive is probably "Cyndi's List of Genealogy Sites on the Internet." Created and maintained by Cyndi Howells, this massive Web page listing contains several tens of thousands of Web links. You will also find free pedigree charts, family group sheets and census forms at the GRS site, labeled "Genealogy Forms." Looking for surnames? The RootsWeb site is impressive, and contains a large variety of content, links and information about how to access surname information on the Internet. The National Genealogical Society's (NGS) Web site is full of great information and links to other sites. "Librarians Serving Genealogists" is a great Web site for librarians. "John's Genealogy Junction" is another great site, with some obscure information. These are but a few of the impressive links in this collection.

- **Getting Started** — You will find several important links in this collection. For the best information about getting started, however, the Courses on the Internet (above) and the forum's **Beginners' Center** are your best resources.

- **Maps** — It is important that you learn how to use maps in your genealogical research. Nothing is more important than finding the right location to search for records. Country, state, province, county, parish, town and city boundaries all have changed a great deal. You can waste significant amounts of time looking for a marriage license in the wrong county. Because you know your ancestors lived in a particular place when they were married doesn't mean that it wasn't part of another county when they were married. The map collection here won't answer all of your questions, but it will get you started. Look for the current location of a town using the U.S. Census Bureau maps, and then consult older maps, such as the 1895 U.S. Atlas.
- **Mayflower Pilgrims** — There are plenty of resources about those who came to this continent aboard the *Mayflower*. This collection contains links to Web pages specifically about Plymouth and the *Mayflower*.
- **Military Resources** — You will find many resources about military records on the Internet. Those referenced on Cyndi Howell's Web site are among the best. The collection offered by the Genealogy Forum contains links to the DAR and SAR, to the American Civil War Home Page and to a site created by the U.S. Army about its role in the Spanish-American War.
- **Online Genealogy Magazines and Newsletters** — There is a growing number of online genealogy-related periodicals available. Regularly-scheduled online columns, such as the ones published at the Ancestry.com Web site, are contributing to the ongoing education of genealogists around the country and world. Newsletters on a variety of topics and tailored to specific audiences are also being published on a regular basis. Here, you will find links to a number of online columns, newsletters and online magazines and journals. This collection continues to grow as members

like you continue to let the Genealogy Forum know about new online materials.

- **Records** — There are a variety of Web sites that provide detailed information about specific records. As genealogical societies and individuals index, catalog and publish materials from courthouses, libraries and other records repositories, the number of these Web sites will proliferate. The forum has compiled some of the better links. The "African American Census Schedules Online" Web page is perhaps the best example of what can be done with publishing records online. Other record links here include the Social Security Death Index and the USGenWeb Census Project. Again, remember to use any information you find online as a pointer to primary records. You must examine, verify and corroborate every piece of information yourself.

- **Societies, Organizations and Clubs** — You will find links to many of the genealogical organizations included here, including the DAR, the SAR and the UDC. In addition, the Federation of Genealogical Societies (FGS) and the Federation of Eastern European Family History Societies (FEEFHS) are represented here. Other organizations are being added as well.

- **Surname Searches** — The forum has centralized the Internet's top three genealogy surname search facilities in one place for you. These are the "Genealogy's Most Wanted, "The African Ancestors Database" and the "RootsWeb/Roots Surname List" facilities. Each is a terrific resource.

- **Surnames/Personal Genealogy Sites** — As a complement to the Surname Searches, this collection contains links to the surname Web pages described in detail in the Surname Center chapter. Individuals who have created a Web page related to one of the Top 1,000 Surnames in the Genealogy Forum can submit a link to the forum. The submitted page is then linked into this collection.

- **Technology and Genealogy** — Do you want to build a Web page? That's just one of the things included in this collection of links that can help you—a link to a site that teaches basic HTML (Hyper-Text Markup Language), the coding used to write Web pages. You also can learn here about all of the genealogy-based online bulletin board services (BBSs).
- **Women and Genealogy** — This collection is relatively new in the forum. It contains a link to an impressive page titled, "Notable Women Ancestors," and was created by one of the Genealogy Forum staff members. This award-winning site is a "must visit."

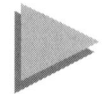

Sites By Region/Ethnic Group

The next button will take you to a great collection of Web sites that deal with genealogy in specific geographical areas or that relate to specific ethnic groups. While there are a number of collections in this area, let's discuss the contents of the major categories. This area continues to grow rapidly, so be sure to check back to make sure you don't miss any new material:

- **African American Web Sites** — This impressive collection consists of more than 130 links to Web sites on the Internet devoted exclusively to African American genealogy. This is the same collection linked into the African American Resource Area in the Resource Center. There are new resources being added periodically as new Web sites are identified by the dedicated members of the African American team in the forum.
- **Canada Genealogy Sites** — If you are researching your Canadian ancestry, you will find literally hundreds of Web sites available in this collection. Not only are there general Web sites available at the national level, but each Canadian province has its own collection of

links. These are the same sets of links found in the Canada section of the Regions of the World in the Resource Center. Be sure to return regularly, as these collections are reviewed and updated periodically.

- **German Genealogy Sites** — This collection contains a relatively small group of resources, including the "German Genealogy Home Page."
- **Jewish Genealogy** — The primary component of this collection is the JewishGen Web site. JewishGen, Inc., is the primary Internet source connecting researchers of Jewish genealogy worldwide. Its most popular components are the JewishGen Discussion Group, the JewishGen Family Finder (a database of over 70,000 surnames and towns), the comprehensive directory of InfoFiles and a variety of databases.
- **Mexico Genealogy** — The area of Hispanic genealogy has been slower to grow than some others. However, you will find several excellent Web sites here. The "Mexico - Address Book Web Page" is a great compilation of Mexican genealogy research. It contains contact information in each of the states for obtaining copies of records.
- **Native American Web Sites** — This is another wonderful collection of Web page links to tribal and cultural resources. There are more than a hundred links here, and the collection continues to grow, thanks to the efforts of the Native American team in the forum.
- **UK/Ireland Genealogy Sites** — This collection boasts links to the Public Records Offices of England, Wales and Northern Ireland, as well as to the National Archives of Ireland.
- **United States Genealogy Sites** — The United States Web collection is a large one, and continues to grow. There is a folder available for each of the 50 states, the District of Columbia and Puerto Rico. Each folder, with the exception of the one for Puerto Rico, contains

a link to its USGenWeb site. (The USGenWeb Project has compiled massive amounts of information for each state, and has stored it on the Internet for easy access.) This is a great place to start your regional research. These state folders are being expanded with other links, so check back often for more Web resources. Among the other Web resources in the United States Genealogy Sites collection are historical sites, links to genealogical society sites, the Library of Congress and the National Archives, maps and much more. These resources are a wonderful starting point for your U.S. research.

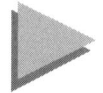

▶ Mailing Lists/Newsgroups

Much like reading an Internet-wide message board, mailing lists and Usenet newsgroups can be very helpful in your research. Let's define each one separately, and then discuss the content of the collection under this button in the Internet Center.

▶ Mailing Lists

Mailing Lists, also referred to as listservs, provide a way for people who share a common interest to exchange information with the entire group via electronic mail (E-mail).

Mailing lists are one of the oldest and most popular resources available on the Internet. There are literally thousands of mailing lists out there. To become involved with one, you must select your topic of interest and then identify a mailing list that discusses it. Once you have located the mailing list, subscribe to it by sending an E-mail message to its administrative address. This is much like subscribing to a traditional, print magazine.

Once you have subscribed to the mailing list, you will receive a welcome message. Be sure to print and save it! This message tells you how to unsubscribe and perform other functions. If you lose the message, you may be stuck on the mailing list.

You should soon start receiving E-mail messages from other subscribers to the mailing list. Some lists are very active, and send scores of messages each day. Others are relatively inactive, and may send no more than a few messages a week.

Read the messages without replying for a while. Get a feel for the content of the list and how people discuss topics. Using a variation on an old adage, "Lurk before you leap" holds true here. After a while, if you are interested in participating, send a message to the posting E-mail address. (The administrative address is strictly for subscribing and unsubscribing; the posting address is strictly for exchanging messages with other subscribers.)

Common rules of Netiquette (Internet etiquette) apply here, including:

- Use thoughtful and descriptive subject lines in your messages. "Help" is not an acceptable subject. "Seeking Passenger List - HMS Morningstar - Manchester 1887" is acceptable. Good subject lines draw attention and get better responses.
- Place surnames in uppercase for ease of location in your text.
- Never type in all uppercase. It is difficult to read, and implies to others that you are shouting.
- Never send a message to the full mailing list that is not of interest to all subscribers. For example, suppose someone posts a query for information about their great-grandfather. If you have information on the name, don't post your reply to the entire mailing list. Instead, send a personal E-mail directly to the person who posted the query.
- Never send commercial advertisements to a mailing list unless it is explicitly clear that they are allowed.

- Never engage in a verbal attack on another person on a mailing list. This is referred to as "flaming," and is considered highly offensive and inappropriate. This type of behavior is never appropriate, either in public or private.

If you decide that the mailing list is not what you want, feel free to unsubscribe. You do this similarly to the way you subscribed. Refer to the welcome message for specific instructions.

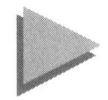

Usenet Newsgroups

Usenet Newsgroups, also referred to as Usenet, Newsgroups or News, are an integral part of communication on the Internet. They differ from mailing lists in that, rather than subscribing and receiving communications via E-mail messages, all messages are posted on electronic bulletin or message boards.

Newsgroups are very similar to the message boards that you find throughout America Online. The major difference is that, since these newsgroups are distributed through the Internet, communication is not limited to AOL members. Rather, the millions of people who use the Internet can access these messages.

There are over 40,000 topics available, and millions of people are constantly participating in these discussions. Newsgroup names usually reflect their focus. For example, aol.new contains discussions about new areas on AOL, while aol.new.internet focuses solely on issues and areas new to AOL's Internet areas. There are scores of genealogy related newsgroups that you can read, and to which you can post. The same rules of Netiquette for mailing lists also apply to newsgroups.

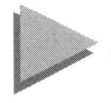

Locating Mailing Lists & Usenet Newsgroups

Your first step in using mailing lists or newsgroups is to locate those of interest to you. Fortunately, there are some wonderful resources available in the Genealogy Forum for locating both mailing lists and newgroups. Let's explore the list of the Mailing List/Newsgroups collection:

- **Genealogy Resources on the Internet** — This site is the best item in the collection. Here, you will find an up-to-date Web page with links available to materials on a variety of Internet tools, including mailing lists and Usenet newsgroups. Instructions on how to subscribe to mailing lists are included here, along with detailed descriptions and the E-mail subscription addresses of literally every genealogy-related mailing list. A current list of all genealogy-related newsgroups, and hyperlinks to each one, is also included. This is the best place available on the Internet for information about genealogy mailing lists and newsgroups!
- **Genealogy Newsgroup Sites** — Here you will find a collection of newsgroups in the form of a Genealogy Forum collection. This collection contains links to each of the newsgroups referenced in the Web site above.
- **Liszt, the Mailing List Site** — Liszt is a clever acronym for the largest one-stop mailing list locator. If your are interested in subscribing to a mailing list about any topic at all, this is the place to check. If you are interested in genealogy, model railroading, music, computing or any other subject, check here for available mailing lists.
- **Cyndi's List of Newsgroups & Mailing Lists** — Cyndi Howells, the prolific Webmaster, maintains her own list of newsgroups and mailing lists here.

There are other articles in this collection that describe specific mailing lists and how to subscribe to them. You will, however, want to rely on the information in the Web sites described above to ensure that you have the most current information about all available mailing lists and newsgroups.

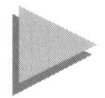

Reading Newsgroups on AOL

When reading newsgroups on AOL, you will use their Usenet Newsgroup screen. To access this screen, go to Keyword: **newsgroup**. The screen shown in Figure 10.2 will be displayed. There are a number of articles available in the listbox that will educate you on how to use the AOL newsgroup facility and how to participate in newsgroups. Take the time to read through these helpful materials.

There are a number of buttons on the screen. Let's discuss each:

- **Parental Controls** — This facility allows you to control what kind of materials are accessed in the newsgroups area. You may only access and set parental controls

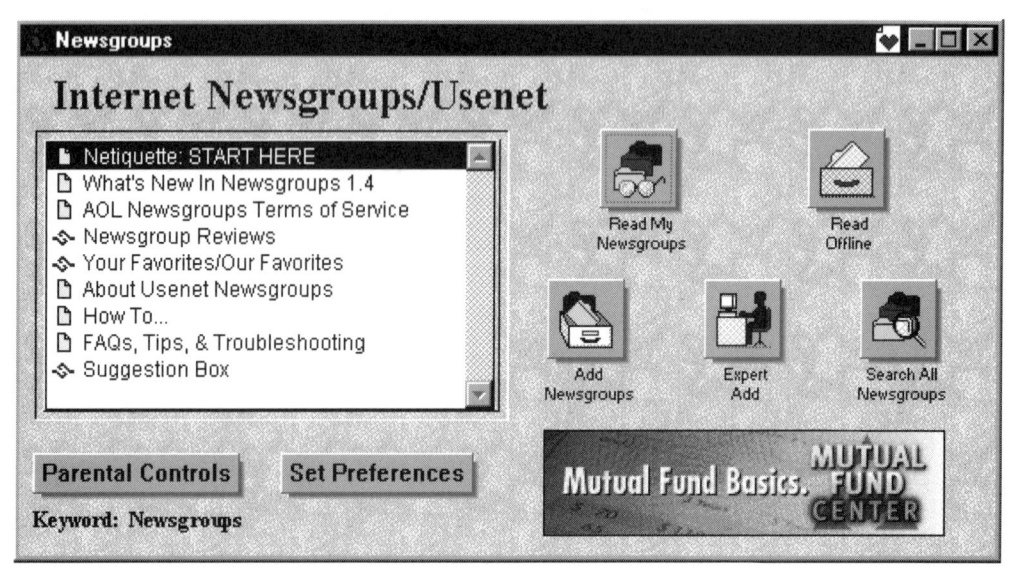

Figure 10.2

212 — The Genealogy Forum on America Online

from your primary account.

- **Preferences** — This button gives you access to set your global preferences that apply to all newsgroups. In particular, you can create or maintain the signature block. This is the information that appears on every newsgroup posting you make, either to a newsgroup or in private replies to those who post messages. Other options available here allow you to control the sequence of messages when they are displayed in the reader—oldest first, newest first or alphabetically by subject.

- **Add Newsgroups** — This is the next button you should use. Here, you will review a list of categories for news groups. Categories are groups in which messages of a similar or related topic are posted. The "comp" category for instance, deals with computer topics; "rec" deals with recreations and hobbies. There are many, many categories available. The genealogy newsgroups are located in the high-level categories "alt" and "soc." Click on the "alt" category and you will see sub-categories. Scroll down to "alt.genealogy." You can look at the content of the newsgroup wherever you see a button labeled "List Subjects" or "Read Messages." If you like what you see, and want to add it to your list of preferred newsgroups, click on the button labeled "Add," and the newsgroup will become part of your collection. The next time you go to the Usenet Newsgroups screen, this newsgroup will be part of your list.

- **Expert Add** — If you already know the name of the newsgroup to which you want to subscribe, simply click on this button and type in the name of the newsgroup. This is a shortcut in the subscription process.

- **Read My Newsgroups** — When you click on this button, a screen similar to the one shown in Figure 10.3 will be displayed. (While the list of newsgroups will differ for each individual, depending on the news

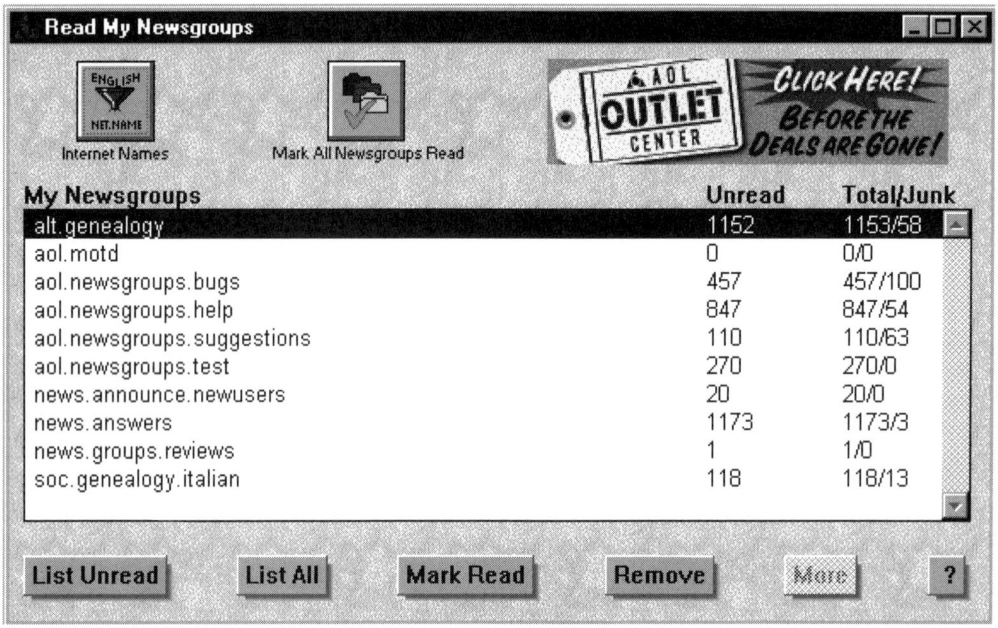

Figure 10.3

groups you have specified, a number of AOL's news groups are already pre-loaded for you.) Each newsgroup is listed, along with a count of how many unread messages are available. If you indicated in your global preferences that you wished junk postings to be filtered, you will now see a count of "good" messages versus junk messages. To view the messages, click on the button labeled "List Unread." To view all the messages available in the newsgroup, including the ones you have already read, click on the button labeled "List All." To mark all the messages in the newsgroup as having been read, click on the button labeled "Mark Read." To mark all the messages in all the newsgroups as read, click on the button at the top of the screen labeled "Mark All Newsgroups Read." To determine what each newsgroup is about, click on the button at the top of the screen labeled "Internet Names." To remove a newsgroup from your customized list, click on the button labeled "Remove."

When you want to read the contents of a newsgroup, double-click on the newsgroup in the listbox. A screen similar to the one shown in Figure 10.4 will be displayed. The subject line of each posted topic (the subject line of the first message) and the number of messages and responses is shown in the listbox. Click on the Read button to read the message. Click on the "List" button to see a list of all the messages about this subject. Click on the "Mark Read" button to mark this message as having been read, even though you haven't read it. Click on the "Mark Unread" button to mark a message you have read as unread; this keeps the message on your list the next time you enter the area to read your messages for this newsgroup. Click the "Preferences" button to set your preferences for this specific newsgroup.

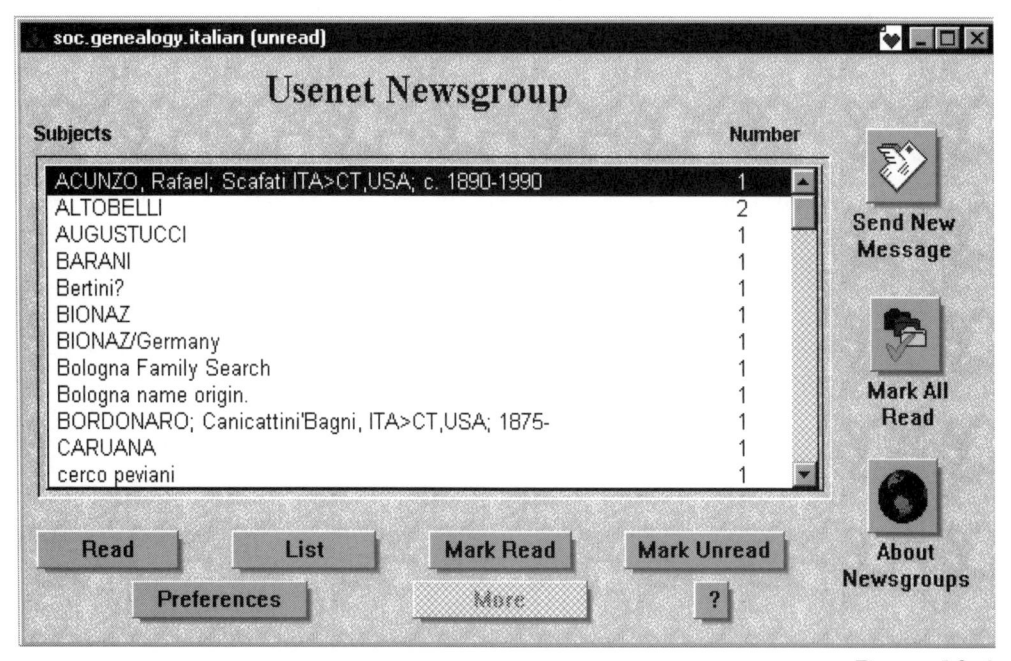

Figure 10.4

Don't forget to use the Find in Top Window feature to scan for specific text or a surname once you have all the topics listed here. (The Find in Top Window feature can be found on the AOL menu under Edit.)

The Genealogy Forum on America Online — 215

To post a message to the newsgroup you are currently in, click on the button labeled "Send New Message." A window will appear that is very much like an E-mail window. Type your message and click on the Send button to send your message to be posted on the newsgroup.

To mark all messages in the entire newsgroup as read, click on the button labeled "Mark All Read."

To locate a newsgroup on a particular topic, click on the button labeled, "Search All Newsgroups." A screen will be displayed in which you can type one or more words. Click the button labeled "List Articles," and any matches on newsgroup names will be listed. You can then double-click on the match in the listbox to either read the newsgroup or to add it to your custom list.

Usenet newsgroups can be treated much the same as the message boards you find in the Genealogy Forum and throughout AOL. Use them to search for messages posted by individuals seeking information about surnames. Post messages yourself and see what responses you get. Newsgroups can be a very effective way to seek information. You will want to save the Usenet Newsgroups screen as one of your Favorite Places, and check it regularly.

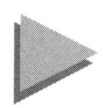

Search Engines

The next button on the Internet Center screen provides you access to an excellent collection of Internet search engines. Search engines are powerful Internet tools used to locate information on the Internet. They are used primarily for locating information on Web pages, although some can also be used to search Usenet newsgroups. By entering a keyword, a combination of words or a phrase in a search engine, you can search the Internet for Web pages that contain the word or phrase. This can be particularly useful if you are searching for a particular surname.

When you use a search engine, it sorts through all of the information it has indexed on the Internet and presents you with a "search results list." The items on that list are ranked in order of relevance—what the search engine "believes" is what you want. The most relevant items are at the top of the list, and those less relevant items are listed below, in descending order. If a search result's list is too large, it could be that your search was too broad. You may want to rephrase your search terms and resubmit. Each of the results will have a blue, underlined hypertext link associated with it. Simply click on the hyperlink to go to the Web page listed.

In addition, some of the search engines may act as directories. In the directory, Web sites are organized into categories, then into sub- categories, and so on, to provide you with a logically organized hierarchy for reference. The process is similar to using the telephone yellow pages.

The Genealogy Forum has collected, in one place, links to the best of the Internet search engines. Click on one, read the Help area for hints and tips, and start searching!

▶ Internet Tour

America Online's Member Services has created a terrific area that explains the ins and outs of the Internet. If you want an explanation of the Internet and detailed instructions about how to use all of its facilities, click on this button and invest some time here to learn more. The Five Minute Tour button on the Member Services site is a great starting point.

Let's finish up the tour of the Internet Center by shifting attention to the items in the listbox in the lower left corner of the screen. Earlier, we discussed the "About the Internet Area" article. Let's focus now on the other important items found here:

- **New Genealogy Sites** — You will remember that, in the **File Libraries Center,** newly uploaded files are held in new libraries located in the listbox to help you easily locate new items. The same thing is done here in the Internet Center. New Web sites are listed in this collection for about a month before they are transferred to their permanent, logical collection. Check here often for new Web sites.
- **World Wide Web Help** — This item provides a link to the same AOL Member Services' Internet site behind the Internet Tour area described above.
- **"The Internet List" Web Site** — This is a link to the "Genealogy Resources on the Internet" Web site described under the Mailing List/Newsgroups button above.
- **Web Sites (Message Board)** — This item will link you to the forum's Web Site Recommendations message board. Other AOL members post messages here to introduce others to their own Web site, or to other particularly noteworthy Web sites. You can post messages with your recommendations here also.

The Genealogy Forum is always looking for great, new Internet resources. Check back often to see what they have added. If you encounter a Web site that you would like to recommend for inclusion in the forum, please feel free to send it via E-mail to gfsbyron@aol.com.

11 ▶ The Reunion Center

*I*T IS NO WONDER THAT SO MANY GENEALOGISTS ARE INVOLVED WITH PLANNING FAMILY REUNIONS. As genealogists, we all have a great respect for family. We generally spend a great deal of time with our families, and older family members provide a tremendous wealth of genealogical information.

A family reunion provides an opportunity to come together to celebrate the bonds of kinship. Distant relatives are brought closer into the fold, and relationships are formed or strengthened, especially between the older and younger generations. Age barriers diminish and people discover or rediscover the things they have in common.

Information is exchanged throughout a reunion. For the family genealogist, a reunion is an invaluable opportunity to gather information about the entire clan. Stories and traditions are recounted, differing recollections are compared and long-forgotten facts and observations are often brought to light. Reunions provide an unparalleled view of the personal interactions between family members. Facets and nuances of individual relationships and family group dynamics are played out.

The family genealogist will seize the opportunities provided by a reunion to:

- Talk with every family member in attendance.
- Obtain and/or confirm vital dates.
- Obtain addresses, telephone numbers and E-mail addresses from everyone in attendance in order to:
    1. Contact them in the future.
    2. Establish for genealogical records where they live at this point in time.
- Gather and document family stories and traditions.
- Take photographs, make tape recordings and/or make videotape recordings of every member of the family, as well as all other attendees.
- Gather handwriting samples.
- Establish relationships with every member of the family and let them know who the family historian is.

These and many, many other details are important parts of a family reunion. It can all be overwhelming if you don't know how to organize a reunion, or if you don't have a plan. Fortunately, the Genealogy Forum has been working on one for you.

One of the newer areas in the Genealogy Forum is the **Reunion Center**, which was developed in response to member requests for guidelines and "how-to" information about organizing reunions. Several members of the forum staff are experts in this area, having organized reunions for their large families, as well as having managed family newsletters.

The purpose of the Reunion Center is to provide:

- "How-to" information about organizing, coordinating and conducting family reunions.
- Information about family associations and links to online associations.

- Instructions about how to organize and produce a family newsletter.
- Information and instructions about scheduling and conducting an online family reunion in the Genealogy Forum's Reunion conference room.

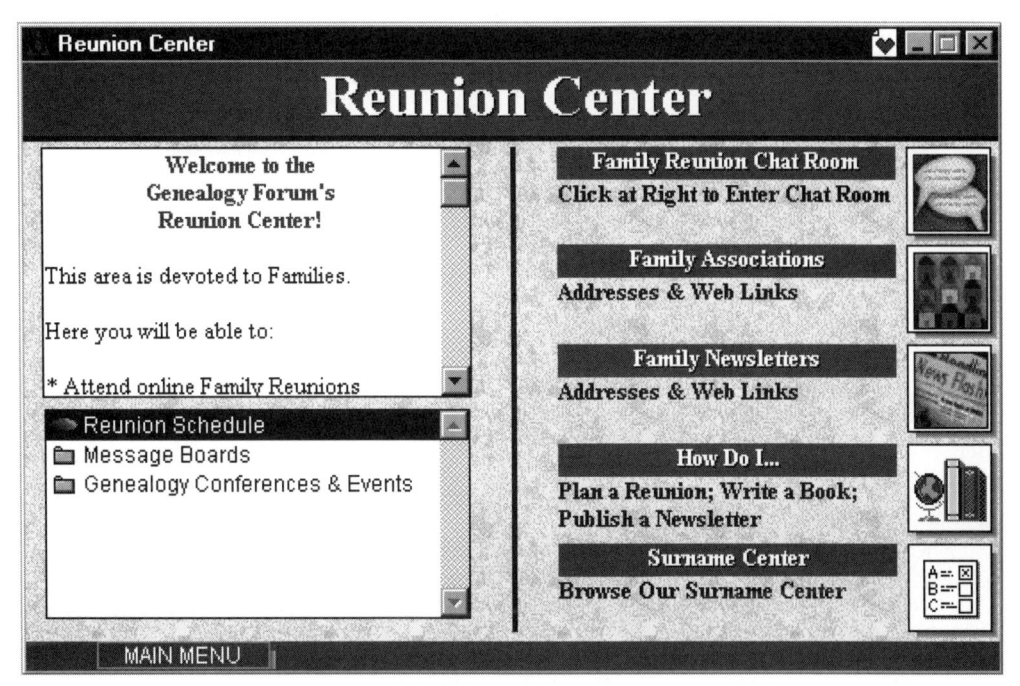

Figure 11.1

The Reunion Center Screen

You access the Reunion Center from the Genealogy Forum's main screen. When you click on the Reunions button, the screen shown in Figure 11.1 is displayed. The materials here are divided into two distinct groups:

- There are five main topic areas with buttons and descriptive text that contain logical groups of related materials. We'll discuss each of these in this chapter.

The Genealogy Forum on America Online — 221

- The listbox in the lower left hand quadrant of the screen contains some important schedules and links that we'll also discuss.

Let's talk about the Reunion Center, starting with the five buttons.

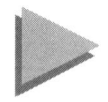

▶ Family Reunion Chat Room

Sometimes it is impossible for the whole family to get together for a family reunion. In this electronic age, more and more people are using E-mail to communicate with one another. Members on AOL not only use E-mail, they also use IMs and private chat rooms to get together on an ad hoc basis. The Genealogy Forum has taken this one step farther: they have provided an electronic conference room called "Family Reunion." This room is used for some of the forum's scheduled chats, particularly those about family reunions. (See the chapter about the **Chat Center**.) It is also used to schedule actual online family reunions.

Some families use the Family Reunion conference room on a regularly scheduled basis. Their family members get together in the conference room to get caught up and share information. Some families use it as a venue for locating distant or lost relatives.

Other families use the facility in a different way. Perhaps your family is holding a reunion and there are relatives who cannot attend. Perhaps the trip is too expensive, the distance is too far or people are physically unable to make the trip. You can schedule the Family Reunion room in the forum on a one-time basis to coincide with your family reunion. You can set up a computer at the family reunion, and absent members can use the conference room to gather and chat with people at the reunion.

To learn more about scheduling events in the Family Reunion conference room, take a look at these two documents in the listbox in the lower left hand quadrant of the screen:

- **Reunion Schedule** — This document contains the day-by-day schedule of family reunions that occur on a regular basis in the Family Reunion conference room.
- **How To Schedule Online Reunions** — This document contains contact information to begin the scheduling process. All you need to do is choose a preferred date and time, send an E-mail, and the process begins.

For detailed information about how the chat rooms operate, please refer to the chapter about **The Chat Center**.

Family Associations

There are tens of thousands of family associations around the world whose primary purpose is to collect and disseminate information about specific surnames. Not all of these groups are of a genealogical nature. They can, however, be a tremendous boon to genealogists who are seeking historical and genealogical information.

When you are planning a family reunion, you might want to consider contacting organizations relating to your surname(s). Depending on the type of reunion you are considering, you might want to ask a family association for information they might have about lost relatives who might be members of their group. Perhaps they can help publicize your reunion if, for instance, you are organizing an event commemorating all persons with a certain surname. Yes, there are such massive reunions!

In the Family Associations area of the Reunion Center, you will find information for thousands of surnames. Some of the information is in the form of links to Web pages. There are also folders containing text files listing family association addresses and contacts. Please be aware that Web pages, addresses and contacts can change. If you encounter a problem with one of these, please be sure to alert the coordinator for this area of the forum. The coordinator's E-mail address appears on the Family Associations collection screen.

▶ Family Newsletters

Another way to contact people who might be interested in your family reunion is by using family newsletters. You also may be interested in subscribing to newsletters regarding the surnames you are researching. You never know where you'll find new information!

Newsletters have historically been published on paper and mailed to subscribers. It is not unusual today, however, for newsletters to be published via E-mail or on an Internet Web page. In most cases, a family's means of receiving information may consist of one or more of these methods. If you decide to publish a newsletter, you should be prepared for some people who want it sent via E-mail, some who will want it on a Web page and others who will want a paper copy mailed to them.

A family newsletter provides a wonderful method of keeping a family in touch. Family members submit information to a focal person who creates and distributes the newsletter. The inclusion of genealogical information in a newsletter often generates a great deal of interest, and family members sometimes respond with more details.

A newsletter is also a convenient way of publicizing a reunion, and asking for help from other family members. Often, other people are reluctant to initiate such a seemingly vast project, but they may be willing to volunteer to help someone else coordinate the event.

The Genealogy Forum has compiled a great, growing collection of newsletters and archives. Most of the newsletters in the collection are Web-based. There are, however, folders available containing information about paper-based newsletters. All of these resources are arranged alphabetically by surname. All you need to do is locate the surname and double-click on the entry in the collection.

If you publish a family newsletter in any format, you can submit information to the coordinator for this area of the forum for inclusion in the Family Newsletter collection. The coordinator's E-mail address appears on the Family Associations collection screen.

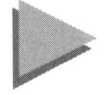

How Do I...

The fourth button on the Reunion Center screen is the crown jewel of the collection. If you want to become the creative focal point of your family, this is the place to start. The three main areas here include information about how to:

- Plan a Family Reunion
- Publish a Family History
- Publish a Family Newsletter

Let's discuss the contents of each of these areas.

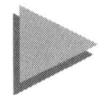

Plan a Family Reunion

Planning and coordinating a family reunion can seem to be a daunting task. First, you select a date and location for the event. You then have to determine who to invite. This often entails compiling a list of every known relative's name, address, phone number, E-mail address or other means of contact. It also may involve locating distant or lost relatives. Invitations have to be created and sent out, responses recorded and follow-ups sent. Reservations for lodging and food may be part of the process. Perhaps you want to prepare special entertainment as well. There seem to be a hundred things to do, and you want to make sure they are all done well.

Never fear! The Genealogy Forum has compiled a collection of information for you to help get the job done. Several members of the forum who are experts at coordinating successful reunions have written articles here that describe how to get the job done. They have had success with their own family events, and have volunteered to share their knowledge with you. In this collection you will find:

- **Planning Your Family Reunion** — This document describes, step by step, how to organize and plan your reunion, how to schedule and coordinate all the tasks to prepare for the event, and how to manage the reunion on-site. From this detailed plan, you can devise a successful master plan and a checklist that fits with your reunion's goals.
- **Reunion Planning Weblinks** — Learn from other people who have coordinated successful family reunions. Here, you will find a selection of Web pages for your reference.
- **Share Your Experiences** — This area is just beginning to grow. Other members have submitted information about their experiences that can help you make the right choices for your group. (Once your family reunion is complete, you can contribute to this area too!)

This collection of reunion planning information is well-written and easy to understand. It includes clear instructions and many excellent suggestions and tips to make your event a real success.

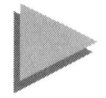

▶ Publish a Family History

Genealogists spend countless hours researching family history. As the work progresses, the ancestors and relatives whose lives we investigate seem to come to life. We learn about their lives, the times in which they lived, their hopes and dreams, their relationships, their happiness and sorrow, and the multitude of details about their daily lives. The more we learn, the more compelled we sometimes become to write a family history.

You may find yourself wanting to write a family history as well. Perhaps, if your family is an historically prominent one, you may want to publish a book for the mass market. If your family is less known, perhaps you would like to publish a limited edition for distribution to family members, people with the same surname, libraries, archives, and genealogical and historical societies. Or, perhaps you simply want to produce a quality family history that can be photocopied and distributed.

No matter what your goals and ambitions are, you will find good advice in this collection in the Reunion Center. There are articles available here about how to organize your material and how to format it. You will find good advice from people who have had experience in writing family histories. In addition, there is available a collection of family history publishers. Here, you will find links to Web sites, as well as name and address information.

This is a great starting point for the family historian who wishes to publish the fruits of his or her research.

Publish a Family Newsletter

We discussed earlier in this chapter the value of family newsletters in keeping communication channels open. People today have a limited amount of time to keep in touch with one another. A well-done newsletter, published on a regular schedule, becomes a welcome and much-anticipated arrival in many households by providing links to other family members and by stimulating communication.

If you want to start a family newsletter, the Genealogy Forum has great information available for you. You will find excellent articles in this collection that can help get you started. Written by experts in the Genealogy Forum who publish their own family newsletters, this collection provides excellent advice about soliciting material, organizing what you compile and formatting the content. It also offers suggestions for the distribution of newsletters in various ways—through paper, E-mail and Web pages.

In addition, the forum has collected some of the best family newsletters as samples. Here you will find ideas on format and layout for your own newsletter. The newsletters are stored in file format in the "Family Newsletters On File" collection. (For detailed information about working with files, please see the chapter about the **File Libraries Center**.) When you publish your newsletter, perhaps you will want to submit yours for inclusion in the Genealogy Forum's collection.

That covers the five buttons. Let's now discuss the major contents of the listbox on the Reunion Center screen.

- **Reunion Schedule** — As discussed earlier in this chapter, the Reunion Schedule lists all the family reunions that meet on a regularly-scheduled basis in the Family Reunion Conference Room.
- **How To Schedule Online Reunions** — This is your starting point for scheduling an online reunion in the Genealogy Forum. The instructions in the document are self explanatory.
- **Message Boards** — Double-click on this item for a collection of links to the forum's message boards related to reunions and publishing. You can discuss the topics listed below with other members there. (For detailed information about how to effectively use the forum's message boards, please see the chapter about the **Message Board Center**.) The topics include:
    - Books and Publications

- Family & Clan Organizations
- Family Name Newsletters
- Family Reunions
- Write/Publish a Family History

- **Genealogy Conferences & Events** — The Genealogy Forum maintains this collection to publicize conferences, lectures, meetings and other events. This is another excellent area in which to publicize your family reunion. Once you have the details worked out, you can submit the information for posting in this collection. Information in this area is listed by date of the event. The collection is usually featured on the main screen of the forum twice a month.

The Surname Center

The last button on the Reunion Center screen will take you to the forum's **Surname Center**. As you begin to plan your family reunion, you will want to look for other people related to your family. The forum has consolidated all kinds of information regarding specific surnames into a single, one-stop area in the Surname center. If yours is one of the top 1,000 surnames in the United States, you will find material including GEDCOM files, links to message boards, Web pages and other materials to help you learn more about your family and its collateral and affiliated lines.

For complete details about these surname resources and how to use them effectively, please read the **Surname Center** chapter.

Summary

A family reunion is a milestone in a family's history. Whether it takes place only once or is an annual event, a reunion provides an unparalleled opportunity to build and reinforce family ties. For the genealogist, it is an exciting venue to gather information from the best possible sources—the family members themselves.

The Reunion Center provides some wonderful reference resources for organizing your family reunion, for joining a family association, for publishing a family newsletter or for writing that family history you've been thinking about for so long.

Don't put it off any longer! With the resources provided in the Genealogy Forum's Reunion Center, you now have access to excellent advice, as well as to an excellent starting point. Now is the time to do it!

12 ▶ The Genealogy Columns

THE GENEALOGY FORUM HAS COMPILED A TREMENDOUS COLLECTION OF MATERIALS FOR YOUR REFERENCE. As you have seen, there are "how-to" and informational articles about all sorts of topics featured in the Genealogy Forum. There are files and Internet links available to help you with your research. The forum's message boards and chats, along with AOL's E-mail and IM facilities, help you communicate with other members and allow you to make connections and exchange information quickly and effectively.

Beyond these materials, however, are the columns that appear in the Genealogy Forum. These provide fresh, new content on a regularly-scheduled basis on a wide variety of subjects. In particular, there are two columns featured in the forum: **"Along Those Lines..."** and the **DearMYRTLE Daily Column**. While each of these has its own specific audience, they complement one another in content and balance, and provide something for everyone. This is not by accident. Not only do the two columnists work together, but they have become good friends as well. In addition, the forum publishes its monthly **Genealogy Forum NEWS**, another excellent communication vehicle. The newsletter is actually a collection of articles (or columns) written by members of the forum's staff, volunteers and members like you.

Between these three online publications, the Genealogy Forum provides fresh and interesting materials on a regularly-scheduled basis. Feedback from readers indicates that these features are a much-anticipated part of members' schedules. People have said that they have added DearMYRTLE and "Along Those Lines..." to their Favorite Places and read them as soon as they are made available. Readers also say that they look forward to the forum's newsletter at the beginning of each month.

With these thoughts in mind, let's explore these areas. You will learn about the authors, as well as the focus and the content of each area.

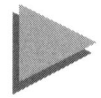

DearMYRTLE Daily Column

DearMYRTLE is one of the better-known and more prolific writers in the genealogy field. She is responsible for the contribution of an impressive body of information in the Genealogy Forum. This includes a wide variety of beginning genealogy materials housed in both the **Beginners' Center** and the **DearMYRTLE Daily Column** areas of the forum.

DearMYRTLE's primary focus is to help and educate beginning genealogists. Her writing style is easy to read and down-to-earth. She has a gift that enables her to describe concepts and procedures so that they can be easily grasped. She receives a great deal of E-mail from her readers, most of which include questions about how to do something specific in the way of genealogical research or organization. Quite often, her daily columns consist of a letter and her explanatory response. And, while she cannot possibly respond to every E-mail she receives, she does read each one, and incorporates her readers' inquiries and informational needs into her column topics. In this respect, she is a sensitive and responsive columnist.

DearMYRTLE started her online genealogy career in 1984, when she began experimenting with Genie and CompuServe. In 1985, she became a regular contributor to "Your Family Tree," the genealogy forum on Q-Link, which was then a forerunner of America Online. She then became the assistant genealogy forum leader there, where she also conducted several weekly online chats/classes. Later, when America Online was formed, she became a member of the Genealogy Forum, where she continues to serve as a senior staff member.

DearMYRTLE received her initial genealogy training at the Washington, DC, Temple LDS Family History Center, and has completed extensive research at the Library of Congress and National Archives. She is the author of numerous articles in print and electronic media, lectures often at local and national genealogical conferences and teaches computer classes at her local community college. In addition to her various online responsibilities, she volunteers weekly at the LDS Family History Center near her home in Bradenton, Florida.

DearMYRTLE's column is accessible from the listbox of Genealogy Forum's main screen. Alternatively, you can access her area directly by going to either of two AOL Keywords: **myrtle** or **dearmyrtle**. When you go to the DearMYRTLE Daily Column area, the screen shown in Figure 12.1 is displayed.

You have here a great many materials available from which to choose. Above the listbox on the left side of the screen, you will see a line of blue, underlined text. This is a hypertext link to a featured collection of material. This link changes periodically, so be certain not to miss MYRT's features here.

The lion's share of MYRTLE's materials are housed in the listbox. There is much to choose from, so let's discuss the key items in the collection.

- **Current Month's Articles** — DearMYRTLE produces a genealogy column every weekday. This collection

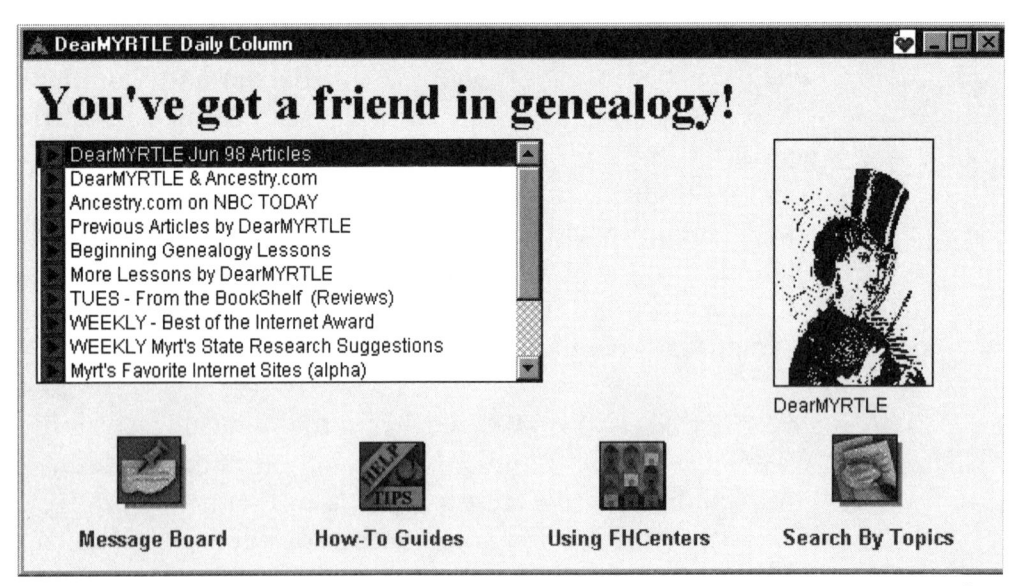

Figure 12.1

includes the articles she has written for the current month.

- **Previous Articles by DearMYRTLE** — All of DearMYRTLE's columns extending from November of 1996 through the previous month's articles are archived in this collection. The previous years' collections contain sub-collections of each month's articles for easy reference. The current year's articles are maintained by month, and are later archived into an annual collection.
- **Beginning Genealogy Lessons** — MYRT's lessons for beginners provide a comprehensive body of training that anyone can use. Easy-to-understand text and examples make them accessible and useful. The lessons are also linked into the forum's **Beginners' Center**.
- **Lessons by DearMYRTLE** — This collection contains several sets of genealogy lessons. In addition to the Beginning Genealogy Lessons, there also are the following lessons:
  - **Finally Getting Organized** — This collection provides a month-by-month regimen for getting all

of those piles of genealogical materials in your home office, bedroom, closet or wherever organized. This collection is also linked into the **Beginners' Center**.

- **Using LDS FHCenters** — A Family History Center (FHC) is part of The Church of Jesus Christ of Latter-Day Saints (LDS). These facilities contain many detailed genealogy resources. They also can serve as a conduit for you to borrow microfilm and other resources from the huge LDS library in Salt Lake City, UT. MYRTLE's extensive experience with FHCs and LDS materials provides her with many insights. You will benefit from her knowledge as you make use of these valuable resources.

- **Writing Personal Histories** — MYRT has begun another collection of materials about creating lasting, written histories. While the art of writing seems to be dying in this electronic age, she encourages you to produce written legacies for future generations of your family. Check out her ideas.

- **From the Bookshelf** — MYRTLE somehow finds time in her schedule for reading. In this area, she shares reviews of books and CD-ROMs. (Please note that the reviews in this area span a period of several years. Some of the books reviewed here may have been updated and reprinted in later editions. Please check with your local bookstore or library for a copy of Books in Print, which will help you confirm the availability of these materials.)

- **Best of the Internet** — With the explosive growth of new Internet sites each month, it is difficult to know where to look for the best of the new crop. While the **Internet Center** is the focal point in the forum for many exciting new Web pages, search engines, mailing lists and Usenet newsgroups, MYRTLE remains ever vigilant in her search for hot, new sites. In this area, she high lights what she considers to be the best of the Web sites.

- **U.S. State Suggestions** — MYRTLE has embarked on

the ambitious project of creating a reference document for each of the 50 states. Each includes some historical background on the state, as well as important addresses, links to resources in the Genealogy Forum, Internet Web links, Internet mailing lists, Usenet newsgroups, descriptions of CD-ROM products (if applicable), LDS FHC resources, maps on the Internet and other valuable resource references. While she focuses primarily on educating beginning genealogists, MYRTLE's State Suggestions are massive collections of materials. Beginners may feel intimidated by such an avalanche of information. Never fear, however, because even the beginner will feel quite comfortable with the materials contained in the State Suggestions documents once they have worked their way through this book.

- **How to Contact DearMYRTLE** — MYRT loves to hear from her readers. You must understand, however, that she receives a huge volume of E-mail each day. While she reads each message, she cannot possibly respond to each individually. Please read the article in this area for more information about how to contact DearMYRTLE.
- **GGM's "Along Those Lines…"** — MYRTLE provides a link available to the "Along Those Lines…" column. You will see later that there is also a link from "Along Those Lines…" to DearMYRTLE's column.

Along the bottom of the screen are four buttons. Let's discuss each:

- **Message Board** — DearMYRTLE has her own message board in the Genealogy Forum where members can discuss her columns. For more information about message boards, please read the chapter about the **Message Board Center**.
- **How-to Guides** — MYRTLE has compiled a copious collection of materials to help the beginning genealogist.

There are a wide variety of topics available here, so be sure to check the contents of this collection. It is also linked to the **Beginners' Center**.

- **Using FHCenters** — This is the same collection as the **Using LDS FHCenters** collection described above.
- **Search By Topics** — This facility enables you to search for materials throughout the Genealogy Forum. Please refer to the chapter about **Search the Forum** for a detailed description of what materials are searchable and how to use the facility.

As you can see, the DearMYRTLE Daily Column area contains a great variety of information. MYRT continues to be a prolific writer, and certainly makes genealogy more accessible to people of all ages and backgrounds. Her columns are highly recommended.

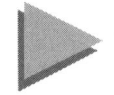

"Along Those Lines..."

"Along Those Lines..." [written by George G. Morgan, author of this book] is published on Friday of each week in the Genealogy Forum. It also is cross-posted at the Ancestry.com Web site (http://www.ancestry.com). The column's audience is a broad one, ranging from beginning to advanced genealogists. The column's focus is to provide information about:

- How and where to locate "alternative" records and information when your primary sources have been lost or destroyed.
- Advanced research methods and techniques using computers, software and the Internet.
- Political developments or situations that impact your ability to gain access to information.
- Discussions of significant developments in the availability of research materials for different ethnic and religious groups.

- Previews of upcoming genealogical conferences, and reviews of significant events at recent conferences.
- Previews and reviews of new and soon-to-be released publications and software products.
- Techniques for the preservation of rare, fragile and ephemeral materials.
- Information about, and links to, Internet Web sites, mailing lists and Usenet newsgroups that can help you locate materials that you might otherwise not know about.

My goal in writing the column is to provide information about the topics above, while using my experiences to help readers relate the topics to their own research. For example, I discussed in one column a table that had been in our family for over 250 years, and how a small envelope, tacked to the underside, contained clues that began my genealogical research down another family surname line. Another column described how my mother's gift to me of my great-grandmother's quilt caused me to learn about textile preservation—and to share it with my readers.

Having started researching my family history at the age of ten, I have now had over 36 years' worth of experience working with various records and materials. That's a lot of research in a lot of different areas. As owner of my own seminar company in the Tampa Bay, Florida, area, I teach workshops across the state. These include high-tech and computer workshops, as well as seminars about genealogical research. Libraries and library consortia comprise a major portion of my clients. Most of the workshops I conduct are presented to librarians, and many of these are librarians who serve genealogy patrons. I have enjoyed the privilege of working with them, and have had the benefit of hearing first-hand about the needs of their genealogy patrons.

The combination of my genealogy background, computer technology experience and training have helped me combine the best of these areas into what I hope is an interesting, helpful and, sometimes, amusing weekly column.

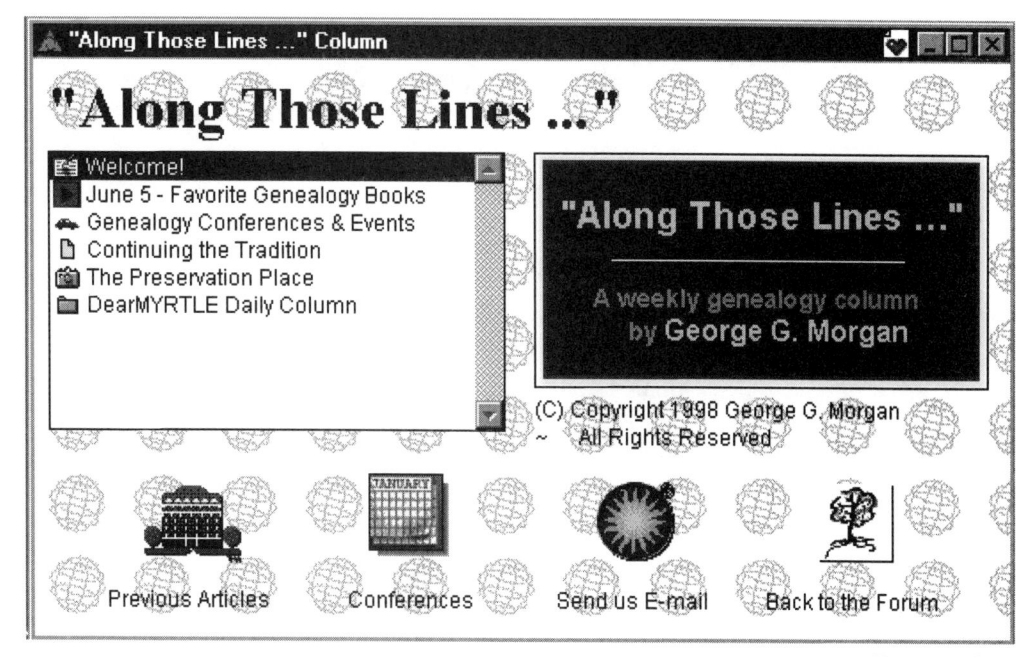

Figure 12.2

The "Along Those Lines…" column area is accessible from the listbox in the Genealogy Forum's main screen. When you go to the column area, the screen shown in Figure 12.2 will be displayed.

You will see a number of items displayed in the listbox on the left side of the screen, and four buttons at the bottom. Let's discuss each of these, starting with the listbox. All items in the listbox are accessible by double-clicking on them with your mouse, or by highlighting the item and pressing Enter or Return on your computer keyboard.

- **Welcome** — The first article in the listbox provides some information about the column and its focus, as well as some biographical information about the author.
- **Weekly Column** — The next item in the listbox is the week's "Along Those Lines …" column. A new column is posted and available every Friday morning at about 1:00 AM Eastern Time. The date of the column and its topic are always included. To read the column, simply

double-click on the column topic in the listbox.
- **Genealogy Conferences & Events** — As a service to members visiting the Genealogy Forum, this site brings you information about conferences, meetings, and other special events related to genealogy. Check this collection for events of interest on a national, state or local level. Events are listed in chronological order, and the location of each is included in the title. The forum is interested in promoting scholarship, and the conferences and other events listed here will help you learn more about genealogical research methods. If you are interested in having a conference, meeting or other genealogy-related event posted, please read the article, "About This Area," which describes how to get started. (**NOTE**: The Genealogy Forum neither endorses, nor recommends, any specific event. Rather, the forum brings these announcements to your attention so you can decide whether to participate in any of the events that seem appropriate to your interests.)
- **Continuing the Tradition** — Your genealogical work is an important part of your family's history. You have invested incalculable hours of travel and effort researching, traveling, compiling and organizing materials. But, what will happen to your work when you join your ancestors? This thought-provoking article will help you make decisions about the fate of your research materials.
- **The Preservation Place** — This collection provides you with a starting point in learning how to preserve family photographs, important newspaper clippings (such as wedding announcements, birth announcements and obituaries), and other family documents. When you access The Preservation Place, the screen shown in Figure 12.3 will be displayed. You can access any of the categories shown on the buttons on the screen.
- **DearMYRTLE Daily Column** — "Along Those Lines..." is pleased to provide a cross-link to MYRTLE's column.

Figure 12.3

The four buttons across the bottom of the screen provide you with access to several areas. Let's discuss each:

- **Previous Articles** — The first button (with the icon of the archive building) will take you to the archive of all previous "Along Those Lines ..." columns. When you click on this button, the screen shown in Figure 12.4 will be displayed. There is an introductory article available in the collection, as well as the history of the photograph shown on this screen—a wedding photograph of the author's maternal grandparents. Take some time to read the weekly columns, and enjoy some of the funny and interesting insights into genealogy available here.
- **Conferences** — This button provides yet another access to the forum's Genealogy Conferences & Events area described above.
- **Send us E-mail** — This button will present you with a pre-addressed E-mail form allowing you to send a

Figure 12.4

message to the author. Please note, though, that he cannot answer every E-mail he receives. Nor can he perform genealogy research for you.

- **Back to the Forum** — This button will take you to the Genealogy Forum's main screen.

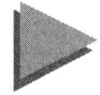

The Genealogy Forum NEWS

There is *always* something going on in the forum, and the Genealogy Forum NEWS is the place to go to keep up with everything. The newsletter is published at the beginning of each month. Each month the editors select a theme for the articles. Staff and volunteers throughout the forum contribute stories or articles relating to the theme. Members, too, contribute written materials. From that perspective, the Genealogy Forum NEWS is a many-authored column.

Along with these "theme" articles, there is always the "Forum Business and Calendar Section" feature, which contains an introduction from the forum's leader, GFL George, and a "Pat on the Back Award" for the forum staff member(s) or volunteer(s) who have contributed in an exceptional manner to the forum. The calendar is an important feature of this section, as well. It lists such things as:

- Special chats/lectures scheduled in specific SIGs for the month
- Birthdays and service anniversaries for your favorite hosts
- Special dates/events on the calendar

A link to the most current Genealogy Forum NEWS is always available in the listbox on the forum's main screen. To access it, all you need to do is double-click on it with your mouse or highlight it and press your Enter or Return key on the computer keyboard. A screen similar to the one shown in Figure 12.5 will be displayed.

The example shown in Figure 12.5 is the Genealogy Forum NEWS from May, 1998. It is typical in that the theme was "Mothers & Grandmothers," in honor of Mothers' Day. There were eleven articles presented on the month's theme. In addition, there were articles about:

- **Beginners' SIG** contains tips and techniques for beginning genealogists by staff and volunteers who host the Beginners' chats.
- **Eastern European SIG** contains mini-articles about locating Jewish resources in Eastern Europe, Austrian resources, and Pfalz and Rhinepalatinate research.
- **German Language SIG** contains an article about the German Red Cross.
- **Internet for Genealogists I & II** contains articles about using new and existing Internet resources in your genealogical research.

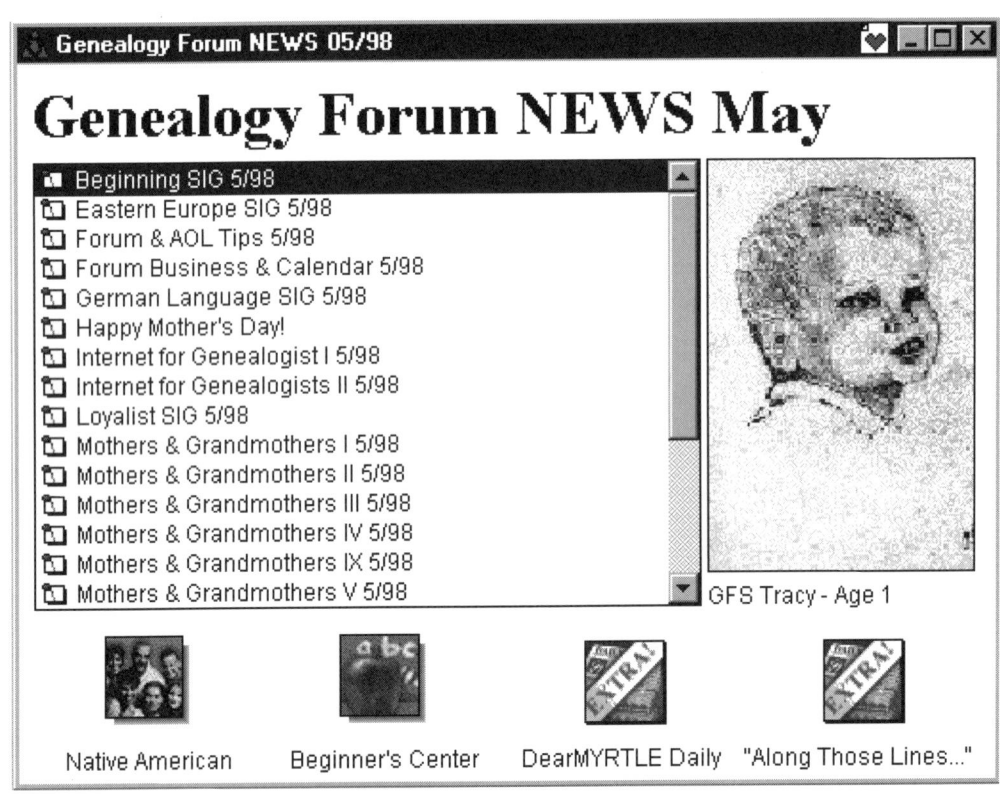

Figure 12.5

- **Loyalist SIG** contains information about a new Loyalist Web site, as well as some rules for researching Loyalist records.
- **Nova Scotia SIG** contains information about ships passenger lists and other Nova Scotia resources.
- **Polish SIG** contains an article about getting started with Polish genealogical research and the fact that your research may require you to look in other countries in addition to Poland.

These are examples of the strength of content that you will find in the Genealogy Forum NEWS. This forum is an online periodical that can provoke your thoughts about how to conduct your research. Learn from the people who have experience by reading the NEWS.

The buttons at the bottom of the screen will take you to several areas. The button on the left in Figure 12.5 will take you to the **Native American Resource Area** in the **Ethnic Area** of the **Resource Center**. This button may change from issue to issue as the NEWS editors choose to feature different areas of the forum. The second button will take you to the **Beginners' Center** discussed earlier in the book. The remaining two buttons will link you directly to the DearMYRTLE and "Along Those Lines..." columns.

Summary

As you have seen, the Genealogy Forum offers three, regularly-scheduled, online feature publications:

- **Daily:** DearMyrtle Daily Column, posted Monday through Friday
- **Weekly:** "Along Those Lines...", published every Friday morning
- **Monthly:** The Genealogy Forum NEWS, posted at the beginning of each month

The quality and diversity of the information in each of these three areas will keep you entertained and informed. Be sure to add DearMYRTLE and "Along Those Lines..." to your Favorite Places list, and look for the Genealogy Forum NEWS at the beginning of each month.

13 ▸ Search the Forum

YOU HAVE SEEN IN PREVIOUS CHAPTERS THE WEALTH OF RESOURCES THAT THE GENEALOGY FORUM HAS TO OFFER. You also have learned where resources are located, as well as how to use them. There are times, however, when you may not be certain what is available and where it might be located. Or, you may be in a hurry to find every possible resource in the forum related to a specific word or phrase.

To help, the Genealogy Forum has a facility available called **Search the Forum**. While this facility provides you the capability to search a vast amount of the materials in the forum, there are limitations, and some materials cannot be searched.

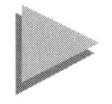

▸ What Determines What is Searchable?

The Genealogy Forum's programming staff is responsible for creating the screens you see, for formatting the articles you read, for managing the message boards and file libraries, for virus-checking all the files and for creating and maintaining the links that help you move from place to place in the forum and elsewhere on AOL and the Internet. They work the behind-the-scenes magic that brings the Genealogy Forum to life.

The forum's programming staff also creates the links that make the forum "searchable." However, they are dependent on the general functionality of America Online to make this happen.

To understand what materials are or are not searchable, it is important that you draw some distinctions between the different types of materials. There are four distinct types of materials in the Genealogy Forum.

- **Articles or Documents** — These are the text materials you see in the various centers and their sub-areas. They are usually shown with a mini-icon of a page or a folder, although other mini-icons may have been used. An article by DearMYRTLE that describes how to organize your genealogical collection is a good example of one of these.
- **Files** — Files contain data. The **File Libraries Center** is devoted to the organization and storage of files for ease of location, download and use. They are usually shown with the mini-icon of a diskette. You will find that files are linked to other areas of the forum as well. For instance, you will find files about the Huguenots linked in the **Resource Center** in the **Huguenots** area of the **Ethnic Resources**. All files, however, are physically stored in the file libraries. They have been linked into other areas to help build the collection and to provide you with another path through which you can access them.
- **Messages** — In the chapter about the **Message Board Center**, you learned that message boards provide a means for members to post electronic messages, queries and announcements for other members to read and to which they may respond. You also learned about the

various categories of message boards, as well as how to effectively create, post and use messages. You can access message boards through the Message Board Center, where all the boards and their contents are stored. However, you will also find links from other areas to individual message boards. For example, if you are in the **Surname Center** and looking at the name BAILEY in the Top 1,000 Surnames area, you will find links to GEDCOM files for that surname. Those files are stored in the file libraries, but a link has been provided to help consolidate BAILEY files together with other BAILEY resources.

- **Internet Links** — In the chapter about the **Internet Center**, you learned about Web pages. The Genealogy Forum provides links to Web pages and places them wherever they are appropriate. Certainly the Internet Center is full of links to Web pages, but you will also find Web links throughout the forum. In the **Resource Center**, in the **Regions of the World** area, under **Canada** and in the collection for **Ontario**, you will find a document titled, "Ontario Internet Web Links." This document contains scores of links to Web pages related to the historical, cultural and genealogical resources of Ontario.

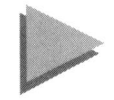

▶ Which Materials are Searchable?

Articles and documents are nearly always searchable. As a matter of course, the programmers set an article or document up to allow the full text of the article to be searchable. That means that if you were searching for the surname WEATHERLY, you would be able to initiate a search of the forum. (We'll discuss how to do this a little later in this chapter.) The "search" would look inside every document in the forum for that word.

In some cases, the programmers are instructed to add searchable keywords to help you locate information when you search the forum. These keywords, however, are not always included in the document. For example, articles about Native Americans might have a keyword "Indian" added to assist in the search. However, don't depend on this type of addition to be the norm.

Files are not always searchable. America Online does not automatically provide a facility to search through file names. Nor does it provide for the contents of a data file to be searched. The Genealogy Forum programmers, however, have expended a huge effort to index the files that you would find most important. These include:

- GEDCOM files
- Lineage files
- Ahnentafel files
- "Tiny Tafel" files

In order to index these files for you, forum programmers have literally opened each file, created a list of the surnames in the files and added the list to each file's descriptive text. Therefore, if you were to use the Search the Forum facility to look for the MORGAN surname, you would have a much greater chance of locating files containing that surname.

Other files, however, have not been indexed. These include maps, recipes, newsletters, history, culture, ethnic resources, records, photographs, chat logs, graphics and software files. You will still need to search the libraries by category to locate specific file titles.

Messages are not searchable. America Online does not provide a facility to search the content of the message boards, or of the messages themselves. In order to do so, AOL would have to commit massive computer memory solely to indexing every word in every message. Because many thousands of messages are being posted every minute, it would be impossible to reindex every message and keep the system up-to-date.

To locate information in the message boards, you will need to review the boards and message titles yourself. Please refer to the chapter about the **Message Board Center** for details about how to effectively use that facility.

Don't forget that you can set your Preferences to alphabetize the subject lines of all the messages on a board. Remember to use the Find in Top Window facility to review all the subject lines. Both of these tools can help you more effectively search the message board contents, even if AOL does not provide the facility to search the content of the messages themselves.

Internet links are searchable only from the standpoint of the title that shows up on the blue title bar of the screen. The programmers refer to this title as the "headline." When they create a link to a Web page, the programmer must provide a headline. While this title is searchable, the content of a Web page linked anywhere in the forum is not.

If you are interested in searching for information in Internet Web pages, you can connect to any of the Internet search engines included in the **Internet Center**, and follow their individual instructions about how to search the Web. (Please check the Help facility at each of the search engine Web sites for detailed information.)

Now that you understand the four types of materials found in the forum, as well as which ones are searchable and why, let's discuss how you can use the Search the Forum facility.

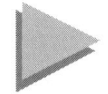

▶ How to Use "Search the Forum"

Search the Forum is accessible from the Genealogy Forum's main screen. Simply click on the "Search the Forum" button. The screen shown in Figure 13.1 will be displayed.

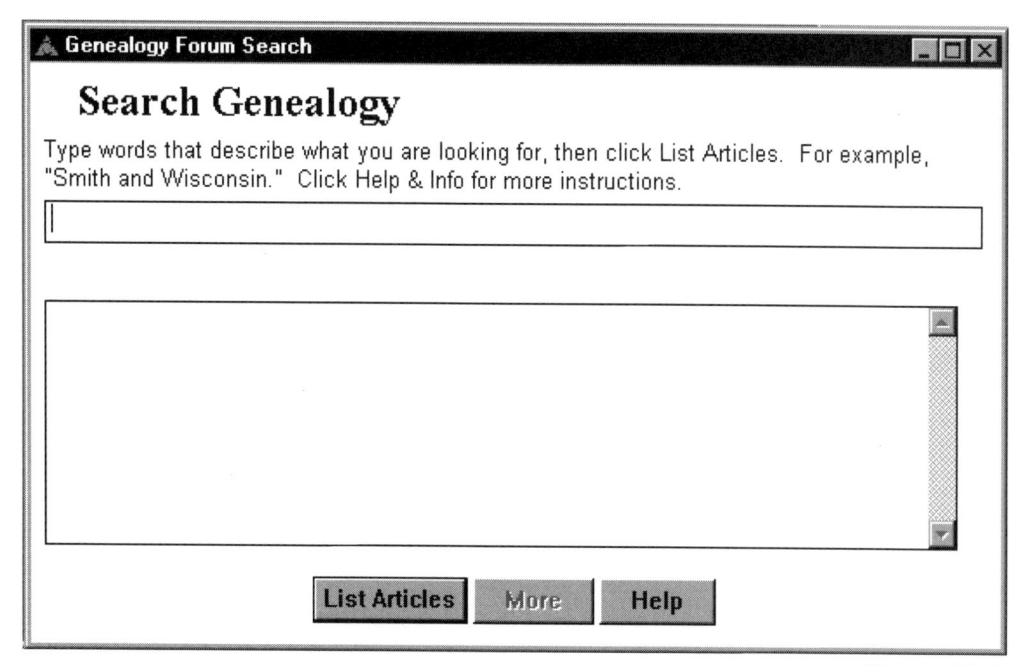

Figure 13.1

    The screen features two boxes and three buttons. The top box is where you type the word(s) which you are searching. This could be a surname, any other word or a combination of words. It makes no difference whether you type the word in all lowercase, uppercase or in mixed case; the search facility locates all matches it finds in any typed case.

    Simply type a surname in the upper box and either click on the List Articles button or press the Enter button on your computer keyboard. Let's try the word "jones." The search results for "jones" are displayed in the lower box, twenty at a time, as shown in Figure 13.2. In this example, the "Items 1 - 20 of 250 out of 886 matches" text appears between the two boxes. Let's discuss what this indicates:

1. The search yielded a total of 886 matches for the word, "jones."
2. AOL's search facility will only allow you to view 250 of these items.

The Genealogy Forum on America Online — 251

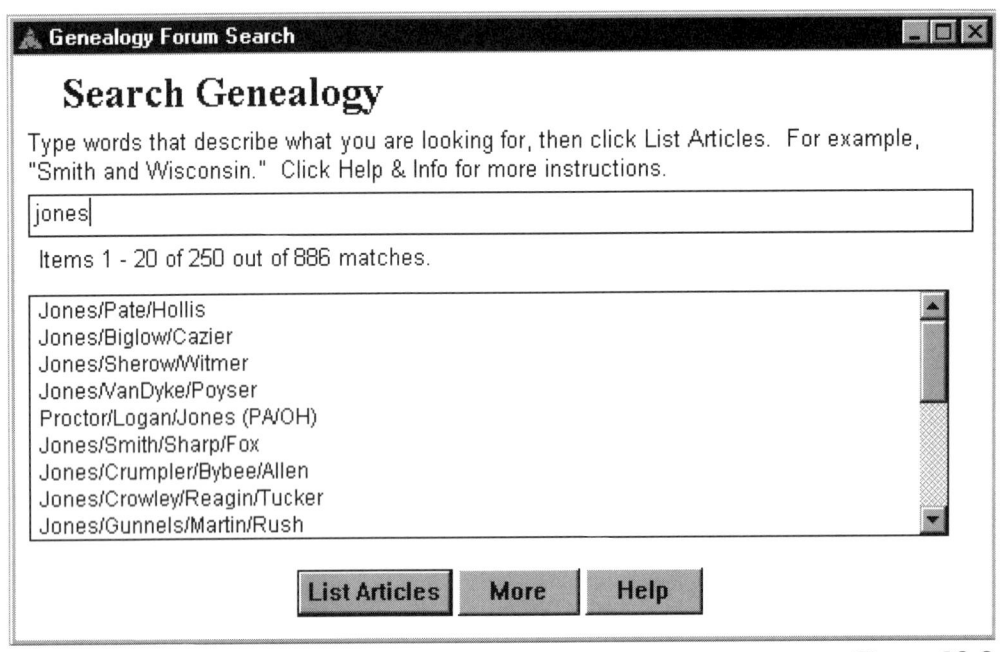

Figure 13.2

3. The first 20 of the matches are loaded into the viewing box.

You can scroll down the list of the first twenty. To view additional matches, twenty more at a time, click on the More button at the bottom of the screen. Remember that you can keep clicking until all 250 are loaded in the view box. At that time, you can use the Find in Top Window facility to search for specific words displayed in the view box. This is especially helpful if you are looking for another surname that might also be in the title of the item shown in the box.

Now, you have all of your matches. They may include files, articles, "Tiny Tafels" and a host of other items. Your work begins when you look at each item to see if you have an interest in the contents.

To view more information about any item on the search results in the view box, double click on the item. If it is an article or document, its full text will be displayed. (Remember to use the Find in Top Window facility to expedite your review for key words in the documents.) If the item is a file, the file description screen will be displayed. You can read the contents and decide whether to download the file or not.

Ways of Narrowing Your Search

In the previous example, there were 886 matches—far too many for AOL to allow to be reviewed. While this can be frustrating in some cases, 886 is a large number. You will probably want to alter your search to obtain a more manageable group of material to review. Fortunately, you can do this by using a Boolean search.

Boolean searches use certain words, called operators, to help you control the scope of your search. The operators are AND, OR and NOT. (There are additional operators, but AOL uses only these three.) Using these, you can cause the Search the Forum facility to look for some words and not others. Let's talk about how each one of the operators works.

NOTE: The operators in the following examples are typed in UPPERCASE, so that you may more easily see them. When using the Search the Forum facility, however, it makes no difference whether you type them in upper- or lowercase.

- AND — You can join words together to cause the search to look for only items that have both the words. For example, if you were looking for items containing the words "jones" and "martin," you would type:

    jones AND martin

    The number of matches was narrowed from 886 to 374 in Figure 13.3. Next, let's add "AND rush" to the list:

    jones AND martin AND rush

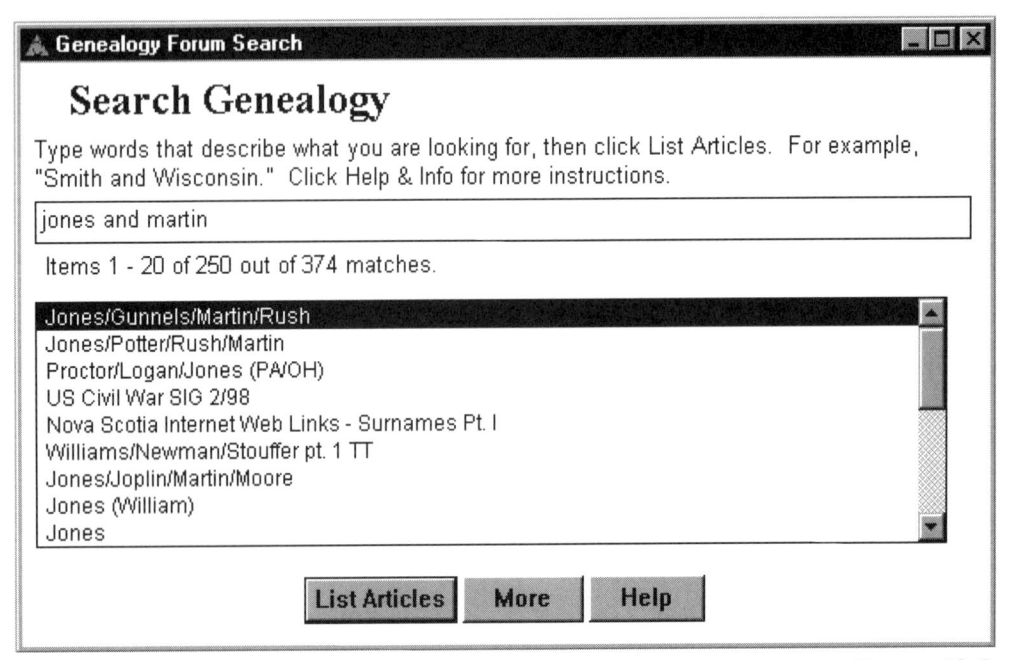

Figure 13.3

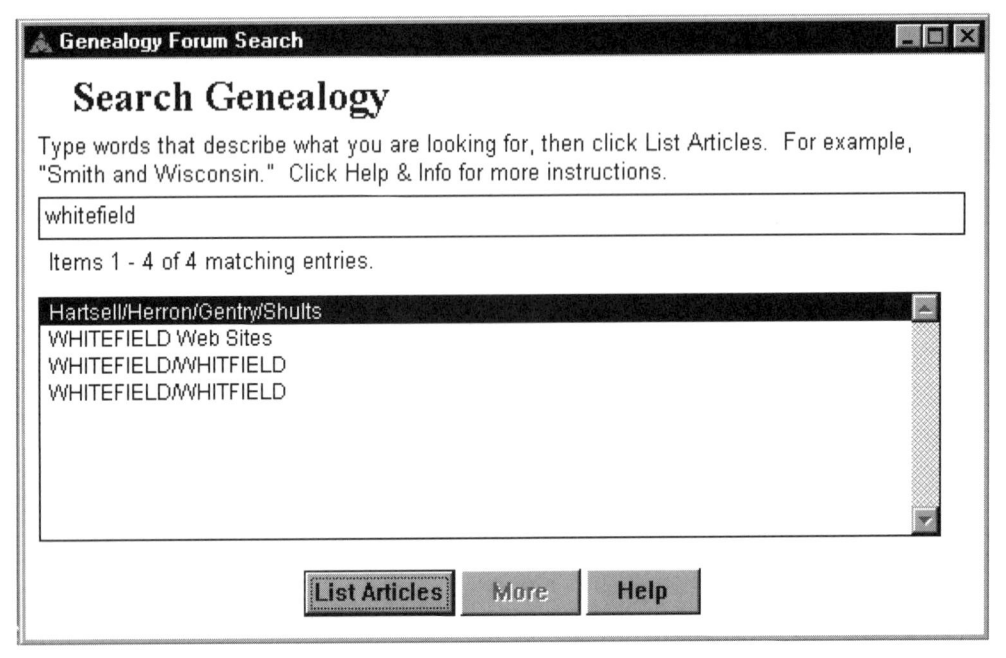

Figure 13.4

254 — *The Genealogy Forum on America Online*

This time, the list was narrowed to only 47 matches—a much easier list to review.

- OR — You can expand your search by using the OR operator. As an example, the surname "whitefield" was used as the search word in Figure 13.4. It yielded four matches.

Recognizing that there may have been a variation of the spelling of the surname, you might type the following:

whitefield OR whitfield

When the search is performed on this combination, you are indicating that you want to see any item with either "whitefield" or "whitfield" in the headline and/or text. In this case, Figure 13.5 shows that there were 32 matches found using the Boolean operator, OR. In this example, too, you will see included in this list of matches

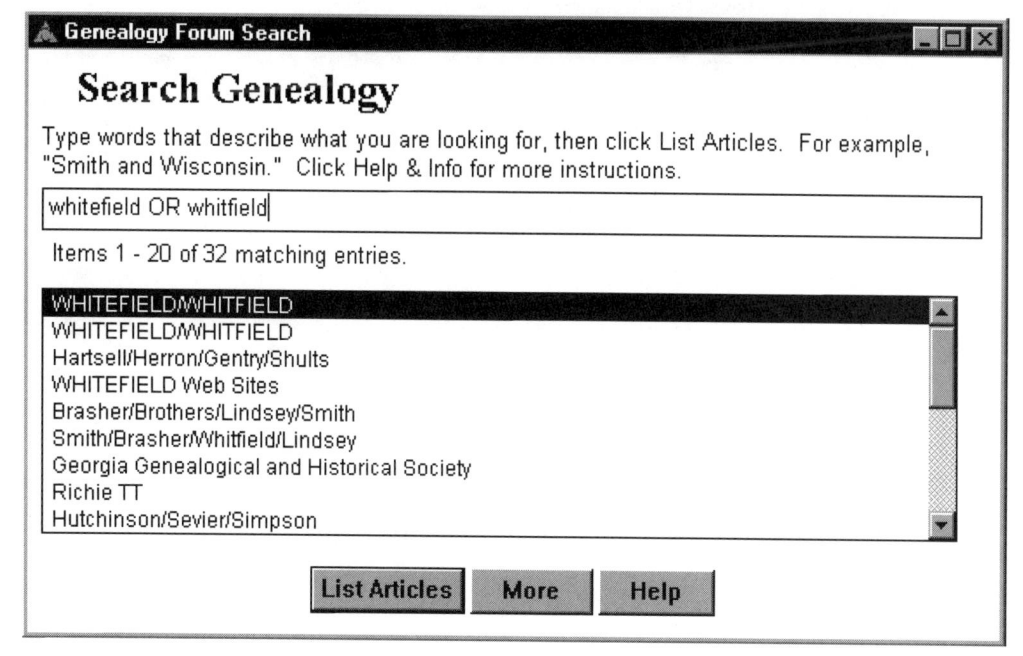

Figure 13.5

The Genealogy Forum on America Online — 255

the "Georgia Genealogical and Historical Society" (Whitfield County and several other references are in this document) and "Richie TT" (a "Tiny Tafel" file, in which Whitfield County is listed).

- NOT — You can limit your search and eliminate items you don't want by using the NOT operator. Let's say you are searching for the surname HOLDER. You recognize that there may be a spelling variant, HOLDEN, but are certain you do not want to see any items with the name HOLDEN. Without limiting the search, you might find 87 matches on the HOLDER surname. You would use the NOT operator, and type:

    holder NOT holden

The results list is shown in Figure 13.6, where only 71 matches were reported. While this seems a small difference, use of the NOT operator can screen out large percentages of unwanted materials.

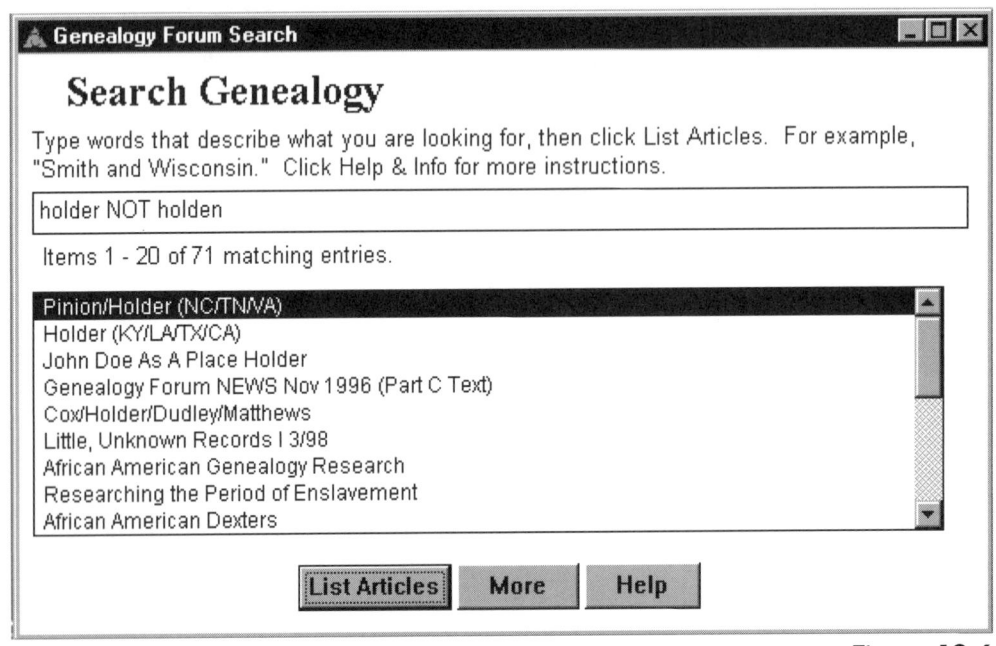

Figure 13.6

Summary

As you can see, the Search the Forum facility can yield great results. The key lies in understanding what materials are searchable, in realizing what materials will not be included in a search results, and in knowing what to do with the material you find.

If you need information about definitions of some of the materials, such as Ahnentafel files and "Tiny Tafels," or working with files of various types, please refer to the index, the glossary, and the chapter about the **File Libraries Center**.

14 ▶ Telephone Search Facilities

SEARCHING FOR PEOPLE IS WHAT GENEALOGY IS ALL ABOUT. Most often, you are probably searching through old records for ancestors and relatives who lived sometime in the past. However, part of your genealogical research should also be directed toward those relatives who are still living. They can be a tremendous source of information. You never know who has that missing family Bible, who knows that special family story, or who is holding on to the memories that might fill in the blanks you need. Interviewing living relatives is a genealogical research project that many people leave until it is too late.

Perhaps you've just lost touch with some relatives, or are planning an elaborate family reunion and want to invite the whole clan. Regardless who you are looking for, one resource you certainly will need is a telephone directory. Fortunately, the Genealogy Forum has collected a variety of resources for you in one place—the **Telephone Search Facility**.

The forum's Telephone Search Facility is a collection of Internet Web sites that provide access to telephone numbers. In

```
Telephone Search Facilities
 Telephone Search Facilities
 Switchboard
 WhoWhere? Phone Numbers & Addresses
 WorldPages: Find the World Here!
 Yahoo! People Search
 Excite People Finder
 Four11 - US Telephone Directory
 Phone & Address - InfoSpace
 The Ultimate White Pages
 Database America People Finder
        Open              More
```

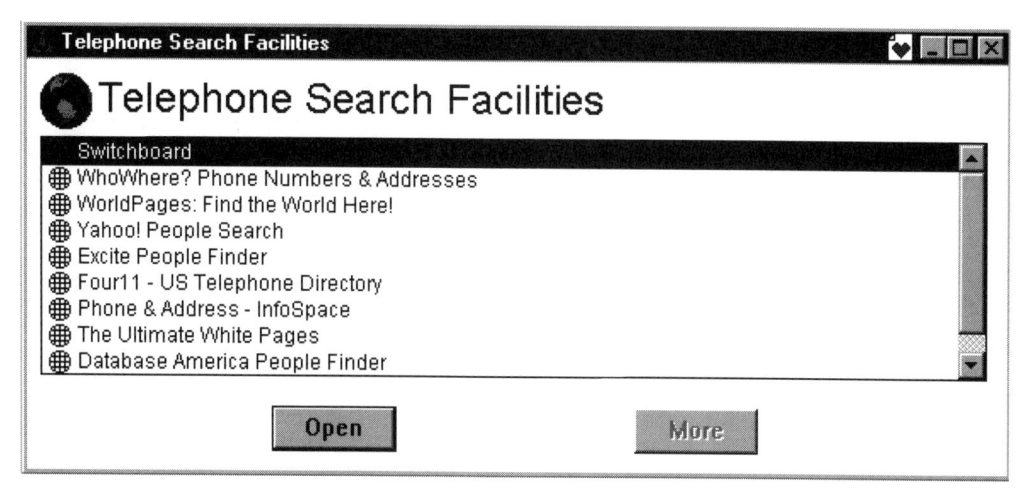

Figure 14.1

many cases, these Web pages also allow you to locate E-mail and/or postal addresses.

Each of these search tools operates differently. Some provide only telephone numbers for residences and businesses. Others may also provide searchable listings for toll-free numbers, or may include E-mail and/or postal addresses. These search tools, however, have one thing in common—they are all able only to locate listed telephone numbers. The search tools are unable to locate unlisted numbers.

The Telephone Search Facility can be accessed from the Genealogy Forum's main screen by clicking on the "Phone Numbers" button. The screen shown in Figure 14.1 will be displayed.

The list of Web sites offering telephone search facilities is displayed in the listbox. This list may, of course, change over time as new facilities become available and others change. Let's discuss a few of these facilities.

- **Switchboard** is an "interactive directory" for locating people and businesses. At the time of this writing, it is AOL's directory of choice. Its People Search facility allows you to search using name and state only. The resulting list will provide names, addresses, cities, states, ZIP codes and phone numbers. (You can even add or modify your own listing.) A similar search option allows you to search for businesses. There is also an E-mail address look-up facility. Locate the right one and send an E-mail!

- **WhoWhere?** provides a similar search facility. An 800 number search facility, as well as business and E-mail searches, is also available. Maps, directories, personal services and other listings are provided here as well.

- **Yahoo! People Search** is provided by the people who maintain the Yahoo! Web site, the preeminent indexed informational directory on the Web. This search facility is probably the easiest to use and the largest of the indexes.

- **Excite People Finder** provides another easy-to-use search facility for addresses, phone numbers and E-mail addresses. It also provides links to Switchboard (described above) and the Lookup USA People Directory (not in the forum's collection).

- **Four11** provides White Pages, Yellow Pages and maps. This facility did not have an E-mail locator facility at the time of this writing.

- **InfoSpace** provides an international phone number search facility in which you can designate the country you wish to search. The U.S., Canada and seven other countries represent the extent of this service at the time of this writing.

- **The Ultimate White Pages** is an exceedingly elegant tool that allows you to search through many of the other telephone search facilities. Also included are two handy reverse search facilities. Perhaps you wrote a telephone number down and don't remember whose it is? Enter the telephone number and the reverse

number search will provide you with the name under which it is listed.
- **Database America People Finder** provides a residential telephone number look-up facility, as well as a reverse number search.

To access any of these Web sites, you can either double-click your mouse on the item in the listbox or highlight it and press the Enter key on your computer keyboard.

All of the sites described above are fairly intuitive to use. Most offer some sort of help text to show you how best to use the facility. You will find these helpful in your genealogical search for living relatives, as well as for many other day-to-day activities.

15 ▶ Other Related Forums on AOL

THROUGHOUT THIS BOOK YOU HAVE BEEN PRESENTED WITH THE WEALTH OF CONTENT OF THE GENEALOGY FORUM. New "centers," message boards and file library areas are constantly being added to the forum. Articles, columns and links to new and exciting Web addresses are added to the forum regularly. New chat topics and additional meeting times for existing chats are added periodically too.

The staff constantly evaluates new functions and features of America Online, and incorporates them into the forum's design. This includes updating the list of related AOL areas that complement the content of the forum, as well as maintaining the links to these areas.

It is important to gain an historical perspective of the places and times in which your ancestors lived. By learning more about the geography of their native lands, the governments that ruled them, the social climates, as well as the economic situations and living conditions under which they lived, you can begin to understand the choices your ancestors made. Their decision to move elsewhere, the places they chose to settle, the occupations they pursued, why they had the number of children they had—these things come into sharper focus when you understand and consider the lives of your ancestors from an historical perspective.

The Genealogy Forum has compiled a collection of links to other areas on AOL to help you make contact with other people, as well as to point you toward other online resources. This collection is located in the Resource Center, behind the Other Resources button, and in the collection named "Other Related Forums on AOL." The links here include such AOL areas as:

- **Maps** (Keyword: **maps**) — There is an impressive collection of cartographic resources available on AOL. You will find here maps of every country of the world and every state in the U.S.
- **Adoption Forum** (Keyword: **adoption**) — This forum focuses on issues related to adoption. Genealogists seeking information about adopted relatives may post messages on the message boards in this area. The Adoption Search message boards are organized by state, plus a board for Native American adoption search information. This forum's library contains archives of many message boards and chat logs.
- **Bistro - Foreign Language Chat** (Keyword: **bistro**, and then proceed to the Foreign Language Chat button) — This area is part of AOL's International Channel. It provides an area to promote cross-cultural understanding in a safe chat environment where members can speak in several different languages, meet people abroad and talk to others who share their cultural background or interest in world affairs.
- **Civil War Forum** (Keyword: **civil war**) — This forum provides information about the period leading up to the U.S. Civil War and its battles. The area is colorful, interesting and contains a wealth of material for Civil War enthusiasts and genealogists. The message boards

in this forum, the scheduled chats and a library of information and photographs available can all add to your understanding of the era.

- **Ethnicity** (Keyword: **ethnicity**) — This area is part of the AOL Lifestyles area. While the primary areas of focus here are African American, Jewish, Hispanic and Native American, there also are available links under the button for many other international groups.

- **German Heritage** (Keyword: **german heritage**) — This area contains many Germanic resources, including articles and materials about German heritage. This material supplements the German Forum found in the International Channel.

- **Hispanic Online** (Keyword: **hispanic online**) — This forum is especially large and informative. It is the gateway to all things Latino on AOL, and serves also as a guide to Latino-interest areas on the Internet, particularly the World Wide Web.

- **History Resources** (Keyword: **history**) — Part of the AOL Research and Learn collection, the History Resources area is full of World and U.S. history references, as well as links to biographical and cultural resources.

- **International Channel** (Keyword: **international**) — AOL has compiled a massive collection of information in its International Channel area. If you go to Keyword: **international** and click on the "Country Information" button, you will be presented with a list of continents. Click on a continent folder and a list will be displayed listing all the countries in that continent for which there are forum areas on AOL. Select a country, click on it, and visit that forum. You will find current events available in all of them, as well as information about travel, traditions, customs and other details. This is a wonderful research area!

- **Japan!** (Keyword: **japan**) — Japan! is a great resource of Japanese art, culture, traditions, current events and other information.

- **Jewish Community Forum** (Keyword: **jewish**) — The Jewish Forum is a vast collection of materials. Available in this area are message boards, libraries, a calendar of events, informational articles, historical and cultural information and much more.
- **Language Dictionaries** (Keyword: **foreign dictionary**) — There are times when you really need to translate words from one language to another. The dictionary facility is a great tool.
- **NetNoir** (Keyword: **netnoir**) — This forum celebrates the African American cultural heritage. You will find a great deal of useful information and discussion for the novice *and* experienced genealogical researcher of African descent in the Heritage and Kinfolks department. In addition to African-American genealogical research information, Heritage and Kinfolks also offers useful tips on planning for a family reunion and how to make it a memorable occasion.
- **Revolutionary War Forum** (Keyword: **rev war**) — This forum is rich with useful information about the Revolutionary War and life during that period. Message boards and scheduled chats can expand your knowledge of the period, helping you better understand the times in which your ancestors lived and the events that influenced their lives.
- **Royalty Forum** (Keyword: **royalty**) — This forum is a great resource if you are interested in royalty. Its message boards contain many interesting discussions of royalty throughout the centuries, as well as information on current reigning monarchs and their families.
- **SeniorNet** (Keyword: **seniornet**) — The SeniorNet area focuses on the international community of computer-using senior citizens. Their Generation to Generation message boards contain wonderful discussions of earlier

times, including the World Wars, the Korean War, the Vietnam War, the Depression, movie nostalgia and other topics of interest.

- **Turtle Island - A Gathering of Nations** (Keyword unassigned at time of printing) — Turtle Island is a forum dedicated to the Native American community. In addition to message boards and scheduled chats, you will find available much information about the Native American heritage of many tribes. This is a great complement to the Genealogy Forum's Native American Resource Area.

The "Other Related Forums on AOL" area offers a great collection of resources about countries of the world, ethnic groups, culture and traditions. Other areas are being added to the collection as they become available on AOL. The Genealogy Forum's staff works closely with AOL, and is always on the alert for new material for this area.

Most members don't even begin to fully mine the vast wealth of information available on AOL that could help their research into history and culture. Don't hesitate to explore the sites the Genealogy Forum staff has assembled for you. You won't be disappointed!

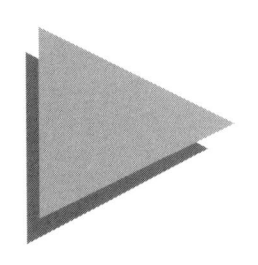

Glossary of Terms

Ahnentafel — German word meaning ancestor file, table or pedigree; a computerized file in the format of an Ahnentafel.

AOL — See America Online.

America Online — The largest, most comprehensive online service available; home of the Genealogy Forum.

Boolean search — A method of combining words, terms and/or phrases to maximize the search of a database by using operators such as AND, OR and/or NOT. Named after English mathematician George Boole.

button — A graphic area on an America Online screen on which you can click your mouse and be connected to another location on the service.

census — An official enumeration of the population of a given area, conducted by a governmental institution, with emphasis on details such as sex, age, occupation, etc.

chat — A real-time meeting held in an electronic conference room, where people discuss topics of common interest. Some chats are hosted Special Interest Groups (SIGs); others are unhosted Drop-In Hours (DIHs). See SIG and DIH.

chat log — A file created during a chat that records all proceedings, including every attendee's comments; helpful for review after the chat is complete. Logs of some important lectures or chats are saved and stored in the File Libraries Center.

citation — A written reference to, or description of, the origin of the source for a piece of genealogical information; a bibliographic or other type of description of the origin of information.

click — To select with one's computer mouse.

database — A collection of computerized information entered into, and stored within, a software program for later retrieval and/or report generation.

diaspora — Any group that is dispersed outside its original or traditional homeland. Applicable to the scattering of the Jews outside Palestine after the Babylonian captivity. Also applicable to any group, including African Americans, dispersed by force from their homeland.

DIH — See Drop-In Hour.

download — The process of copying a file from a remote computer, or system of computers, such as America Online, to your local computer.

Drop-In Hour — An unhosted chat in the Genealogy Forum during which time members drop in and discuss a topic of common interest.

electronic mail — An electronic message sent from one computer user to another.

E-Mail — See electronic mail.

family group sheet — A chart showing all genealogical information about a single family unit (father, mother and all children).

FAQs — Frequently Asked Questions; common questions that are asked by new members; includes answers.

Favorite Place — A facility on America Online that acts as a bookmark; you may add an area on America Online to your Favorite Places list so that you can click on it and go directly to that place on the service.

FHC — Family History Center; a genealogical records repository of The Church of Jesus Christ of Latter-day Saints where research may be performed.

file — A collection of related computer data stored in a single electronic storage unit with a filename and extension.

Find in Top Window — A useful facility available on America Online that allows you to search for text in a window. Provides an easy-to-use facility to locate text when contents of the window cannot be sorted. Accessed through File/Edit or by pressing the CTL+F keys on the computer keyboard.

GEDCOM — Acronym for Genealogy Electronic Data COMmunication; a standard electronic file format used to format data from a genealogical software program for exchange of data with others.

genealogy — The study of the line of descent of a family, or the study of a family's history.

genealogy software program — A computerized database program used for entering and storing genealogical information, as well as for producing charts, reports and extract files.

GFH — Screen name prefix for a Genealogy Forum chat host in training.

GFS — Screen name prefix for a Genealogy Forum chat host.

GSP — See Genealogy Software Program.

heraldry — The study of armorial bearings, coats of arms and other family insignia.

hosted chat — See SIG and chat.

hotspot — An area of a computer screen that is linked to another location. A hotspot on a screen can easily be identified: when you move your mouse pointer over a hotspot, the pointer arrow changes to a small hand with a pointing index finger. By clicking your mouse on the hotspot, you will be connected to another area.

hypertext link — A blue, underscored line of text in a document or on a screen that, when clicked on with your mouse, connects you to another place on America Online or to an Internet Web site. Similar to hotspot.

IM — See Instant Message.

Instant Message — An America Online facility that allows members to exchange real-time, short messages with one another. See real time.

Internet — The world-wide network of computers whose primary function is to share information.

keyword — A facility on America Online that provides a shortcut to another location on the service.

LDS — Abbreviation for The Church of Jesus Christ of Latter-day Saints; the Mormons.

link — A connection between two places in the electronic environment. Links may be made between two points on America Online, two points on the Internet or between one point on America Online and one point on the Internet.

listbox — A component of a screen on America Online; contains articles, folders, links to other places on AOL, Web links or any combination of materials.

listserv — Another term for a mailing list.

log — A file created during an event that captures all activities that occurred within that forum or environment. See chat log.

mailing list — An electronic, subscription-based facility on the Internet that allows you to participate in the sharing of E-mail messages with a large group of other people who have the same interests.

member — A subscriber to America Online.

Member Directory — The facility on America Online where you can search for, and locate, other members by searching for information they have entered into their user profile.

message — An electronic posting on a message board.

message board — An electronic bulletin board on America Online on which members post messages and others respond.

Netiquette — The rules of conduct governing participation in the electronic environment.

pedigree chart — A genealogical chart that represents the lineage of an individual and all direct ancestors; a family tree chart.

posting — The act of placing a message on an electronic message board, bulletin board or Usenet newsgroup; a message placed on such an electronic medium.

primary source — An original piece of genealogical documentation, usually created at the time an event occurred. An example would be a birth certificate.

profile — A descriptive file on America Online containing a member's personal information.

protocol — The structured, orderly method used for conducting hosted lectures or chats. Members type "?" to indicate they wish to ask a question or "!" to indicate they wish to make a comment. The chat hosts maintain a queue and call on members in sequence to allow them to ask questions or make comments.

query — A question or inquiry made for information about an individual, a surname or other data for purposes of genealogical research. In genealogy, most often posted on an electronic message board, in a magazine or in a newspaper.

real-time — A component of certain computer applications that allows for immediate responses to user input; the period of time wherein people participate in, or share, an experience via computer as it is happening. Participation in a chat is a real-time experience; the exchange of E-mail is not.

reunion — The gathering of relatives, kinsmen and friends after a period of separation, or on a regular basis.

search engine — A tool that allows you to search vast areas of the Internet in order to locate Web pages or Usenet newsgroups related to a specific topic.

secondary source — A piece of genealogical documentation that was not created at the time an event occurred. Secondary sources should be corroborated whenever possible with primary sources.

SIG — Special Interest Group. In the Genealogy Forum, this term refers to a hosted chat.

surname — The name that one shares with other family members; a last name.

thread — A group of related messages following the same subject on a message board or in a Usenet newsgroup.

"Tiny Tafel" — A file that is an abbreviated version of an Ahnentafel. See Ahnentafel.

TOS — See Terms of Service.

Terms of Service — The rules of conduct to which every member agrees when becoming an America Online member. Violation of these rules can cause a member's account to be terminated.

unhosted chat — See DIH and chat.

upload — To copy an electronic file from your local computer to another, remote computer, such as America Online.

URL — Universal Resource Locator; a Web address.

Usenet newsgroup — A computerized tool on the Internet that acts like an electronic bulletin board. Users post messages for others to read and to respond to, either on the newsgroup or via private E-mail.

user profile — See Profile.

vital record — In genealogy, a vital record is typically a birth-, marriage- or death-certificate.

Web — See World Wide Web.

Web address — The Uniform Resource Locator (URL) or address of a Web page. An example: http://www.ancestry.com

Web page — An electronic document on the World Wide Web, most often consisting of text and graphics.

Web site — An address or location on the World Wide Web where a Web page is stored; a URL.

window — A small box on a computer screen, generated by the application program for the purpose of providing information or of obtaining input from the user.

World Wide Web — An Internet tool that facilitates the delivery of information in the form of Web pages.

Index

A

Acadia research, 79
addresses, for genealogical research, 111–12, 170–71
Adoption Forum, 263
African American research
African Diaspora Library, 99, 160
    family research hints, 97
    Internet web sites, 99, 206
    listbox resources, 101
    NetNoir forum, 265
    networking through message boards, 99–101
    understanding African American history, 98
    using Resource Center information, 96–97
African Diaspora Library, downloading/uploading, 99
Ahnentafel Library, 158
Albania research, 93–94
Alberta research, 79
"Along Those Lines…" column
    author of, 238–39
    Back to the Forum button, 242
    Conferences button, 241–42
    description of, 51
    focus of, 237–38
    getting to the screen, 239
    listbox resources, 239–41
    Previous Articles button, 241
    publication schedule, 245
    Send Us E-mail button, 242
    view of screen, 239
    See also DearMYRTLE Daily Column;
Genealogy Forum NEWS
American Legion, 111
American research. *See* United States research
America Online, key features of
    E-mail (electronic mail), 26–31
    Favorite Places, 24–25
    importance of understanding, 19
    IMs (Instant Messages), 31–32
    Keywords, 22–24
    layering screens, 38
    Member Directory, 33–34
    Member Services Online Help, 20
    Offline Help, 20–21
    using buttons, 38–39
Ancestor Photos and Graphics file library, 164
Ancestral Digs chat room, 192
Ancestral Seasonings, 113–14
AOL. *See* America Online, key features of
archives, addresses for, 112
associations, family, 170–71, 223–24
Austria research, 88
Azores research, 89–90

B

Beginners' Center
    Beginners' Center button, 55
    Beginners' Tool Kit button, 59–63
    DearMYRTLE's Lessons button, 58–59
    description of, 39
    FAQ/Ask the Staff button, 56–57
    5-step Research Process button, 57–58

Beginners' Center *(Cont.)*
   Genealogy Quick Start Guide, 39, 54–55
   getting to the screen, 54–55
   Introduce Yourself! button, 39–40, 55
   listbox resources, 64–68
   screen contents, 56
   For Starters Conference Room button, 63–64
   view of screen, 55
Beginners Chats, 64
Beginners' Tool Kit, 59–63
Belarus research, 90–93
Belgium research, 88
Bible, Birth and Marriage Records file library, 161
Bistro-Foreign Language Chat, 263
Black research. *See* African American research
BOBO Roots Cellar, 164
book reviews, 235
Bosnia research, 93–94
British Columbia research, 80
British Isles research
   England, 84, 207
   Internet links, 207
   Ireland, 84–86, 207
   Scotland, 86
   Wales, 87, 207
Bulgaria research, 93–94
buttons, 38–39

C

calendar, perpetual, 114
calendar systems, 60
Canada research
   Acadia, 79
   Alberta, 79
   British Columbia, 80
   downloading newsletters, 78
   Internet links, 206–7
   Labrador, 80–81
   Manitoba, 80
   maps, 78
   New Brunswick, 80
   Newfoundland, 80–81
   Northwest Territories, 81
   Nova Scotia, 81
   Ontario, 81–82
   Prince Edward Island, 82
   Quebec, 82
   Saskatchewan, 83
   using Resource Center information, 78–79
   Yukon, 83
Cape Verde Islands research, 89–90
CD-ROM reviews, 235
Channel Islands research, 88
Chat Center
   chat etiquette, 194–95
   chat logging, 195–97
   Chat Preferences button, 191
   chat protocol, 193–94
   chat rooms available, 192, 222–23
   checking for scheduled chats, 185–87
   dealing with objectionable behavior, 191
   description of, 42
   Drop-In Hours (DIHs), 184
   effective use of chats, 197–98
   entering a chat room, 187–88, 193
   Get Profile button, 190
   getting to the screen, 184
   Help button, 192
   Home button, 192
   Ignore Member button, 190
   lecture chats, 193–94
   Member Directory button, 191–92
   Notify AOL button, 191
   participating in a conversation, 188–90
   Private Chat button, 191
   recording a chat, 195–97
   screen contents, 184–85
   Send Message button, 190
   Special Interest Groups (SIGs), 183–84
   types of chats, 183–84
   view of screen, 185
chat rooms. *See* Chat Center
citations, electronic, 16
citing information sources, 15–16
Civil War file libraries, 160
Civil War Forum, 263–64

classes, genealogy
    Courses Online, 65
    DearMYRTLE lessons, 58–59, 62, 234–35
    on the Genealogy Forum main screen, 52–53
    Internet links, 202–3
    Keyword for, 65
columns. *See* "Along Those Lines..." column; DearMYRTLE Daily Column; Genealogy Forum NEWS
Complete Genealogy Message Boards, 125
computer technology Internet links, 206
Computer Tools and Techniques message boards, 124–25, 137
computer viruses. See viruses, computer
conference rooms, 183
conferences and events, genealogy, 51–52, 114, 203, 240, 241–42
corroborating information, 9–10, 16–17, 200
Countries of the World message boards, 123
Courses Online, Keyword for, 65
Croatia research, 93–94
Czech Republic research, 90–93

D

Database America People Finder, 261
days of the week, translation table for, 60
DearMYRTLE Daily Column
    author of, 233
    contacting DearMYRTLE, 236
    description of, 50
    focus of, 232
    getting to the screen, 233
    How-to Guides button, 236–37
    Keywords for, 233
    Message Board button, 236
    publication schedule, 245
    resources available, 233–36
    Search by Topics button, 237
    Using FHCenters button, 237
    view of screen, 234
    See also "Along Those Lines..." column; Genealogy Forum NEWS
DearMYRTLE lessons
    Beginning Genealogy Lessons, 58–59, 234
    Finally Getting Organized Lessons, 62, 234–35
    Using LDS FHCenter Lessons, 235
    Writing Personal Histories Lessons, 235
Death Records, Obits and Wills file library, 161
Denmark research, 87–88
dictionaries, 265
DIHs (Drop-In Hours), 42, 184
documents
    assessing reliability, 12–13
    importance of original, 10
downloading files
    AOL files, 34–35
    E-mail attachments, 35–36
    to floppy disks, 35
    from the File Libraries Center
        Download Later button, 154–56
        Download Now button, 152–54
        List More Files button, 156
        Read Description button, 152
        searching for files, 150–52
    protecting against viruses, 35–36
    See also uploading files, to the File Libraries Center
Drop-In Hours (DIHs), 42, 184

E

electronic mail. *See* E-mail
E-mail
    Address Book, 30
    addresses, 27–28
    attachments, 29
    blind courtesy copies (BCCs), 28–29
    etiquette, 29, 209–10
    listservs, 208–10
    Mail Center, 30
    Mail Extras, 30
    mailing lists, 30–31, 208–10
    multiple addressees, 28–29
    reading, 26
    sending, 27–28, 30
    writing, 26–29
England research, 84, 207

Estonia research, 90–93
Ethnic and Special Groups message boards, 123–24, 137
Ethnicity area, 264
etiquette
   chat room, 194–95
   E-mail, 29, 209–10
European Message Archives, 160
Europe (Eastern) research
   challenges of, 90–91
   countries included in collection, 92
   maps, 91
   place name locations, 91–92
   using Resource Center information, 92–93
Europe (Southeastern) research
   challenges of, 93
   countries included in collection, 94
   using Resource Center information, 93–94
Europe (Western) research
   Austria, 88
   Belgium, 88
   Channel Islands, 88–89
   France, 89
   Germany, 89, 207, 264
   Italy, 88
   Netherlands, 88
   Portugal and related areas, 89–90
   Spain, 90
   Switzerland, 88
Excite People Finder, 260

F

family associations, 170–71, 223–24
Family Folklore Questionnaire, downloading, 61
family histories, compiling, 63, 226–27
Family History Centers, LDS Church, 235
family newsletters, 224–25, 227–28
Family Reunion chat room, 222–23
family reunions
   online, 222–23, 228
   planning, 225–26
   value of, 219–20, 229–30
Family Treehouse chat room, 192
Favorite Places, 24–25

file downloading and uploading. *See* downloading files; uploading files, to the File Libraries Center
File Libraries Center
   Ancestors button, 157–59
   decompressing files, 157
   description of, 42–43, 140
   downloading files
      Download Later button, 154–56
      Download Now button, 152–54
      List More Files button, 156
      Read Description button, 152
      searching for files, 150–52
   effective use of, 165–66
   getting files into libraries, 141–42
   getting to the screen, 140
   History and Culture button, 159–61
   Logs, Newsletters and More button, 163–64
   New File Uploads GEDCOM library, 141–42
   New File Uploads library, 141–42
   Records button, 161–62
   screen contents, 140
   Software and Tools button, 164–65
   uploading files
      guidelines for, 148–49
      procedures for, 143–48
      reasons for, 142–43
      Upload button, 156
   view of screen, 140
file transfer, 15
Finland research, 87–88
5-step Research Process, 57–58
For Starters chat room, 63–64, 192
Four11, 260
France research, 89

G

GEDCOM file libraries, 158
GEDCOM format, 158
Genealogical Records file library, 161–62
genealogical research, basic
   assessing document reliability, 12–13
   bibliographies for, 67–68

genealogical research *(Cont.)*
    for children, 66–67
    citing information sources, 15–16
    corroborating information, 9–10, 16–17, 200
    5-step research process, 57–58
    getting started, 8–9, 59–63
    importance of good research skills, 7
    importance of original documents, 10
    in the online environment, 7–8, 12, 14–15, 16–17
    organizing information, 61–62
    primary sources, 10–11
    recording information, 14
    secondary sources, 11–12, 200
    verifying information, 9, 16–17, 200
genealogical societies
    addresses for, 112
    Internet links, 205
genealogy
    for children, 66–67
    definition of, 1
    impact of online services and the Internet on, 2
    reasons for popularity, 1–2
    software for, 62, 164–65
    and women, 206
genealogy classes. *See* classes, genealogy
Genealogy Forum
    main screen
        advertisement box, 53
        "Along Those Lines..." Column, 51
        Beginners button, 39–41
        Chats button, 42
        DearMYRTLE Daily Column, 50
        Feature button, 48
        Files button, 42–43
        Genealogy Classes, 52–53
        Genealogy Conferences and Events, 51–52
        Genealogy Forum NEWS, 50
        getting to the screen, 37
        Golden Gate Store button, 46
        Help button, 48
        Internet button, 44–45
        Keywords for, 22, 36, 53
        listbox resources, 49
        Main button, 47–48
        Members' Choice button, 46
        Member Welcome Center, 49
        Messages button, 41
        Phone Numbers button, 47
        Resources button, 43–44
        Reunions button, 46
        Search the Forum button, 47
        Surnames button, 45
        view of, 38
    related forums, 262–66
    searchable materials, 248–50
    staff of, 2, 3
    types of materials available, 247–48
Genealogy Forum NEWS
    buttons, 245
    description of, 50, 242–45
    publication schedule, 245
    view of screen, 244
    See also "Along Those Lines..." column; DearMYRTLE Daily Column
Genealogy Forum Newsletter, 163
Genealogy Forum Newsletters collection, 114–15
Genealogy Lectures file libraries, 163
Genealogy Meeting Logs file library, 163
genealogy software programs (GSPs), 62, 164–65
General Genealogy message boards, 125
Georgia research, 74–77
German Heritage area, 264
Germany research, 89, 207, 264
Global Preferences, 119–21
Golden Gates chat room, 192
Golden Gate Store, 46
Greece research, 93–94
GSPs (genealogy software programs), 62, 164–65

H

Hawaiian Islands research, 89–90
Help
    Member Services Online Help, 20

Help *(cont.)*
    Offline Help, 20–21
    World Wide Web Help Internet link, 218
Herzegovina research, 93–94
Hispanic file libraries, 160
Hispanic Online forum, 102, 264
Hispanic research, 101–2, 264
historical information file libraries, 159–61
historical societies, addresses for, 112
histories, compiling family, 63, 226–27
History Lectures and Meeting Logs file libraries, 159–60, 163
History Resources area, 264
Huguenot research, 110
Hungary research, 90–93

I

IMs (Instant Messages), 31–32
Indian research. *See* Native American research
InfoSpace, 260
Instant Messages (IMs), 31–32
International Channel, 264
Internet Center
    description of, 44–45
    getting to the screen, 201
    impact of Internet on genealogical research, 2, 199–200
    Internet information as secondary source, 200
    Internet Tour button, 217–18
    listbox resources, 217–18
    Mailing Lists/Newsgroups button, 208–16
    screen contents, 201–2
    Search Engines button, 216–17
    Sites by Region/Ethnic Group button, 206–8
    Sites by Topic button, 202–6
    view of screen, 202
    See also Internet links
Internet links
    African American Web Sites, 206
    Canada Genealogy Sites, 206–7
    Courses on the Internet, 202–3
    Cyndi's List of Newsgroups & Mailing Lists, 211
    Events, 203
    Genealogy Newsgroup Sites, 211
    Genealogy Resources on the Internet, 211
    General Genealogy Internet Sites, 203
    German Genealogy Sites, 207
    Getting Started, 203–4
    Jewish Genealogy, 207
    Liszt, the Mailing List Site, 211
    Maps, 204
    Mayflower Pilgrims, 204
    Mexico Genealogy, 207
    Military Resources, 204
    Native American Web Sites, 207
    New Genealogy Sites, 218
    Online Genealogy Magazines and Newsletters, 204–5
    Records, 205
    Reunion Planning Weblinks, 226
    Societies, Organizations and Clubs, 205
    Surname Searches, 205
    Technology and Genealogy, 206
    Telephone Search Facility, 259–61
    "The Internet List" Web Site, 218
    UK/Ireland Genealogy Sites, 207
    United States Genealogy Sites, 207–8
    Web Sites (Message Board), 218
    Women and Genealogy, 206
    World Wide Web Help, 218
Internet Relay Chats (IRCs), 15
Internet search engines, 216–17
Internet Tour, 217
IRCs (Internet Relay Chats), 15
Ireland research
    downloading files, 84–85
    Internet links, 207
    resources available, 84–86
I&S Newsletter, 164
Italy research, 88

J

Japan!, 264–65
Jewish Community Forum, 103, 265
Jewish file library, 160
Jewish research, 103, 160, 207, 265
journals, 62–63

K

Keywords
- adoption, 263
- bistro, 263
- civil war, 263–64
- courses, 65
- dearmyrtle, 233
- ethnicity, 264
- foreign dictionary, 265
- genealogy forum, 22
- german heritage, 264
- help, 48
- hispanic online, 264
- history, 264
- international, 264
- japan, 264–65
- jewish, 103, 265
- latino, 102
- Mail Center, 30
- mail extras, 133
- map, 72
- maps, 263
- members, 33
- myrtle, 233
- netnoir, 265
- newsgroup, 212
- rev war, 265
- roots, 22, 36, 53
- royalty, 265
- seniornet, 265
- using Keywords, 22–24

L

Labrador research, 80–81
Latvia research, 90–93
lecture chats. *See* Chat Center
letters of request, 61
libraries, addresses for, 112
listservs, 208–10, 211–12
Lithuania research, 90–93
logging, chat, 195–97

M

Macedonia research, 93–94
Madeira research, 89–90
magazines, genealogy, 204–5
Mail Center
- Keyword for, 30
- using, 30–31

mailing lists, 208–10, 211–12
Manitoba research, 80
maps
- Internet links, 204
- Keyword for, 72, 263

Maps file library, 160–61
Mayflower Internet links, 204
Mayflower surnames, 179–80
Member Directory
- Keyword for, 33
- using, 33–34

Members' Choice Award, AOL, 46
Member Services Online Help, 20
Member Welcome Center, 49
Message Board Center
- Computer and General button, 124–25
- Countries of the World button, 123
- creating a new subject, 134–36
- description of, 116–17
- Ethnic and Special Groups button, 123–24
- examples of effective use, 136–38
- getting to the screen, 118
- Keyword for changing text, 133
- reading messages, 130–32
- replying to messages, 132–33
- screen contents, 118–19
- setting personal preferences, 119–21
- Surnames button, 121–22
- threads, 126
- United States button, 122–23
- view of screen, 118
- working with list messages, 126–30

message boards, 41
Mexico research, 83, 207
military research, 204, 263–64, 265
Moldova research, 93–94
months, translation table for, 60

MYRTLE. *See* DearMYRTLE Daily Column; DearMYRTLE lessons

N

National Archives and Records Administration (NARA), addresses for, 111–12
National Archives file library, 162
Native American research
   family research helps, 105
   file libraries, 108
   historical resources, 105–8
   Internet web sites, 108–9, 207
   networking through message boards, 109
   Turtle Island — A Gathering of Nations forum, 266
   using Resource Center information, 104–5, 108
Netherlands research, 88
Netiquette, 29, 209–10
NetNoir forum, 265
New Brunswick research, 80
Newfoundland research, 80–81
News. *See* Usenet Newsgroups
NEWS, Genealogy Forum. *See* Genealogy Forum NEWS
Newsgroups. See Usenet Newsgroups
newsletters, family, 224–25, 227–28
newsletters, genealogy, 114–15, 204–5
Northwest Territories research, 81
Norway research, 87–88
Nova Scotia research, 81

O

Offline Help, 20–21
online environments, types of, 14–15
online services, 2, 14
Ontario research
   downloading files, 81–82
   resources available, 81–82
original documents, 10

P

perpetual calendar, 114
personal histories, 235
personal preferences, 119–21
photographs file libraries, 159
Poland research, 90–93
Portugal research, 89–90
Portuguese SIG Newsletter, 164
preferences, personal, 119–21
preponderance of evidence, 9–10
preservation, 240–41
primary information sources, 10–11
Prince Edward Island, 82
Profiles, member, 33–34
protocol, chat, 193–94

Q

Quebec research, 82

R

recipes, family, 113–14
Recipes file library, 161
Recipes Message Board, 138
Regional and Ethnic [Message] Archives, 160
relationship terms, 61
Research Tips and Resources file library, 162
Resource Center
   Addresses button, 111–12
   description of, 43–44
   Ethnic Resources button
      African American Resource Area folder, 96–101
      Hispanic Resources folder, 101–2
      Huguenot Information folder, 110
      Jewish Resources folder, 103
      Native American Resource Area folder, 104–9
   getting to the screen, 69
   listbox resources, 114–15
   Other Resources button, 113
   Regions of the World button
      British Isles folder, 83–87
      Canada folder, 77–83
      description of resources, 70–71
      Eastern Europe folder, 90–93
      Mexico folder, 83
      Scandinavia folder, 87–88

Southeastern Europe folder, 93–94
United States folder, 72–77
view of screen, 71
Western Europe folder, 88–90
screen contents, 69–70
view of screen, 70
Vital Records/Other Records button, 110–11
Reunion Center
description of, 46
Family Associations button, 223–24
Family Newsletters button, 224–25
Family Reunion Chat Room button, 222–23
getting to the screen, 221
How Do I...button, 225
listbox resources, 228–29
purposes of, 220–21
screen contents, 221–22
Surname Center button, 229
view of screen, 221
Revolutionary War Forum, 265
Romania research, 93–94
Root Cellar chat room, 192
Royalty Forum, 265
Russia research, 90–93

S

Sandwich Islands research, 89–90
Saskatchewan research, 83
Scandinavia research, 87–88
Scotland research, 86
screens, layering, 38
search engines, Internet, 216–17
Search the Forum facility
description of, 47
determining what is searchable, 246–48
expanding your search, 255
getting to the screen, 250
narrowing your search, 253–55, 256
searchable materials, 248–50
using the facility, 250–56
view of screen, 251
secondary information sources, 11–12, 200
SeniorNet area, 265–66
Ships Passenger Lists message boards, 137–38

SIGs (Special Interest Groups), 42, 183–84
Slovakia research, 90–93
Slovenia research, 93–94
software, genealogy, 62, 164–65
Spain research, 90
Special Interest Groups (SIGs), 42, 183–84
Surname Center
description of, 45, 167–68
family association addresses, 170–71
GEDCOM files, 171–73, 178–79
getting to the screen, 168
Input Surname Web Sites button, 180–82
Internet web sites, 177–78, 180–82, 205–6
Mayflower Surnames button, 179–80
Message Board Center button, 180
message boards, 173
screen contents, 168
Surname Areas button, 168–69
Tiny Tafels, 173–77
Top 100 U.S. Surnames button, 179
uploading GEDCOM files, 178–79
view of screen, 168
Surnames Archives file libraries, 158–59
Surnames message boards, 121–22, 136, 173
Sweden research, 87–88
Switchboard, 259–60
Switzerland research, 88

T

Tafel Libraries
in the File Libraries Center, 159
in the Surname Center, 173–77
Telephone Search Facility
description of, 47, 258–59
getting to the screen, 259
search facilities available, 259–61
view of screen, 259
Tiny Tafels. *See* Tafel Libraries
Turtle Island — A Gathering of Nations forum, 266

U

Ukraine research, 90–93
Ultimate White Pages, 260–61
United States message boards, 122–23, 136–37

United States research
    DearMYRTLE materials, 235–36
    Internet links, 207–8
    Keyword for maps, 72
    maps, 72
    by region, 72–73
    by state, 73–75
    using Resource Center information, 75–77
uploading files, to the File Libraries Center
    guidelines for, 148–49
    procedures for, 143–48, 178–79
    reasons for, 142–43, 178
    Upload button, 156
    See also downloading files
U.S. State Message Archives file library, 162
Usenet. *See* Usenet Newsgroups
Usenet Newsgroups
    collection contents, 211–12
    description of, 210
    Keyword for, 212
    reading newsgroups on AOL
        Add Newsgroups button, 213
        Expert Add button, 213
        locating newsgroups, 216
        Parental Controls button, 212–13
        posting messages, 216
        Preferences button, 213
        reading newsgroup contents, 215–16
        Read My Newsgroups button, 213–14
USGenWeb Project, 199, 208

V

verifying information, 9, 16–17, 200
viruses, computer
    in AOL files, 35
    in E-mail attachments, 35–36
    and virus protection programs, 35
vital records
    Bible, Birth and Marriage Records file library, 161
    Death Records, Obits and Wills file library, 161
    Internet links, 205
    in the Resource Center, 110–11

W

Wales research, 87, 207
WhoWhere?, 260
women and genealogy, 206
World Wide Web Help Internet link, 218

Y

Yahoo!, 260
Yugoslavia research, 93–94
Yukon research, 83

George G. Morgan began working on his family's genealogy at the age of ten. One rainy afternoon, he discovered a number of boxes of old family papers and Bibles dating back to the mid-1700s at his aunt and grandmother's home in North Carolina. He's been hooked on genealogy ever since.

He joined the Genealogy Forum on America Online several years ago as a volunteer, serving as a member of its senior staff and as a programmer, developing new screens and writing articles to add to the content of the forum.

George is a noted genealogical writer, having published materials in several publications including *Genealogical Computing*, for which he has written cover articles about the sophisticated electronic database, NAIL, at the National Archives and Records Administration and the Electronic Search System (ESS) at the Library of Congress.

He is also internationally recognized as the author of the weekly online genealogy column, "Along Those Lines...", which appears every Friday in the Genealogy Forum of America Online. In addition, he is published at the *Ancestry* Web site (http://www.ancestry.com).

George owns and operates Aha! Seminars, Inc., a Tampa Bay-based seminar company that teaches workshops about the Internet, Web page design and management, several software programs, time management and, of course, genealogy. He works closely with library consortia and cooperatives in Florida to deliver continuing education to library personnel. He is an adjunct instructor for the School of Library and Information Science at the University of South Florida in Tampa.

He lives in Odessa, Florida, a suburb of Tampa, and is researching the surnames Morgan, Weatherly, Holder, Swords, Wilson, Alexander, Ball, Morrison, Monfort, Potts, and Whitfield/Whitefield.